SPYING FOR HITLER

SPYING FOR HITLER

NAZIS WHO INFILTRATED AMERICA

NORMAN RIDLEY

FRONTLINE
BOOKS

First published in Great Britain in 2024
by Frontline Books
An imprint of
Pen & Sword Books Ltd
Yorkshire - Philadelphia

Copyright © Norman Ridley, 2024

ISBN 978 1 03611 219 6

The right of Norman Ridley to be identified as Author of this work has been asserted by him in accordance with the Copyright, Designs and Patents Act 1988.
A CIP catalogue record for this book is available from the British Library

All rights reserved. No part of this book may be reproduced or transmitted in any form or by any means, electronic or mechanical including photocopying, recording or by any information storage and retrieval system, without permission from the Publisher in writing.

Typeset by Lapiz Digital
Printed and bound in the UK by CPI Group (UK) Ltd,
Croydon, CR0 4YY.

Printed on paper from a sustainable source by
CPI Group (UK) Ltd, Croydon, CR0 4YY

Pen & Sword Books Limited incorporates the imprints of Archaeology, Atlas, Aviation, Battleground, Digital, Discovery, Family History, Fiction, History, Local, Local History, Maritime, Military, Military Classics, Politics, Select, Transport, True Crime, After the Battle, Air World, Claymore Press, Frontline Publishing, Leo Cooper, Remember When, Seaforth Publishing, The Praetorian Press, Wharncliffe Books, Wharncliffe Local History, Wharncliffe Transport, Wharncliffe True Crime and White Owl.

For a complete list of Pen & Sword titles please contact:

PEN & SWORD BOOKS LTD
47 Church Street, Barnsley, South Yorkshire, S70 2AS, England
E-mail: enquiries@pen-and-sword.co.uk
Website: www.pen-and-sword.co.uk
or
PEN & SWORD BOOKS
1950 Lawrence Rd, Havertown, PA 19083, USA
E-mail: uspen-and-sword@casematepublishers.com

CONTENTS

Introduction vii

Chapter 1 The First World War 1
Chapter 2 German Propaganda 38
Chapter 3 FBI Background 56
Chapter 4 The Griebl-Lonkowski Spy Ring 61
Chapter 5 Nazis on the West Coast 95
Chapter 6 Financial Espionage 102
Chapter 7 Torkild Rieber 105
Chapter 8 Ritter, Duquesne and Sebold 108
Chapter 9 Sleepers 127
Chapter 10 The Ludwig Spy Ring 131
Chapter 11 Operation Pastorius 141
Chapter 12 Wilhelm Albrecht von Pressentin genannt von Rautter 156
Chapter 13 Gimpel and Colepaugh 161
Chapter 14 Double Agents 166
Postscript 183

Appendix 1 The German Intelligence Services 185
Appendix 2 Members of the Duquesne Spy Ring 190
Appendix 3 Members of the Ludwig Spy Ring 198
Appendix 4 Coding Radio Messages 200
Notes 205
Sources 214
Index 217

INTRODUCTION

On the evening of 12 June 1942, Lieutenant Commander Hans-Heinz Lindner, commander of the type VIIC U-boat *U-202* 'Innsbruck' was taking bearings which he hoped would confirm his position just off Long Island at East Hampton, New York. In fact, the German submarine was actually three miles away from there lying a few hundred metres off Amagansett. Nevertheless, the minor discrepancy underscored a quite remarkable feat of navigation because he had brought his ship across three thousand miles of the Atlantic Ocean from Lorient in Brittany running along the surface by night and submerged by day. His main problem on this night was much more serious. His U-boat was stuck on a sandbank making it visible to anyone on the shore and a sitting target for American guns when dawn broke.

Lindner had found himself in this most unnatural position for a submarine because he had been assigned to approach as close as possible to shore and carry out a mission to put four German saboteurs on American soil. These men, all of whom had spent years living and working in the United States had been recruited by the Abwehr military intelligence and returned to Germany a year previously. There they had been given false identities and meticulously trained to blow up railroad bridges, power plants and tunnels to paralyze industrial facilities vital to the American war effort, all of which was designed to demoralize the American civilian population.

Fortunately, the tide was rising and eventually, under full power with the ship shuddering and straining, it found buoyancy and slipped free but remained on the surface. In the minutes before dawn, the four secret agents, wearing German military uniforms so that if they were caught setting foot on US soil they would be interned as prisoners of war and not shot as spies, slid, one by one, down the U-boat hull and manhandled by two crewmen into a dirigible lurching awkwardly in a heavy sea. Along with the four men, came four waterproof crates loaded with explosives, incendiaries and timing devices.

This in itself was a terrifying ordeal for non-mariners. The saboteurs were far from being a close-knit group and had not bonded well during their training, so they found little strength in each other's company as they had endured the daily emergency drills when the U-boat crash-dived with all crewmen rushing to action stations while the klaxons wailed.

The heavy mist that lay over the Newfoundland Banks was a blessing of concealment but held a gothic portent of danger. After fifteen days cooped up in the U-boat suffering seasickness and claustrophobia, however, the men breathed in the cool, damp night air with something bordering relief. This was only half of the mission, however. Two days later another four men were landed from U-boat *U-584* onto Ponte Vedra beach at Jacksonville, Florida. Their short passage from U-boat to shore was over calmer water but their ship had been lucky to survive a bombing attack by British aircraft during its more southerly transit.

All eight saboteurs were the personnel of Operation Pastorius that had been hatched soon after the United States had entered the Second World War by Walter Kappe, head of a small, somewhat independent, unit of Abteilung II working out of a third-floor office at Rankestraße 8, Berlin. The plan was for them all to meet up in New York, settle back into the American mainstream and begin laying the foundations for a campaign of terror.

Chapter 1

THE FIRST WORLD WAR

> 'The country is honeycombed with German intrigue and infested with German spies, [*sic*] The evidence of these things [are] multiplying every day.'
>
> President Woodrow Wilson[1]

When the First World War broke out in August 1914, the economic importance of the United States (US) to the warring nations was obvious. Although not a belligerent in the European war and, as far as the majority of Americans were concerned never would be, it was free to trade with the warring nations. Inevitably its civilian economy and capacity for mass-production meant that it was bound to play a major role, however, and Germany had taken steps to exploit that. With efficiency unmatched by any other belligerent, the *Bundesministerium des Innern und für Heimat* (Federal Ministry of the Interior) had set up the *Zentral-Einkaufsgenossenschaft mbH* (Central Purchasing Corporation) to aid both the Department of War purchasing agency and German industry's war commission to procure important strategic materials such as cotton, dye and rubber, as well as arms, munitions, explosives, and related chemicals from neutral countries including the US. Gerson von Bleichröder, Deutsche Bank, Disconto-Gesellschaft and Dresdner Bank, provided the funding while Germany's main commercial shipping lines, the *Hamburg-Amerikanische Paketfahrt-Aktien-Gesellschaft* (Hamburg-American Line – HAPAG) and the *Norddeutscher* (North German Lloyd), as well as additional leased merchantmen, arranged for shipping.[2] Germany's preparations for war had seen them stockpile strategic materials and foodstuffs, but only enough for a relatively short war, which the military had predicted. The priorities for German diplomats in the US, with their extensive contacts, were to ensure that shipments of foodstuffs and raw materials continued flowing to Germany from the US and, where possible, to interfere with US trade with the Entente Powers (Britain, France and Russia) either by adversely affecting production of supplies to them or preventing their shipment by sea.

The US was to become an intelligence and economic battleground for British and German agents but its legal framework governing their activities within the country was signally ill-suited to deal with all the plots and subterfuges that ensued. Federal agents of the various secret services of the US government actually had no legal powers to interfere in the activities of foreign agents and, as a result of general lack of supervision, German military attachés had been fully engaged in illegal operations long before the outbreak of the First World War in 1914.

The German ambassador to the US was Count Johann Heinrich Andreas Hermann Albrecht von Bernstorff, a statesman whose ancestors for generations had been Saxon diplomats. Although he had overall responsibility for German citizens in the US, he remained aloof from the worst excesses of German espionage agents which suited him since his main preoccupation was living the high life and enjoying the company of glamorous young women.

Contrary to most published sources, von Bernstorff was not recalled to Germany in June 1914 but had been taking a holiday there when he was summoned to a meeting with State Secretary of Foreign Affairs Gottlieb von Jagow.[3] He was told that Jewish banker Bernhard Dernburg would join him in the US to arrange with him a loan of $150 million for the purchase of American goods for export to Germany. He would also give all necessary assistance in organising the sale of German war bonds there, and all the money raised from the bonds sale would be added to the pot. Unfortunately for the military attaché, Captain Franz Joseph Hermann Michael Maria von Papen, the war bonds scheme with which Germany had hoped to finance much of its intelligence work in the US would be an unmitigated failure. After the halting of the German armies on the Marne in September 1914 nullifying the Kaiser's boast that his troops would be 'home before the leaves have fallen off the trees', American investors lost confidence in the bonds and the sinking of the SS *Lusitania* on 7 May 1915 put the final nail in their coffin.

A heavily-built man with full beard and clear blue eyes, Dernburg had spent time working for Ladenburg Thalmann in New York, US. Von Bernstorff and Dernburg travelled back to the US together and were joined two days later by the man who would become the chief controller of German espionage activities in the US, Heinrich Friedrich Albert.

Albert was reserved, non-descript and youthful looking for a man in his late thirties but he was distinguished by a duelling scar which clearly indicated Prussian heritage. Born into a wealthy banking family, he had studied law although never actually qualifying for the title of 'Doctor' which is often ascribed to him. His career up until 1914 had been as *Geheimer Oberregierungsrat* (Privy Chancellor) in the Federal Ministry of the Interior although it is almost certain that this was only a cover for various intelligence missions. Without prior experience in covert operations, it is unlikely that he would have had at his disposal the entire resources of HAPAG when he arrived in the US along with his two bosses from *Abteilung III b*, the German military counterintelligence division, Otto Ecker and Albert Polis. Once there he contacted Hans Tauscher, the US representative of Krupp, Mauser, and other German arms manufacturers. Albert's role encompassed *Reichseinkauf* (purchasing), *Geldbeschaffung* (fund-raising), *Aufklärungsarbeit* (propaganda) and *Schädigung des Feindes* (espionage). In the performance of this last role, he was assisted by the military attaché, von Papen, and the naval attaché, Captain Karl Boy-Ed. Both men were members of what became Albert's Secret War Council, which had been set up by Germany to combine the interests of the military and commercial organisations. Other members were Bernhard Dernburg and Karl Alexander Fuehr, both involved with propaganda.[4]

Despite his cavalry background and the significant wealth he had acquired through marriage, von Papen had spent most of his career posing as a civilian and travelling widely in the pay of *Abteilung III b*. His duties had taken him to the Republic of Ireland and later to Mexico, a country in the throes of almost constant revolution, where he had made a close study of rebel espionage operations especially against railways using mines and explosives.

Under orders from *Abteilung III b*, he went to New York in March 1914 and set up the *Kriegsnachrichtendienst* (War Intelligence Agency), under the charge of New York banker Wolf Walter Franz von Igel, to report on politico-military developments on the North American continent. He returned to Mexico but was rushed to Washington DC days before the outbreak of the First World War bringing with him German agents from Mexico, and others drafted in from different parts of the world. To these he added a number of experts such as chemists and lawyers, already living in neighbourhoods all across the US that were still proudly Germanic in speech and culture, who were more than willing to serve the Kaiser. Several hundred German language newspapers catered for these neighbourhoods loudly calling for a swift German victory in the First World War. Many recent German immigrants, now working in a wide range of industries at various levels, were military reservists who were still under German military oaths.

Von Papen's overbearing, arrogant attitude in all things had made him few friends and may have accounted for how he now found himself in what he considered to be a diplomatic backwater but, under direct orders from the military in Berlin, Germany and not Ambassador von Bernstorff, he soon began organising his network of spies and saboteurs. He anticipated a relatively easy ride. It was entirely in keeping with von Papen's arrogant approach that, throughout his espionage activities in the US, he made few efforts to cover his tracks. His scorn for US intelligence agencies was profound. Instead of going about his business quietly and efficiently, von Papen made a point of organising these reservists in parades singing 'Deutschland, Deutschland ūber alles!', which brought out French protestors singing the 'Marseillaise'; the whole thing generally erupting into street battles. This habit of showing off soon had US authorities in Washington DC 'very much excited' over his antics and had 'a constant watch kept on him'.[5]

The impressive Boy-Ed was the epitome of a Prussian naval officer despite being the son of a German mother and a Turkish father. Amusing, intelligent, cosmopolitan and extremely well read, he was popular and respected by the US naval officials he came into contact with. He had been the naval attaché in Washington DC in 1913 with peace-time duties to study all aspects of the US Navy from personnel to coastal defences. In March 1914, he was given extra resources in the form of a new organisation, *Nachrichtenabteilung des Admiralstabes* (Department of Naval Intelligence).

Under von Papen and Boy-Ed, Washington DC and New York became the headquarters of German intelligence operations in the Western world. In New York, Boy-Ed had his offices in Room 809 at 11 Broadway, Albert could be found in the Hamburg-American building at 45 Broadway and von Papen had offices on the twenty-fifth floor of 60 Wall Street. Within a triangle formed by these points were the building of J.P. Morgan & Co., chief bankers for the Entente Powers, the New York Stock Exchange and the offices of the Standard Oil Company, Inc. Albert and his assistant, von Igel, supervised the collection and dissemination of intelligence, as well as the dispatch and payment of secret agents but overall financial control rested with Albert and no plot or scheme of any importance went ahead without his approval.[6]

As part of Britain's economic blockade, the German merchant shipping fleet had virtually disappeared from the high seas. Of its 1,500 ships, 245 were captured, 1,059 were confined in neutral ports, and 221 were restricted to the Baltic.[7] In the Hudson River alone there were more than eighty German vessels tied up and going nowhere with their crews left free to roam around the city. In 1914, the personnel of German ships in US ports totalled 476 officers and 4,980 men. Most of the sailors on the HAPAG and North German Lloyd ships became war draftees at the outbreak of the First World War and so *de facto* had become what amounted to a virtual German army, albeit unarmed, on American soil under the German navy's command. Responsibility for paying the stranded crews in the US fell on Boy-Ed who ran his own accounts separate from Albert. Crew wages amounted to about $3,000 every week and funds for this, totalling $300,000, came from the Bayer chemical company, whose virtual world monopoly on dyestuffs had accrued for them large currency reserves in the US. The money was transferred through the Warburg Bank to Boy-Ed's account in the German Embassy in Washington DC and the German government reimbursed Bayer in Germany. The man who coordinated these transactions was, at the time, a relatively non-descript administrator in the German *Reichsmarineamt* (German Imperial Navy Office), Department B.I.2., Lieutenant Commander Franz Dagobert Johannes von Rintelen who would go on to play a much greater role in the following years. Another $750,000 went into Boy-Ed's embassy accounts put there by Gustav B. Kuhlenkampff, a commodity broker in New York who was also working for *Abteilung III b.* He later claimed to have received it 'out of the blue' from the Deutsche Bank and told to pass it on to Boy-Ed.

Almost all international financial transactions passed through London in one way or another and the British kept a close eye on funds going into and out of the US. They quickly stopped virtually all transfers of funds between Germany and neutral trading partners, such as the US and made it illegal for any British merchant ship to transport goods for any enemy country. The Royal Navy had also put an economic stranglehold on Germany with its naval blockade cutting off supplies. Having failed to break the blockade at the Battle of Jutland, the German fleet retired to Kiel and remained there for most of the First World War. By the end of 1914, almost the whole of the German naval fleet was either anchored or destroyed.

However, the director of the Deutsche Bank in the US, Hugo Schmidt, and his assistant, Frederico Stallforth, proved to be experts at finding ways around the tight controls using dummy accounts and became a lifeline for secret German operations there. G. Amsinck & Co., Inc received $250,000 from the Disconto-Gesellschaft via the National City Bank in New York on 22 August 1914 and another $500,000 two days later all of which were the initial funds with which Albert established the Secret War Council. Von Rintelen sent $1 million directly to Karl Boy-Ed via the New York banking house of J. & W. Seligman and Co. on 12 September 1914 to pay for food and fuel leaving US ports to re-supply the German Atlantic and Pacific fleets. Schmidt arrived in the US in October 1914 tasked with ensuring that arrangements for extensive money transfers that had been authorised to agents all across the US, Mexico and South America were in place. Through this work he established a large number of contacts with financiers and businessmen all sympathetic to the German cause.[8]

Although wages for the crews stranded in US ports were met, maintenance and mooring fees still had to be paid by HAPAG and North German Lloyd for their ships in harbour and this together with a virtual cessation of any income threatened to bankrupt the shipping lines. Of HAPAG's 175 large passenger and cargo ships, 80 were docked at German ports at the beginning of the First World War, 12 liners were in enemy ports and confiscated and the other 83, to avoid being impounded by British warships on the open sea, had taken refuge in neutral ports, mostly in the US. Albert despaired that his whole mission was falling apart before it had even begun but he could not allow himself the luxury of self-pity.

He turned to the urgent issue of supplying food to Germany from the US. Von Bernstorff, Ecker and Polis were quick to endorse his plan to create an organisation that could source and ship meat, flour and grain to Germany without the knowledge of either the US or the British governments. Initially he contacted Paul Tietgens, a German commodities broker from Chicago, Illinois, US who set up a company called Henius & Co. based in Copenhagen, Denmark. Next he made a deal with K. & E. Neumond, a German company with representation in New York that had been awarded a $3 million contract to supply 40,000 tons of cereal for the German army. K. & E. Neumond managed to ship the bulk of this order through a neutral Scandinavian America Line using the Guaranty Trust Company of New York as a guarantor. During all the time he was operating, only three out of twenty of Neumond's shipments were intercepted and impounded.

Next Albert addressed the issue of trade with the US. Britain, unlike Germany, had only a small munitions manufacturing base and was particularly dependent on US supplies but both sides of the European conflict looked to the US to supply critical raw materials, such as wood pulp, rubber, cotton, wool and non-ferrous ores such as copper. It was soon clear just how critical this trade would be when all indications were that the war was now going to be a long drawn-out affair.

The American economy faced great challenges. The British sea blockade effectively cut the traditional trade links between the US and Central Europe causing the New York Stock Exchange to panic. The American South was unable to export the 2.5 million bales of cotton that German usually bought annually and the import of German dyestuffs and artificial fertilisers that should have been crossing the Atlantic in the opposite direction were stalled. The First World War, however, had also resulted in a huge increase in trade with Britain and France with demand for munitions, in particular, promising to ignite a boom in US production with new factories springing up all across the country taking up the slack and bringing down employment figures. Whilst President Wilson had declared the US to be neutral on 19 August 1914, it was clear that, although adhering to the letter of that declaration, American corporations spotted opportunities for huge profits and saw the government's task as being able to facilitate that. The war in Europe was hauling the American economy out of recession and the spirit of neutrality was dissipating in the face of realpolitik with America turning into an export-based economic powerhouse. This emergence of the US as a critical economic lifeline to the Entente Powers convinced German officials there that they were now justified in operating outside American laws to do all they could to sabotage these new US trading links with their enemy.

In reality, maintaining trading links between Germany and the US had never been Albert's primary concern. It was obvious from the start that the Royal Navy would severely limit scope for that and, given the restrictions on payment structures because of the British dominance of international financial institutions, the few operations that he was able to set up with Paul Tietgens and K. & E. Neumond was pretty much all that was possible under the circumstances. It was some consolation that he had been able to insure his 'neutral' cargos against loss and was able to claim against US insurance companies for every ship that the British impounded. Little more than $10 million of goods ever found their way to Germany, but a significant benefit of these operations to Albert was the establishment, by the end of 1914, of a formidable network of confidential agents, dummy firms, shippers, and fake companies that would give him intelligence contacts deep within the US financial and commercial sectors. These would soon form the backbone of his intelligence gathering operations and commercial ventures that would encompass propaganda, espionage, sabotage, and attempts to corner the output of specific US industries.

Attention now turned towards propaganda. Every incident in which the British stopped and searched ships on the high seas, sometimes impounding cargos, was heavily publicised by German agents in the US who spread stories of German children going hungry and looking emaciated in the streets. The US government was flooded with complaints from inside and outside the US. Cotton growers in the American South had seen their exports cut almost in half and they exerted huge pressure on their government to exclude cotton from the list of contraband materials. It had been banned because it was not only used to make uniforms but was also a vital component of artillery shells. They then pushed the government to re-flag more than sixty German ships as US merchantmen to carry the cotton to Europe. The fact that only eight ships ever made it to Germany was of much less importance to Albert than success in driving a wedge between a large part of the American business community and the British government.

A large part of Germany's naval strength lay blockaded by the British in the Kiel Canal, where they remained for more than three years but there were still German warships at sea that required provisioning. The *Emden, Dresden, Scharnhorst, Gneisenau* and *Nurnberg* were all at large in the southern oceans. The Hamburg-America Line had been contracted to the Admiralty division of the German government to provision them during wartime using the US as a base but that was becoming increasingly difficult. It was Boy-Ed's responsibility, however, to make sure that the contract was adhered to but Hamburg-American Line ships leaving American ports were liable to be intercepted by British naval vessels and US authorities refused to let German warships use American ports as supply stations for conducting war operations. Boy-Ed got round this by leasing a fleet of merchant ships then loading them with supplies and submitting false manifests and misleading sailing schedules allowing them to supply ships in the German battle fleet on the high seas with coal and other supplies, including arms. Each of these ships would have on board a German agent who had authority even over the ship's captain and the whole operation would later be shown to have had a spectacularly high rate of success. Gustav B. Kuhlenkampff had been particularly useful as a conduit for finance. It was not to last, however. Apart from the fact that Admiral von Spee's German Pacific Fleet had been decimated in the South Atlantic off the Falkland Islands, the whole operation had come out into the open in spring 1915. Boy-Ed's diplomatic immunity saved him but the 72-year-old HAPAG managing director Dr Karl Buenz was tried in November 1915 on charges of defrauding the US and sentenced to two years' imprisonment. He died a few short months later, but in contrast to the way that the US had responded to the German blockade running, British cruisers patrolling both the East and West coasts of the US were openly receiving supplies from US ports which said much about supposed US neutrality.

When the war started, large numbers of German and Austrian reservists living in the US were called up by their governments. Some 60,000 had followed von Papen's instructions and flocked into New York but they had no way of crossing the Atlantic. The US refused to allow them to board ships under their neutrality stance and in any case if the ships had been allowed to sail they would be rounded up by British warships and their occupants interned in PoW camps. Von Papen suddenly found himself responsible for housing and feeding these reservists. While there was little chance of overcoming the administrative hurdle to facilitate the passage of all these men to Germany, von Papen looked for ways of getting a few of the more important individuals back to Germany. His solution was to provide them with false passports and pay for passage on neutral passenger liners. German immigrants who had acquired American citizenship were persuaded to hand over their legal US passports which were then modified with new photographs.

The ruse worked for a short while but no more than 1,000 reservists managed to leave on false passports before the scam was detected and shut down. The US authorities made sure that the plot was given maximum publicity, which began to focus public attention on the activities of not only German diplomats but German-Americans who had been complicit in the subterfuge. It turned out to be something of a public relations disaster for the Germans, the negative effects of which were felt by the whole German-American community.

At the outset of the First World War, von Papen had looked for potential agents and one of the first he chose was a German citizen, Paul W. Koenig. Since 1912, the brutal, sadistic PK, as he was commonly referred to, had been head of the Bureau of Investigation of the Atlas Line, a subsidiary of the Hamburg-America Line. With his small force of some twenty-five detectives, many of whom were former Pinkerton men, he was charged with combatting smuggling, theft and stowaways. In his role, he was also responsible for vetting ship's crews and monitoring their activities while on shore. For him and his men, violence was by no means a last resort when seeking information and there was little he did not know about the sailors, tug-skippers, wharf-rats and longshoremen all along the waterfronts of Boston and New York where he was feared and disliked in equal measure. As well as being brutal, Koenig was also a wily operator. He had a vast array of several hundred spies and informants comprising army reservists, both German-American and American, clerks, scientists and Federal employees. He had eavesdroppers in hotels, and on busy telephone switchboards. He employed porters, window-cleaners, bank clerks, corporation employees and even a member of the police department. All had suitable aliases and passed information using coded messages. Koenig chose a few of his toughest men and formed what he called his *Geheimdienst* (Secret Service) through which he kept von Papen informed about shipments of war material to Europe. The *Kriegsnachrichtendienst* (Federal Intelligence Service) employed similar groups of agents in the other harbour cities such as Baltimore.

In 1914, the US armament industry was relatively small. Exports of munitions to the Entente Powers were limited and German agents were well placed to keep von Papen updated about quantities and types of cargos. Theodore Otto, with contacts in many steel-making plants in Allentown, was probably the most productive source. Otto Heins, General Manager of Robert Bosch Magneto Company, was another but it was not only industrialists. Many of the contracts placed by the Entente Powers for munitions and other supplies went through the Rockefeller-owned National City Bank of New York and Koenig even had informants there too.

In order for German saboteurs to target munitions factories and arms shipments, they needed information about where, when and what. The man ideally placed to provide this was Frederick Schleindl, a 26-year-old German from Wildenstein, Bavaria who had served in the 11th Bavarian Infantry Regiment and who now worked as a clerk in the commercial credit department of the National City Bank. Here he had access to records of munition deals from purchase to transportation to harbours and ships. He was instructed by the German consul in New York to go to the Hotel Manhattan where Koenig arranged with him to supply confidential information in return for a $25 per week reward. On his way home in the evening, Schleindl would drop off documents to the offices of the Hamburg-American shipping lines and collect them again on his way to work the next day.

What von Papen learned about the relatively small volume of trade in arms convinced him that it might be possible to buy up the total US production of munitions and explosives to prevent them being exported to the Entente Powers. He estimated that it could be done for around $20 million. It would not matter if only a small part of it could find its way to Germany, there was a ready market for guns and ammunition in Central and South America. The whole of US production could be diverted there all of which could be arranged through the German-Jewish naval intelligence agent, Felix A. Sommerfeld. It was an ambitious project but one that had not been properly thought through by von Papen. Berlin took one look and refused to sanction it. Whilst it might have had some initial success, it would undoubtedly have stimulated US munitions factories to expand production to meet the demand which, is exactly what happened anyway as the war in Europe started to show signs of dragging on for years.

Only a few miles from New York, a huge mobilisation programme had got under way to send Canadian troops to Europe to fight on the side of the Entente Powers. In October 1914, a fleet of ships containing 31,000 men and supplies passed out into the Gulf of St Lawrence and more were soon to follow. The relatively small population of Canada included about 100,000 Germans and Austrians who had arrived since the turn of the century. Von Papen calculated that many of these could be activated as agents to sabotage the Canadian military effort and sent Koenig on a reconnaissance mission across the border to ascertain what might be done in that regard.

For five weeks, Koenig and his men mixed with the dock workers in Quebec harbour and reconnoitred the shipping lanes through the Great Lakes and down the St Lawrence river working out exactly what sort of numbers were involved in the Canadian mobilization and the routes their transports would take on the way to the coast. Valcartier military camp was where troops of the Canadian Expeditionary Force were massed before transferring to Quebec but ships from there would have to pass through the narrow channels either side of Orleans Island and it was here that Koenig believed that by blowing up bridges and sinking barges, the shipping lanes could be temporarily blocked.

Franz R. Wachendorf was something of an enigma in German intelligence. He had worked in German intelligence under Colonel Walter Nicolai on assignments ranging from burglary to blackmail. At the early age of 16, he had already been deported from Britain for forgery. He claims to have travelled to the US as a steward on the SS *Kroonland* in May 1912 but there is no record of an entry into the country under any of his known work names at that time. However, Franz R. Wachendorf is listed as having served as a private in the 19th Infantry in Galveston later that year. According to his own account, he was ordered by a German agent to abscond and cross the border to Mexico where he was recruited by Sommerfeld, who had been a German army veteran of the Boxer Rebellion and a reservist who had served as the head of Mexico's secret service under President Madero from 1911 to 1913.

There is no documentary evidence to support Wachendorf's claim that, in the revolutionary environment of the time, he was taken prisoner and tried as a spy. Despite being sentenced to death, he claimed that Otto Kueck, the German consul in Chihuahua, Mexico was able to intervene on his behalf and arrange a deal that saw him deported to the US instead.[9] He was directed to New York where, acting on instructions from Sommerfeld, he got in touch with von Papen who soon found work for him utilising his experience of handling explosives.

As early as 12 August 1914, four armed Germans had been arrested while crossing the St Lawrence river in a small boat which first alerted the Canadian security services to the danger of US-based espionage. This had been the first tentative step in what would become a major operation launched against Canada and Wachendorf was to take the next one. Carrying a passport in the name of Bridgeman H. Taylor, he was sent to Baltimore to act as liaison and cut-out between von Papen and an existing cell of trained saboteurs, run by Karl A. Luederitz. These were Charles Tuchendler, alias Charles J. Tucker, Alfred E. Fritzen, a Latvian-born intelligence agent, Frederick J. Busse, and the Italian, Constante Covani. They were to execute a plan first put forward by two leading members of the Sinn Féin Irish resistance movement, Thomas P. Tuite and John Devoy to dynamite railway junctions, grain elevators at Fort William, and the locks of the Welland Canal that joined Lake Erie to the western end of Lake Ontario.

Hans Tauscher arranged for the purchase of 100 kilograms of dynamite from DuPont on 5 September 1914 and monitored its transfer from a barge on the Hudson River near Black Tom Island not far from the Statue of Liberty. The explosive was then taken and stored at the home of Tuite while final plans were worked out. Ten days later, Koenig, Frederick Metzler and an Irishman, Edmund Justice, left for Burlington, Vermont with half of the dynamite while Fritzen, Busse, Covani, Wachendorf and Tuchendler went to Buffalo with the rest. Koenig's team was assigned to target Valcartier military camp and Quebec harbour.

Wachendorf received $400 to pay the wages of his team who were paid on a daily basis to keep them on a tight rein. He sat back and waited for instructions to proceed with the operation. It was known that it was planned that a large contingent of Canadian troops was scheduled for transport at the beginning of October but the plotters had not counted on the large Canadian security operation that had been put in place to protect them in transit. That was not all, the Canadians were acutely aware of the critical importance of the Welland Canal and had increased security all along its banks with 1,000 extra guards. It was clear that any attempt to carry out the operation was now fraught with complications. The troops were leaving camp and proceeding to Quebec harbour and still no word from von Papen. For some unexplained reason, Wachendorf and Covani returned to New York and when Koenig heard about that he pulled his team out also.

Whatever the reason for abandoning the Canadian operation, it had unnerved von Papen. He may have suspected that the Canadian police had got wind of it in which case he needed to cover his tracks in case they passed on the information to US authorities. He made a final payment to Wachendorf and put him on the SS *Duca d'Aosta* on 8 October 1914 for passage to Germany via Genoa but from then on, Wachendorf's account of what happened is suspect. He claims to have gone straight to Berlin and reported to the *Auswärtiges Amt* (German Foreign Office) on the 'conditions in Mexico and the United States' rather than *Abteilung III b* which is where he had been instructed to go by von Papen.[10] There he claims to have been debriefed and ordered to go back to the US via Rotterdam posing as an officer in the Mexican army but when he docked in England on the return trip, he decided to hand himself over to British intelligence. Why he should have done this is a mystery especially since he goes on to say that the British refused his offer to work for them and threw him into Pentonville prison instead. This story seems to be part of a smokescreen to obscure the events that saw Wachendorf become a double agent working for the British. The likelihood is that British agents had become aware that he was on the SS *Duca d'Aosta* and intercepted him before he got anywhere near Berlin. By means unspecified, they persuaded him to become a British agent and concocted a story to cover their tracks. Records show that he registered in a London hotel on 4 November 1914 in the name of Bridgeman Taylor from El Paso, Texas, US and that he was arrested ten days later as an unregistered alien. The Germans would have no way of knowing that he had been turned. He would be eventually handed over to the US courts to which he testified in great detail about German espionage operations in that country.

It is worth mentioning at this point an operation that had been supposedly planned by von Papen in which German reservists were to be mobilised to attack a number of communication hubs in Canada. Hundreds of thousands of rifles and hundreds of rounds of ammunition were said to have been in storage in German-American brewery warehouses in New York, Chicago, Buffalo, Philadelphia, Detroit, Milwaukee and other cities on the border. At 200 West Houston Street, New York, alone, were 2,000 45-calibre Colt revolvers, 10 Colt automatic guns, 7,000 Springfield rifles, 3 million revolver cartridges and 2.5 million rifle cartridges.[11] For this operation, Albert had apparently allocated a fund of $10 million and given it to Max Lynar Louden (aka

Max Scheimangk) to finance a force of 150,000 reservists divided into four divisions, with six sections. The first two divisions were to have assembled at Silver Creek, Michigan the seize the Welland Canal and Wind Mill Point, Ontario, Canada. The third was to go from Wilson, New York to Port Hope and the fourth was to proceed to Kingston, Ontario. The fifth was to assemble near Detroit and land near Windsor while the sixth section was to leave Cornwall and take possession of Ottawa.

There is not a scrap of evidence to support this invasion story but it is often included in accounts of German intelligence operations during the First World War essentially because after Louden's trial at which he proudly gave details of the supposed plot, it was made much of by the US and British press to get full propaganda value from it.[12] When Louden came to the attention of US intelligence agents, it was not long before they discovered that he had three wives, Amelia Wendt, Rose O'Brien and Nella Florence Allendorf. He already had a criminal record for stealing money collected for a charity and he was given three years in Sing Sing prison for bigamy.

The collapse of the Welland Canal operation forced von Papen to think again but it was still to Canada that he looked to strike a telling blow to the Entente Powers' war effort. On 3 January 1915, he received a telegram from Arthur Zimmermann at the *Auswärtiges Amt*. It read,

> With reference to my telegram, No. 257, Secret, The General Staff is anxious that vigorous measures should be taken to destroy the Canadian Pacific in several places for the purpose of causing a lengthy interruption of traffic. Captain BOEHM who is well known in America and who will shortly return to that country is furnished with expert information on that subject. Acquaint the Military Attaché with the above and furnish the sums required for the enterprise.[13]

Then on 23 January 1915, in a move that clearly authorised acts of war against the US, Rudolf Nadolny, Chief of the Political Section of the Imperial General Staff instructed the *Auswärtiges Amt,*

> To find suitable personnel for sabotage in the United States and Canada inquire with the following persons:

1) Joseph Mac Garrity [*sic*], 5412 Springfield Philadelphia, Pa.,
2) John P. Keating, Maryland Avenue Chicago,
3) Jeremia [*sic*] O'Leary, Park row [*sic*], New York.

> No. 1 and 2 completely reliable and discreet, No. 3 reliable, not always discreet. Persons have been named by Sir Roger Casement. In the United States sabotage can cover all kinds of factories for military supplies; railroads, dams, bridges there cannot be touched. Embassy can under no circumstances be compromised, neither can Irish-German propaganda.[14]

A report furnished by Albert in February 1915 shows just how much detailed information he had about war shipments in the US. He writes that the Bethlehem Steel Works were shipping 200 heavy naval guns on SS *Transylvania 2*, the Savage Arms Company were sending to Europe 50 Lewis machine guns every week, the Bridgeport Brass Company had an order for 1 million bullets for the French army and the Curtiss Aeroplane and Motor Company was supplying 400 aircraft to the British while the Russians were getting 25 locomotives shipped through Vladivostok.[15]

For this mission, von Papen chose a first lieutenant of the reserve in the German army, Werner Horn, who had been working in Guatemala. He had come to New York from Mexico on Boxing Day 1914 determined to do his bit for the fatherland. Had von Papen been aware at the time of Horn's deep psychological problems, said to stem from advanced syphilis, he might have been less enthusiastic about instructing Koenig to provide Horn with sixty vials of nitro-glycerine for the purpose of blowing up the 110-foot strategically important rail bridge over the Saint Croix River between Vanceboro, Maine and St Croix, New Brunswick.

On 1 February 1915, while Horn was staying at the Vanceboro Exchange Hotel, he laid the explosives over the border on the Canadian side of the bridge, getting his hands badly frost-bitten in the process. When they detonated, he was arrested but could not be charged with any crime because he was in the US and neither was he eligible for extradition. The explosions caused superficial damage to some iron beams on the bridge and it was only out of service for a few days.

Albert Carl Kaltschmidt was a leading light and prosperous factory owner in the German community in Detroit. On 27 January 1915, $2,000 had been deposited in his bank account from the banking firm of Knauth, Nachod and Kuhne, by von Igel, the German military attaché's secretary. This was a down payment for Kaltschmidt to set in motion an enterprise that is best described by the indictment that was later read out at his trial:

- To blow up the factory of the Peabody's Company Limited at Walkerville, Ontario [which was] engaged in the manufacture of uniforms, clothing and military supplies.
- To blow up … the building known as Windsor Armouries in the city of Windsor.
- To blow up and destroy other plants and buildings in said Dominion of Canada which were used for the manufacture of … munitions.
- To blow up and destroy the great railway bridges of the Canadian Pacific Railroad Company at Nipigon.
- To employ and to send into said Dominion of Canada spies to obtain military information.[16]

He took on two German reservists, Richard Herman and William Jarosch who had been sent to him by the German consul general in Chicago, Count Kurt von Reiswitz. Their task was to go to Duluth and buy explosives which they brought back to Detroit to make bombs to blow up the Detroit Screw Works, the St Clair tunnel running under the Detroit River from Port Huron, Michigan, to Sarnia, Ontario, and tunnels of the Canadian Pacific Railroad in the Selkirk mountains. Kaltschmidt then hired Charles Francis Respa and showed him two elaborate time-clock devices for detonating the bombs. Respa took the clocks to Windsor, Ontario where they met up with William Lefler, the night watchman of the Peabody Overall factory in Walkerville. Lefler already had the dynamite which had been taken over the border under the front seat of Kaltschmidt's car. Respa attached the clocks and set the charges before taking the last ferry back to Detroit. The factory bomb exploded but the other charge failed to explode. The Canadian provincial detectives arrested Lefler and through him learned about Respa's role. Respa was extradited, tried and sentenced to life imprisonment. Lefler got ten years.[17] Others complicit in the plot, all of whom were later given prison sentences were Franz Bopp, German consul in San Francisco, US Baron Eckhart H. von Schack, German vice consul, Lieutenant Wilhelm von Brincken, attaché of German Consulate, Charles C. Crowley, detective for German consul, and Mrs Margaret W. Cornell, secretary to Crowley. At his later trial, Kaltschmidt was found guilty on three counts, sentenced to four years in Leavenworth Penitentiary and fined $20,000.

Having spent a small fortune, von Bernstorff and his crew had proved to be spectacularly incompetent so far with almost nothing to show for their travails. Albert, Dernburg, Boy-Ed and von Papen's efforts up to the end of 1914 had had virtually no impact on the war effort. Albert's

Secret War Council had been starved of funds that might have made a difference and, crucially, there had been no strategic plan governing their activities. The Imperial General Staff arrived at the conclusion that von Papen did not recruit the right people, did not manage his projects well, and took too much time. They had seen enough and decided to send someone from Germany to work alongside Albert but, crucially, a man who would not hesitate to work independently on his own initiative if the occasion demanded it. The man they chose was a naval intelligence officer, Franz von Rintelen who arrived in New York on 3 April 1915.

He had first visited the US ten years earlier as a representative of the Disconto-Gesellschaft one of Germany's biggest banks and he had already spent time in London working for the Deutsche Bank where he had perfected his spoken and written English. Tall, thin and athletic looking, von Rintelen was popular and made many important contacts when he spent three years in New York working for one of the most powerful investment banks in the US, Kuhn, Loeb & Co., in Manhattan.[18] Through these contacts he acquired membership of the prestigious New York Yacht Club in 1906. He went from New York to Mexico before returning to Germany to work for the Disconto-Gesellschaft, a large Berlin-based commercial bank with far-reaching international connections. He married Emilie 'Milly' von Kaufmann, the daughter of a Jewish-German university professor.

By January 1915, he was a director of the Nationalbank für Deutschland as well as working as a consultant financial expert for the *Deutscher Flottenverein* (German Navy League) in charge of publicity with the rank of lieutenant commander and working directly for Grand Admiral Alfred von Tirpitz. Apart from von Papen, he was well acquainted with all the other members of the Secret War Council in New York and was familiar with their mission and problems. Boy-Ed had known and worked closely with him since the start of the First World War and Albert knew of him through funding of his operations.

On paper, von Rintelen seemed to be a perfect choice to revitalise the US espionage programme, but he was reckless and something of a braggart. When he arrived in New York his mission was to interfere with the flow of munitions going from the US to the Entente Powers, especially Russia. He was carrying two important documents: a Swiss passport that identified him as Emil Victor Gasché and a *Kaiserpass* signed by the Federal Minister of Foreign Affairs, which requested that all German representatives in the US give the bearer whatever assistance he called for. The latter document was particularly galling for von Bernstorff, von Papen and Boy-Ed who were less than pleased to see this man coming in and apparently taking over the espionage network. The disdain was mutual, von Rintelen decided that he would have as little as possible to do with these resident agents and proceeded to set up his own 'Manhattan Front'. By day he prowled the waterfronts making contacts amongst the idle crews of the eighty or so impounded German ships and Irish stevedores whose hatred for the British easily matched that of the Germans but by night, he dressed up and socialised with the business community where he was remembered with fondness and still had many acquaintances.

Once he had settled in, he opened an account with the Transatlantic Trust Company in the name of von Rintelen and had $800,000 transferred into it from Berlin. Millions more were deposited in various banks across the country. He registered a company, E.V. Gibbon, Inc., importers and exporters, through which he began purchasing supplies with the intention of sending them to Germany. With the help of Captain Gustave Steinberg, a naval reservist, he chartered ships and dispatched them under false manifests to Italy and Norway, where their cargoes could be readily smuggled into Germany. One of his contacts from whom he bought supplies was Walter Scheele, described as 'a quiet, reserved man, who is constantly in deep thought, and very preoccupied' who was still retained by the German army as an intelligence officer.[19]

Scheele had been born in Cologne in 1865 and had earned a doctorate in chemistry from the University of Freiburg. He emigrated to the US in 1890. He worked initially for the Bayer chemical company but had branched out and formed his own company, the New Jersey Agricultural and Chemical Company of Bogota (New Jersey) with a $10,000 donation from Albert. Here he was able to implement new processes that he had invented for solidifying oils and lubricants, which could be packaged and shipped to Germany falsely manifested as artificial fertiliser. He had also devised methods of producing artificial rubber and concealing it much the same way. Much of this found its way to Germany in contravention of US government restrictions. A tireless inventor, he had also created new explosives, rapidly accelerating incendiary chemicals, timed incendiary devices and artillery missiles propelled by compressed air. Scheele had been approached by von Papen after the German Consulate had received orders, on 6 January 1915, to restrict the shipment of munitions from the US to the Entente Powers in Europe.

Realising that bombs big enough to cause significant damage to ships would need to be very large and difficult to carry and put in place, under cover of his own factory, Scheele now invented a small incendiary device that was quickly nicknamed the 'cigar bomb' because of its shape and size. Because it could be timed to detonate after so many days, this device could easily be smuggled onto ships and hidden in the holds so that it would explode after the ship had set sail. The shell of the bomb was made of lead, which could be easily moulded into shape. Inside a copper disc bisected the bomb vertically. Sulphuric acid filled the upper compartment and when a seal was broken, it would start to eat through the disc and come into contact with potassium chlorate in the lower compartment producing chloric acid and potassium sulphate, which spontaneously ignite with an intensely hot flame melting the lead casing leaving no trace. The timing of the bomb could be regulated from two to fifteen days by the thickness or thinness of the copper disk. The device was inexpensive, dependable, easily concealed and untraceable. Cargos of sugar were especially susceptible to these firebombs.

Much to von Papen's chagrin, von Rintelen now recruited Scheele to the Manhattan Front and gave him enough money to go back and start manufacturing his cigar bombs in quantity. Another of his recruits was Ernst Becker, an electrician on the North German Lloyd liner *Friedrich der Grosse*, tied up at Hoboken, who worked in collusion with Captain Enno Bode, pier superintendent of the Hamburg-American Line and Captain Otto Wolpert, pier superintendent of the Atlas Line, to turn the ship into a veritable bomb-making factory. Quantities of lead and copper sheets from Scheele's factory in Hoboken were smuggled on board where they were cut, shaped and soldered together by teams of sailors before being returned to Scheele who completed the highly dangerous process of filling them with the chemicals. Once the wax seals were in place each device became a ticking time bomb with the copper plate eroding inexorably towards the moment of detonation. It is estimated that well over 1,000 of these cigar bombs were produced in 1915 and yet more in 1916 according to records showing more purchases of lead in January.[20]

Scheele's device had already been tested before von Rintelen's arrival. As early as 3 January 1915, there was an explosion on board the munitions ship *Orton*, lying in Erie Basin, a part of New York Harbor. On 6 February 1915, a bomb was found in the cargo of the *Hannington*. On 27 February 1915, the *Carlton* caught fire at sea.

On 7 February 1915, the British freighter SS *Grindon Hall* caught on fire in Norfolk harbour. Ten days later, the Italian steamer *Regina d'Italia* loaded with oil, kerosene and cotton burst into flames at Pier B in Jersey City, New Jersey. On 27 February 1915, the *Carlton* caught fire at sea, on 17 March 1915 the SS *La Touraine* caught fire in mid-Atlantic

500 miles off the coast of Ireland and on 11 April 1915 Italian steamer SS *San Guglielmo* burst into flames in Naples harbour, all having sailed from New York. The list of target ships had been drawn up by a German lawyer, Karl Max Schimmel and many other informants in banks, shipping offices and harbour workers.

Serious fires also severely damaged the American warship USS *Oklahoma* in the Camden, New Jersey, shipyard and two more US Navy ships mysteriously caught on fire in the Philadelphia navy shipyard a few weeks later. The US government claimed that these were the result of accidents but the *Philadelphia Evening Ledger* quoted unofficial government spokesmen in Washington DC as saying, 'The fire on the *Oklahoma* strengthened the suspicion that the United States is being subjected to the hostile activities of partisans of the war in Europe.'[21]

It was not only ships that caught fire. On 18 January 1915, a large steel mill of the and the Roebling's Sons Company in Trenton, New Jersey, that specialised in steel wires and produced anti-submarine netting and artillery chains for the Entente Powers, caught on fire and burned to the ground. In addition, authorities suspected that seventeen major fires that occurred in Pennsylvania, New Jersey and Maryland in 1915 were the handiwork of German agents. Several munitions plants of DuPont, the Aetna factory in Grove Run, New York, Bethlehem Steel in Pennsylvania, the Baldwin Locomotive Company in Eddystone, New Jersey, John A. Roebling and Sons in Trenton for a second time all blew up or caught on fire that year. On 10 December 1915, enormous quantities of wheat were destroyed by fire in grain elevators at Erie and on the same day an explosion had occurred at the Hopewell plant of the DuPont works. Investigations showed that in many cases Germans, under assumed names, had obtained work in the factory; and then, shortly after the fire or explosion, had disappeared. When Federal agents tried to track them down they were found to have escaped to Germany or Mexico.

Scheele's group did not escape detection, however but he managed to flee to Havana, Cuba at the start of 1916 but after US agents intercepted letters he had sent to his wife still in the US, he was tracked down living under a false name and extradited in March 1918. He subsequently agreed to switch sides and proceeded to work for the US on multiple bomb designs and air propelled artillery shells and agreed make available a host of other inventions he had in his repertoire. As part of the deal he was obliged to transfer his firebomb patents to the United States Navy. The elimination of Scheele did not, however, prevent further incendiary attacks in 1916 when there were a dozen major explosions in DuPont factories alone with many casualties.

Two armaments plants at Bridgeport, Connecticut were blown up and an explosion in May wiped out a large chemical plant in Cadillac, Michigan. A munitions works of the Bethlehem Steel Company at Newcastle, Pennsylvania was also destroyed. It is important to note that many explosions in munitions factories were not caused by sabotage but simply by poor management. New factories had sprung up in response to the demand for products that were inherently dangerous and many accidents were the result of poor management and inexperienced, poorly-trained workers.

Before 1914, the German government had maintained well-placed secret agents within the Mexican ruling elites and in the revolutionary leadership, the most important of which was Felix Sommerfeld. Born into a wealthy Jewish family in Schneidemühl he joined the German Secret Service and moved to Chihuahua, Mexico in 1908. He manoeuvred himself into a close relationship with Mexican President Francisco Madero and became an intelligence asset for the German ambassador in Mexico, Rear Admiral Paul von Hintze establishing a network of agents along the Mexican-US border. When Mexican army general Victoriano Huerta launched the violent Decena Trágica coup d'état and killed Madero. Sommerfeld joined his secret service organization in the battle against the usurper. He worked closely with the American military and the US Department of Justice (DOJ), as well as the US Department of State and became a vital link in the revolutionary supply chain of smuggled arms and ammunition to for both rebel leaders Venustiano Carranza and Pancho Villa while his contacts in the highest echelons of the American and German governments shut off credit and supplies for Huerta's government. He eventually sided with Villa and became his unofficial diplomatic envoy in the US. In this role he became well known and generally well liked by the American public and cultivated friendships in the highest reaches of the US government.[22] He was to lay the foundation of future collaboration with US munitions manufacturers by brokering arms deals between the German and Mexican governments apparently with the approval of the US government who turned a blind eye to the blatant violations of US laws.

Up until the start of the First World War, Sommerfeld had managed to maintain productive relations between his Mexican employers, the Imperial German Empire, and the US government but he would need all his wits about him to steer his way through the diplomatic storms ahead. Noted for his intelligent and bravado, his daredevil and reckless persona had seen him at various times in the roles of soldier, prospector, revolutionary, businessman and spy. Whilst being the sort of heroic character that attracted admiration from some, he was not necessarily the sort of man that they might want to follow into battle. As the largest oil-producing country in the world and one engulfed in violent revolution, Mexico was of strategic importance to Germany and it was to Sommerfeld, with his close connection to Villa, that they turned to implement German clandestine missions in Mexico now that he was firmly ensconced in his extravagantly expensive three-room suite at the Hotel Astor in New York and both Sommerfeld and Stallforth reporting to Boy-Ed. His extensive contacts in Mexico as well as amongst the large contingent of Mexican exiles in the US made him the ideal choice but meanwhile the situation in Mexico was becoming dire. Huerta's government forces were facing defeat by the Carranza-Villa coalition, but the two revolutionary leaders were on the point of falling out with each other and the US pondered which horse to back. Huerta had enjoyed a close working relationship with Kaiser Wilhelm II and when his position became untenable in July 1914 it was to Jamaica that he fled on the Germany light cruiser, the SS *Dresden* before eventually going into exile in Spain.

Sommerfeld now found himself in the role of a trusted adviser and liaison between Mexico and the US government. He would frequently be called on by Secretary of War Lindley Miller Garrison and Secretary of State William Jennings Bryan for advice, which put him in a position to influence US foreign policy and military strategy. This changed dramatically in summer 1914 when the war in Europe completely overshadowed events in Mexico, which now became consigned to the back pages of the newspapers. Russian, French and British agents swarmed into the US throwing money at the relatively small munitions industry there causing a massive price-hike. US arms manufacturers forgot about Mexico, and Sommerfeld could not even get supplies from the German arms trading agency of Hans Tauscher in New York. His lucrative source of income dried up overnight.

Because of his contacts with Carranza, the acting president, and Villa, Sommerfeld was now drawn into negotiations to broker peace between the two warring factions whose activities were threatening to spill over onto US soil. A series of border raids were launched from Mexico along the lower Rio Grande Valley with the ambitious but unlikely objective of recovering 'Texas, New Mexico, Arizona, and upper California [US] of which states the Republic of Mexico was robbed in a most perfidious manner by North American imperialism.'[23] This clear threat to US sovereignty had required the US government to station more than 7,000 troops along its Mexican border at the end of 1914.

Over the previous twelve months, Sommerfeld had the seen the US teeter on the brink of war with Mexico three times. The first episode resulted from the murder of William S. Benton in February 1914, possibly on Villa's orders when Sommerfeld had brokered a deal with Villa that had alienated Carranza. Then when an arms delivery on the German steamship SS *Ypiranga* in April 1915 precipitated a full-scale US invasion of the port city of Veracruz, Sommerfeld was again called in to diffuse the tension. Now he had been so instrumental in calming things and finding grounds for compromise that General Scott had noted in his memoirs that 'I owe him gratitude for services to our Government in Mexico that he freely and faithfully rendered without thought of compensation, as a duty to our Government and in friendliness to me.'[24]

Now that tensions in Europe were drawing the continent closer to war, Sommerfeld saw President Wilson's dilemma by having to commit the majority of his available regular forces to the Mexican theatre and this became the basis of his subsequent strategy in 1915 and 1916. The border remained a powder keg that he would be able to ignite with little effort. It would be relatively easy for him to precipitate an armed incursion of Mexican raiders with the unavoidable consequence of American civilian deaths. German war planners understood perfectly well that the US-Mexican border was a prime opportunity for creating trouble for the US government by diverting its attention away from Europe. This was especially true of the oil-producing region around Tampico which fuelled the sizeable British fleet in Atlantic waters but plans to dynamite the oilfields was called off by Berlin at the last minute.

An Irish-American businessman called Andrew Meloy now came into the picture. Like Stallforth, he had lost a fortune after the rebels had ousted Huerta and he now travelled to Berlin to put to the Germans a plan to form a coalition of Mexican exiles, Manuel Mondragón, General Aureliano Blanquet and Felix Díaz with the intention of reinstating Huerta to the presidency. Amazingly, he had also contacted Carranza's representatives in the US and Villa's man, Sommerfeld. He hoped that with the full support of the US government backed up with German cash, he could find a solution to please them all. Sensing that the time was ripe for a counterrevolution, Huerta left Spain in late March 1915 on the Spanish steamer *Lopez* and despite urgent calls from the Mexican government to deny him entry, landed in New York on 12 April 1915. Carranza and Villas were unreconciled, but Sommerfeld and Stallforth had encouraged Meloy in his belief that he could broker a peace deal primarily so that they could maximise the amount of intelligence that could be gleaned from talks between the different factions.

According to British intelligence Sommerfeld, who worked closely with Boy-Ed agreed with him in early May 1915 that the Huerta plot was not worth supporting and decided instead to manipulate it to bring about a state of war between the US and Mexico. Meloy had been foolish enough to involve von Rintelen, who was now operating under the alias of 'Hansen' so the first thing Sommerfeld did was to quietly inform *The New York Herald* of Hansen's true identity. The full glare of publicity curbed von Rintelen's activities somewhat but he could never resist boasting about how important he was and how he had access to 'unlimited funds', which only increased the level of surveillance he was now placed under by US intelligence.[25]

Meloy's plot started to unravel when Carranza backed out and refused to negotiate causing Huerta's man, Mondragón, upon whom Meloy had placed so much hope, to remove himself from the talks also. Huerta did not lose faith, however, and Sommerfeld was buying up huge quantities of arms and ammunition from Western Cartridge Company, Peters Cartridge Company and Winchester Arms Company all of which found their way to the various competing factions on both sides of the Mexican border.[26] On 24 June 1915, Huerta and a group of his closest advisers boarded a train for San Francisco but changed at Chicago and, instead, took a train to Kansas City, where they changed again and headed for El Paso. In the early hours of 27 June 1915, the train stopped at Newman in New Mexico where Huerta had arranged to meet the businessman Pascual Orozco. Even before the train had arrived, newspapers were reporting that Huerta was on his way to Mexico to start a new revolution. DOJ agents and federal troops were waiting at the station to arrest him and Orozco. Huerta was formally charged with conspiracy to violate United States neutrality laws. Both were released on bail, but Orozco fled and went into hiding before US marshals hunted him down and killed him in a gunfight on 30 August 1915. Huerta, who had become dependent on alcohol during his exile, became ill with liver problems. He underwent two unsuccessful operations in Fort Bliss Military Hospital and died of complications on 13 January 1916.

It has been accepted as fact that Huerta's plot was financed with German money as reported in *The Providence Journal* at the time but no evidence had come to light in any archive to support this claim.[27] The story of German patrons buying 8 million rounds of ammunition in St Louis, Missouri, US depositing a total of $895,000 in various Cuban and Mexican bank accounts in Huerta's name and promising to supply the Mexicans with 10,000 rifles which would be dropped off along the Mexican coast by German U-boats should be considered fiction. The accounts of von der Golz and von Rintelen's involvement come mostly from books written by them and, as with much of what they wrote, is of dubious value. For instance von der Golz's claim that he was given 'authority to spend almost unlimited sums of money for the purchase of arms, for the bribery of officials-for anything in fact that would cause trouble in Mexico,' should be treated with caution.[28] The only money von Rintelen is known to have disbursed for the Huerta-Orozco-Mondragón conspiracy is a cheque for $10,000 paid to Meloy on 16 July 1915. The general consensus is that Huerta financed his coup attempt with money that he had taken with him when he had fled Mexico in 1914.[29]

Even while von Rintelen was heavily engaged in the Mexican conspiracy, he was planning yet more, this time to restrict the sale of arms to the Allies in Europe. His target now was American labour and in this intrigue he elicited the cooperation of a totally unscrupulous confidence trickster called David Lamar, who had been only recently released after having served a term of imprisonment for impersonating a congressman. Lamar had at one time swindled John Rockefeller Jr out of $1 million.

The idea was to persuade union leaders to bring out munition workers on strike on the pretext of keeping the US out of the First World War. Two of von Rintelen's agents offered Samuel Gompers, president of the National Federation of Labour, $500,000 to endorse and finance a peace propaganda campaign but he turned them down. In June 1915, a big advertising campaign had been started in newspapers across the country promoting the idea of US neutrality; Lamar was able to convince politicians such as Congressman Frank Buchanan and H. Robert Fowler to support the cause. Soon thousands of invitations were sent to labour leaders, small and large, and to heads of farmers' granges, to attend a national convention. All railroad fares, hotel expenses and a liberal allowance for spending money were promised. The conference adopted resolutions to promote peace and called on the US government to administer and regulate all businesses associated with arms manufacture and export.

Huge sums of money were regularly being drawn from von Rintelen's Transatlantic Trust Company account and in some instances, handed over in suitcases. In an expensive but fruitless operation, lawsuits were filed against banks, manufacturers, shipping companies and port authorities accused of violating US neutrality laws but all were dismissed. Underneath this cloak, however, von Rintelen's real purpose was playing out.

By means of what was later termed 'solicitation, persuasion and exhortation [and] other means and methods ... decided as the occasion arose', he attempted to bribe officers of labour unions to call out their men on strike. They were successful with regard to the Standard Oil plant in Bayonne, New Jersey, the General Electrics Plant in Schenectady and the Remington Arms Company in Bridgeport, Connecticut. On the docks, over $1 million was paid out to longshoremen all along the Pacific and Atlantic coasts to walk out and stay out for one month and bring all shipping to a halt. Not content with that, von Rintelen also devised other schemes in munition factories to stop or delay the production of materials destined for Europe. He sent trained German reservists to get employment in factories with orders to collect information and do what they could to cause trouble. He also employed organised criminal gangs to steal from and cause damage to ships being loaded with supplies in New York Harbor.

When his funds had dwindled to about $40,000 with little to show for it, von Rintelen questioned Lamar about the effectiveness of the latter's management of some of the projects but von Rintelen was rapidly running out of friends in the US. His incessant indiscretion and inferiority complex that caused him to constantly exaggerate his importance was bringing far too much attention from the US press and intelligence services. He told anyone who wanted to listen that his powers exceeded those of the German ambassador. Boy-Ed persuaded Berlin that it was high time to recall him, which they did and he boarded SS *Noordam* in early August 1915. Meloy and his wife accompanied him. Because of constant surveillance, however, von Rintelen was unable to get a new passport and had to use his Gasché one. A routine search of the ship in Ramsgate harbour alerted British intelligence who removed von Rintelen, arrested him and took him to a prison camp at Donnington Hall. Stallforth could hardly contain his pleasure telling Berlin how much better things were after the collapse of the Mexican plot. He also urged Berlin to hang on to Meloy 'on some pretext or other so that he will not again make such a furore here'.[30] In the US, von Rintelen was indicted on the charge of forgery on the passport application, and upon that basis, an application was made to the English authorities for his extradition. Over a year later, he was extradited to the US tried and found guilty in a Federal court in New York, and imprisoned for four years. He stands out as the most reckless, most extravagant and most extraordinary German agent sent to the US. Boy-Ed and von Papen conveniently claimed that von Rintelen was the root cause of all German intelligence failures in the US ever since he set foot there. Spending an enormous amount of money, he had tried to foment war between the United States and Mexico, had violated many American neutrality laws and had attacked American institutions with the aim of causing industrial stagnation but his record of achievement was limited. His Mexican plans were a failure. The few strikes he started were quickly settled.

On 4 February 1915, Germany authorised a campaign designed to completely eliminate the export of munitions to Europe from the US by announcing unrestricted submarine warfare against commercial shipping. The waters around Great Britain and Ireland were designated as a war zone where neutral shipping may be attacked if they were suspected of carrying war materials. This threw the German diplomatic mission in Washington DC into turmoil and risked drawing the US into the First World War directly as a belligerent but the gamble was that direct US involvement would not materially affect the war in Europe whilst the submarine blockade restricting US munition to Europe would be hugely beneficial to Germany. President Wilson objected to the submarine blockade in the strongest terms but he was in no position to do anything about it. Meanwhile, Koenig's men knew exactly which passenger ships leaving US ports were carrying contraband munitions and consequently so did the U-boat commanders. Some British ships such as the Cunard liner RMS *Lusitania* flew US flags to avoid becoming targets as they entered the designated war zone, even though many carried munitions, and this infuriating many US politicians.

In April 1915, a total of thirty-seven ships were sunk by U-boats causing the British government to institute effective countermeasures. Mine fields were laid to protect British shipping lanes and the use of false flagging continued. Large passenger liners could easily outpace submarines and the US and British press mocked German attempts to strike at them. After the sinking of the British steamer SS *Cambank, The New York Times,* however cautioned on 21 February 1915 that 'the presence of a German submarine near the route which the Atlantic liners take on their way to and from Liverpool, and along which many steamers pass daily, is bound to cause uneasiness.'[31] Von Bernstorff placed an advertisement in that same newspaper on 1 May 1915 advising passengers planning to board the RMS *Lusitania* at Pier 54 in New York to think twice. It was not normal for von Bernstorff to give such warnings, which suggests he may have had some foreknowledge of what followed. The Cunard press agent responded to his caution by saying 'I have no fear of [submarines] whatever'.[32] According to its manifest, the ship set sail with 1,257 passengers and 702 crew members but it also carried over 4,200 cases of small arms munitions, 1,000 rounds each, and 1,250 cases of empty shrapnel casings in her hold.

The *Lusitania* would normally have docked in Liverpool within five days but for some reason she fired up only three of her four boilers and was still at sea on 6 May 1915 when the German submarine *U-20* under the command of the 30-year-old Walter Schwieger found itself cruising near the Old Head of Kinsale on its way to patrol off Liverpool. *U-20* had already sunk the British steamers, SS *Centurion* and SS *Candidate,* two cargo ships, without warning. Despite specific warnings sent to the RMS *Lusitania* after these *U-20* attacks, her Captain Bill Turner, took his ship straight into the Channel at reduced speed taking no evasive measures. Thick fog on the following morning caused him to sound her fog horns once every minute broadcasting her position for miles around. The ship was essentially a sitting target for any lurking U-boat. It may be that Turner thought the fog would protect him.

Just after noon, Schwieger intercepted the liner and launched a torpedo from 700 metres distance striking her and creating an explosion, which was closely followed by a second more massive one. Traditionally it has been accepted that one of the ship's boilers exploded but surveys of the wreck now indicate that the point of impact was the forward coal bunker that had been converted into a secondary magazine. The loss of fuel storage may also have been the reason for the ship's slow progress. Eighteen minutes after the torpedo struck, the *Lusitania* disappeared beneath the waves with the loss of 1,198 lives, 128 of whom were Americans.

Speculation is rife, but with no conclusive evidence either way there is no consensus, over whether Schwieger came upon the *Lusitania* as a result of happenstance or whether the sinking of a passenger ship was a premeditated act authorised by the High Command of the German navy. The circumstantial evidence supporting premeditation is described by Heribert von Feilitzsch in his book *The Secret War on the United States in 1915* as overwhelming.

Spontaneous demonstrations against Germany broke out in New York and other large cities. Insurance premiums for neutral shippers soared. The US demanded that Germany cease all submarine attacks on unarmed merchant ships. Germany expressed its deepest sympathy at the loss of American lives but insisted that the ship had been carrying munitions for the Entente Powers and was therefore a legitimate target. President Wilson came under extreme pressure to respond but insisted that he should 'do nothing that might by any possibility involve us in the war'.[33] Instead he ordered his secret service to begin surveillance on German and Austrian embassy staff. Wire taps were set up and extra federal agents were brought into Washington DC and New York. There was now a twenty-man team employed full time trailing suspected German agents.

One of the men they followed was George Sylvester Viereck, an American publisher of a fiercely pro-German newspaper *The Fatherland*. He also wrote articles for the *German-American Economic Bulletin* and *Today's Challenge* in which he reminisced about his personal encounters with Adolf Hitler. His personal strategy was to keep a low profile and work behind the scenes persuading pro-isolationist campaigners to set up organizations such as the Make Europe Pay Its War Debt Committee and the Islands for War Debt Committee.

Viereck was born in Munich but had lived in the US since graduating from the College of the City of New York in 1906. He was a man of 'many talents and enormous energies',[34] and quickly earned a reputation as a poet, at one point called 'the most widely discussed young literary man in the United States'.[35] He became a devoted Germanophile, so much so that by 1915 he was being called 'the soul of pro-German propaganda in the United States.'

A series of government post-First World War investigations into German propaganda efforts would later reveal that Viereck benefitted financially from his pro-German activities, but he rode out the storm of his public disgrace in relative calm apart from an incident where he narrowly escaped from a lynch mob.

When Viereck met up with another man on 24 July 1915 at the offices of the Hamburg-American Line, they were followed by two detectives and all four men took the elevated train at 6th Avenue station. Viereck got off first, followed by one of the detectives, W.H. Houghton, and the other, Frank Burke, stayed with the second man.

Burke version of what happened next was given in *The Milwaukee Journal* of 20 July 1942 in an article entitled 'The Man Who Revealed German Plan in First War Leaves Secret Service.'

> a young woman boarded the car and took the vacant seat beside Dr. Albert and began reading a book. To reach his home, Albert had to take another car at 59th str., but when the train reached that point he was reading and was not aware that the train had halted until it was about to proceed again. The stuffed brief case [*sic*] was between Dr. Albert and the side of the car. When it occurred to him that he must get off, he jumped up and told the guard to wait a minute. As he got to the platform, the young woman called that he had forgotten his brief case [*sic*]. Burke told the girl the case was his, grabbed it up and headed for the station platform by another exit from the car … Dr. Albert meanwhile was

> struggling to get back into the car, his passage impeded by a fat woman in the doorway. By this time Burke had reached the platform, looked back and saw that Dr. Albert was visibly agitated. Other passengers on the platform provided Burke with some concealment, but the stairway leading to the street was beyond the excited German. Sparring for time, Burke partially concealed the briefcase under his coat, and leaning against the platform wall, acted as if he were having trouble lighting a cigar. Dr. Albert glanced hastily about the platform, then dashed downstairs to the street below. Burke followed him. Dr. Albert was in an increasingly disturbed frame of mind. He walked out into the street, the better to scan the line of pedestrians. As an open trolley car clanged past, Burke ran out and leaped on its running board. But Dr. Albert had seen him and began pursuit. Burke told the trolley conductor the man pursuing them was deranged, so the car did not stop for him.[36]

The man who lost his briefcase was none other than Heinrich Albert who rode the train between his office at 45 Broadway and his Ritz-Carlton hotel room every day and had no reason to believe that his briefcase had been taken by anyone other than an opportunist thief. Unaware that it was now in the possession of US federal agents, more in hope than expectation, he placed an advertisement in the *New York Evening Telegram* on 27 July 1915. It read: 'Lost on Saturday. On 3:30 [pm] Harlem Elevated Train, at 50th St. Station, Brown Leather Bag, Containing Documents. Deliver to G.H. Hoffman, 5 E. 47th St., Against $20. Reward.'

Burke had taken the briefcase to his boss, William Flynn, who sent a message to the Secretary of the Treasury William Gibbs McAdoo who had for some time been trying to uncover German espionage rings. When President Wilson was informed, he was left in no doubt about the extent to which German consular officials were violating neutrality laws but he could not go public with the information due to the way in which it had been acquired. To cause maximum embarrassment to the German government, however, Wilson gave permission for the *New York World* newspaper to publish of the contents of the briefcase.

The paper duly identified Albert as a German master spy, who, along with von Papen, had arranged many of the sabotage operations with the approval of the German military general staff. Other documents showed how Germany had set up a proxy company, the Bridgeport Projectile Company in Connecticut, to buy up large quantities of raw materials for the manufacture of munitions. They would then sign contracts with British purchasing agents to supply armaments but then prevaricate and delay endlessly so that the orders were never fulfilled. Other bogus companies had bought up large quantities of chlorine gas and carbolic acid to prevent their export. Almost the whole of German secret service activities in the US were made public. To divert attention from their role, the US authorities, however, claimed that the briefcase had been stolen by British agents. Albert did not have diplomatic immunity at the time, so to save him from prosecution, von Bernstorff quickly made him a commercial attaché. Later, von Papen would write to his wife saying that 'Albert could hardly have chosen a more unfortunate set of documents to carry about with him and lose.'[37] The press now swarmed all over the German diplomats asking awkward questions and vilifying them in print but more worrying for them was that the US secret service now pulled out all the stops and the twenty-man surveillance team soon became a small army.

It was on 27 September 1915 that Koenig took two of his best men, Richard Emil Leyendecker and Frederick Metzler, to Buffalo and made a thorough reconnoitre of the Welland Canal and its numerous locks. He had earlier sent George Fuchs who had reported back that the most vulnerable spot where most damage would be done was where Chippewa River joined the canal. The plan was to row a boatload of dynamite across the upper Niagara River into Canada. US agents had followed them all, however, and extra guards were posted all along the canal. While waiting for Koenig to decide on a date for the attack, Fuchs became ill with flu and went missing for a few days. Fuchs was furious when Koenig withheld some of his wages and, under the pretext of his constant arguing, drinking and disorderly habits, fired him.

US agents who had been keeping a close eye on Koenig and his associates, recognised that Fuchs was now a weak link and one that should be broken. They picked him up and persuaded him to talk in return for amnesty. A search of Koenig's house turned up a little black, loose-leaf book in which he had meticulously kept a record of all his agents and their assignments right up to the previous day. The notebook was a virtual operational history of the *Abteilung III b* network in America and was described by the New York police department as 'unquestionably one of the richest prizes of the spy hunt in America.'[38] Schleindl was one of those caught in the net. His arrest sent shock waves through Manhattan's financial district where hurried measures were taken to ensure that details of munition deals were much more closely guarded.

Koenig was indicted for violating Section 13 of the Penal Code. He was charged, along with Leyendecker, with a 'military enterprise' to cause damage or destruction to the Welland Canal and also charged with an Irishman Edmund Justice, with 'attempting to obtain military information in Canada for the German government to use against the

King of Great Britain and Ireland'. All charges against Metzler were dropped and he appeared as a witness for the prosecution. Koenig was not brought to trial but simply interned as an enemy alien.[39]

Von Rintelen had been exposed through questioning of the Austrian banker with the Transatlantic Trust Company, George Plochmann. His three-month stay in the US might, with some justification, be seen as a disaster. His Prussian arrogance, almost total lack of discretion and inflated ego had brought him to the attention of the US intelligence almost immediately upon his arrival and thereafter all with whom he came into contact also came under suspicion. It had been his transfer of $508,000 to Boy-Ed that exposed the naval attaché and led to his eventual recall to Germany. The ship-bombing plot had been uncovered and further evidence of German government involvement in the organising, financing, and execution of espionage was overwhelming. In November 1915, President Wilson announced an increase in the size of the US Army by 140,000, the embryonic Central Intelligence Agency (CIA) was created, and the government decided it was time to bring German agents to trial. Robert Fay, Paul Daeche and Walter Scholz were convicted of sabotaging ships and while Boy-Ed and von Papen were clearly implicated alongside them, they were protected by diplomatic immunity. That didn't prevent US Secretary of State Robert Lansing demanding that Berlin recall them.

That was far from the end of German espionage, however. These high-profile cases may have succeeded but the US security organs were still poorly coordinated and there was still a serious lack of legal means to combat clandestine activity. There were plenty of German agents still at large and the one who now stepped up to fill the void left by von Rintelen was the banker Frederico Stallforth. Although by no means experienced in espionage, he was the best they could come up with. Stallforth had for some time been making himself useful to Albert by finding couriers and establishing links with German-American businessmen who were willing to finance clandestine operations and nobody else could match his knowledge of operational finances or agent networks. One of the advantages of using Stallforth was that he seemed to fly very much under the radar of US intelligence who obviously knew about him through his connection with von Rintelen but thought him to be fairly harmless. He was called up before a Grand Jury in March 1916 but his lawyer told him that

> the authorities of the United States [are] satisfied that you were not connected with nor guilty of any violation of any laws of the United States, and of your thorough and sincere desire to promote the friendly

> relations between this country and Germany, and that you have to that end made every effort in good faith.[40]

Stallforth took control of $75,000 that von Rintelen had left behind and continued to fund the firebombing of ships but there is evidence that some of it went towards relieving his own somewhat straitened financial situation that had existed since losing his personal fortune in the Mexican revolution. One of Stallforth's first operations was to finance the work of a young American doctor, Anton Dilger. At von Rintelen's suggestion, *Abteilung III b*, had recruited Dilger, to carry out an act of sabotage to stem the flow of horses and mules going to the war front. Dilger had been born to German immigrants in 1884 on a farm in Front Royal, Virginia. He had studied medicine at Johns Hopkins University in Maryland and later went to the University of Heidelberg in Germany to complete his medical degree specialising in bacterial infections in animals. While there, he had served in the German army in Serbia and Bulgaria as a volunteer surgeon in German field hospitals. It was while he was in Germany that he was identified as a perfect candidate for recruitment by German intelligence to work in the US. He returned to the US on 7 October 1915 on the Dutch liner SS *Noordam* carrying four vials containing gelatinous cultures. Two contained *bacillus anthracis*, from which the serious infectious animal disease anthrax can be derived, and the other *pseudomonas mallei*, a microbe known to cause glanders, a contagious disease deadly to horses and mules.

In the US Dilger settled into a two-story white brick house in the 5500 block of 33rd Street, NW, near Connecticut Avenue, not far from Chevy Chase Circle. Here, along with his brother Carl, he assembled a laboratory for producing his deadly biological weapon. The anthrax and glanders cultures were then supplied to another of von Rintelen's agents, Frederick Hinsch, captain of an interned German ship in Baltimore, who recruited pro-German dockhands and longshoremen to infect the horses and mules while they were in corrals in the East Coast ports awaiting shipment. One of Hinsch's men later testified,

> The germs were given to me by Capt. Hinsch in glass bottles about an inch and a half or two inches long, and three-quarters of an inch in diameter, with a cork stopper. The bottles were usually contained in a round wooden box with a lid that screwed on the top. There was cotton in the top and bottom to protect the bottles from breaking. A piece of steel in the form of a needle with a sharp point was stuck in the under

> side [*sic*] of the cork, and the steel needle extended down in the liquid where the germs were. We used rubber gloves and would put the germs in the horses by pulling out the stopper and jabbing the horses with the sharp point of the needle that had been down among the germs ... We did a good bit of the work by walking along the fences that enclosed the horses and jabbing them when they would come up along the fence or lean over where we could get at them. We also spread the germs sometimes on their food and water that they were drinking ...[41]

As with much testimony offered up by German agents, it is hard to separate truth from fiction and there is no doubt that any sort of evidence pointing to German espionage operations was exaggerated by both US intelligence, who did it for political reasons, and the press whose motives may have had more to do with circulation figures. There is no doubt that many horses died in transit but they are animals that often do not react well to stress and natural causes probably accounted for most casualties. It is impossible to say just how extensive or effective Dilger's operation was but statistics show that for a number of months during 1915, the export of horses and mules was significantly reduced.

At the beginning of 1916, von Kleist, Wolpert, Bode, Becker, the three sailors on the *Kaiser Friedrich der Grosse* and their supervisor, First Engineer Carl Schmidt all had to appear before the magistrate in handcuffs.

The US security services had been lulled into a false sense of security by this and the high-profile arrests and deportation of German agents at the end of 1915. Unfortunately for them, this allowed the next and most damaging German espionage operation to evolve undetected.

Paul Hilken Jr was a German-American businessman in charge of the North German Lloyd in Baltimore who had been actively involved in firebombing operations with Koenig and in Dilger's horse-poisoning venture. Together with another German agent Frederick L. Hermann, Hilken and Dilger were recalled to Berlin in spring 1916 to receive new instructions. They were instructed to blow up the Lehigh Valley Railroad Company's loading terminals on Black Tom Island, under the cover of establishing a commercial submarine service between Germany and the United States.[42] Stallforth would be the link between Albert and this saboteur cell.

All German acts of sabotage would pale into insignificance, after 30 July 1916 when, on Black Tom Island in New York Harbor, barges and freight cars, reportedly filled with over 1 million tons of shrapnel, black powder, TNT, and dynamite were tied up and waiting to be loaded onto ships for transport to Russia. The depot, which was unfenced, easily accessible from land or water and virtually unguarded.

A number of small fires had been lit along the pier, probably by vagrants sleeping rough, and, as firefighters were trying to put them out, shortly after 2.00 am, there occurred one of the biggest artificial non-nuclear explosions ever recorded equivalent to an earthquake measuring between 5.0 and 5.5 on the Richter Scale. This tremendous blast shattered glass windows throughout Manhattan and Brooklyn, New York. It was heard and felt as far away as Philadelphia, and in Baltimore. The explosions destroyed more than 100 railroad trucks, 13 warehouses, and left a 110 by 50 metre crater. At least five people were reported to have been killed, but the death toll was likely to have been much higher given that barges and buildings in the vicinity were commonly used as night-time shelters by vagrants and recent immigrants. Artillery shells and other munitions continued to explode for days afterwards. The authorities were forced to evacuate hundreds of terrified immigrants from the nearby Ellis Island to the mainland and the Statue of Liberty suffered severe shrapnel damage. The shock wave from a second blast was so powerful that it pushed the torch arm against the crown of the statue, damaging the structure's internal framework.

Investigations showed that, despite regulations stipulating a twenty-four-hour time limit for storage of dynamite and keeping railroad cars with explosives at the terminal, the workload was so backed up that it sometimes took up to one week before cargo was loaded from trucks onto barges before being transferred to ships waiting offshore. Hudson County prosecutors would later accuse the Lehigh Valley Railroad Company and the Central Railroad of New Jersey of criminal and gross negligence.

At first it was accepted that the disaster was the result of an accident. US investigators were lacking even the rudimentary resources to investigate in depth at the time but the culprits were later identified as Michael Kristoff, Kurt Jahnke and Lothar Witzke, all working under the orders of von Papen. Links to the Irish Republican movement were also uncovered. After the First World War the joint German-US Mixed Claims Commission investigated the blast and concluded that German saboteurs, under orders from the German government had been responsible and ordered them to pay $50 million damages.

Kristoff was arrested by the Jersey City police on suspicion of involvement in the blast, but later released for lack of evidence. Jahnke and Witzke fled to Mexico in 1917 and were among the German agents who stirred anti-American sentiment and organised sabotage operations from across the border. Witzke (aka Harry Waberski, Hugo Olsen, Pablo Davis) was tracked by US security agents and later captured at Nogales on the Mexican border on 1 February 1918. He was put on trial in August 1918 charged with inciting mutiny within the US Army and various labour unions, conducting sabotage and plotting to assassinate American officials. A military court found him guilty of espionage and sentenced him to death, the only German spy who was given this sentence in the US during the First World War. President Wilson later commuted his sentence to life in prison, but he was pardoned and released to the German government in 1923. Jahnke was never caught. He returned to Germany in 1921 and later served as an intelligence agent for the Nazis before being captured and executed by the Soviets in 1945. Boy-Ed and von Papen had to answer for the activities of the German Consulate. Both were accused by the US of 'conducting improper activities in military and naval affairs' and 'violating the courtesies extended to them as diplomatic agents'. Von Papen sailed for Germany just before Christmas 1915 and Boy-Ed left a couple of weeks later.

When the passenger liner, the SS *Arabic* was sunk by the German U-boat, *U-24,* in August 1916, with three Americans killed, the US threatened to enter the war against Germany unless the submarines were restricted to attacking only armed vessels. Dozens of American factories had been blown up, ships had been fire-bombed, and workers in critical industries brought out on strike using secret German funding and agitation. After Black Tom, the New York Harbor lay in shambles, and much of the US Army was occupied trying to keep the peace along the Mexican border. Then in early 1917, the British intercepted and deciphered a coded German communication from the German State Secretary for Foreign Affairs Arthur Zimmermann intended for Heinrich von Eckardt, the German ambassador to Mexico. The telegram stated that if the neutral US entered the war on the side of the Entente Powers, von Eckardt was to offer to forge a secret wartime alliance with Mexico. The Germans would provide military and financial support for a Mexican attack on the United States, and in exchange, Mexico would be free to annex territory in Texas, New Mexico and Arizona.

On 1 February 1917, tension was ratcheted up to near breaking point when Germany announced that it would resume its policy of unrestricted submarine warfare and sink, without warning, any neutral ships suspected of carrying arms and ammunition to Britain, France or Russia. They had decided that American neutrality had outlived its usefulness. Diplomatic relations between the US and Germany were severed and von Bernstorff was ordered home with all his staff.

Then on 2 April 1917, President Wilson asked Congress to approve a decision to declare war against Germany.

One German who was accused of being a spy and actually was put to death was Robert Prager. It was, however, an ex-judicial lynching that took place in Collinsville, St Louis on 4 April 1918. Prager was a socialist and union activist working in the coal mines who got into an argument with a drunken mob. They stripped him totally naked, put a rope around his neck, and paraded him down Main Street, making him sing US patriotic songs. Beer bottles were smashed under his feet. He was taken to the edge of town to a hanging tree and murdered. Eleven men were put on trial for the lynching, but all were acquitted. The local newspaper reported:

> The community is well convinced he was disloyal. The city does not miss him. The lesson of his death has had a wholesome effect on the Germanists of Collinsville and the rest of the nation.[43]

Chapter 2

GERMAN PROPAGANDA

'come and see... my country, which is a land of peace and work'[1]

The First World War had left Germany physically and culturally devastated, and politically riven between right and left activists who battled for control of the streets while, 3,000 miles away, the US was a peaceful, booming industrial giant and a land of opportunity. It was an enticing prospect for young men of ambition to look to the US as a place of opportunity. Many would have some family members there and would have some knowledge of the country. After the First World War there had, however, been a backlash against German culture in the US. Anti-German sentiment had been on the rise since 1917 when the US declared war on Germany and German-American institutions came under attack. Some discrimination was little more than cosmetic with the German names of schools, foods, streets and towns often changed, and music written by Wagner and Mendelssohn had been removed from concert programs and even weddings. It was the German language and education that suffered most, however. German-language newspapers were closed, German-language books were burned, and occasionally Americans who spoke German were threatened with violence or boycotts. German-language classes were discontinued. Age-old German traditions and culture were pushed to the margins of national life. Things had settled down after the Armistice but it would take a few years before the animosity was forgotten.

Nazism had emerged out of the chaos of early Weimar government and came to the US in the 1920s in the hearts and minds of German émigrés, mostly single young men between the ages of 21 and 35. Many were semi- or unskilled workers who had suffered under the harsh economic depression that hit Germany after the First World War. Language difficulties meant that they did not fit easily into American society and relied heavily upon established German-American communities but within these groups it was politics that caused friction. Many of the new arrivals were members of the new *Nationalsozialistische Deutsche Arbeiterpartei* (National Socialist Democratic Workers' Party – NSDAP) that had sprung up in Germany and saw their American adventure as an interim phase before returning home when economic circumstances improved. Settled German-Americans, however, saw themselves first and foremost as Americans. Except for the few who managed to assimilate, the new immigrants were forced to find solace in their own distinctive social clubs and political groups.

When the Nazis achieved power in Germany, despite Hitler's indifference to the US, the German military and intelligence services fully understood that, although separated from Europe by 3,000 miles of ocean the US would play a significant role in European politics and would be a useful ally in any future war. It was vitally important, therefore, that Germany not only get its message across, especially to Americans with German connections, to present itself as a positive, dynamic and non-belligerent nation but also to generate a movement within the US to promote a non-interventionist policy in the event of a European war. The Nazis also had ambitions to 'pick the brains' of US industry for the most up-to-date information about new military technologies being developed there. While espionage was little more than an aspiration in 1933, propaganda was a different matter. A campaign could be initiated with little preparation and minimal cost to prepare the ground within the German-American community to support and populate an espionage network.

The *Reichsministerium für Volksaufklärung und Propaganda* (Nazi Ministry of Public Enlightenment and Propaganda – RMVP), under the guidance of Joseph Goebbels, set out an approach to propaganda in the US with four main goals:

- Broadcast a positive image of Nazi Germany.
- Consolidate the support of German-Americans.
- Create divisions between Americans.
- In the case of a war, prevent them from joining the conflict at all costs.[2]

As early as 1933 they sent Colonel Edwin Emerson, a 'soldier of fortune, mediocre author and fairly competent war correspondent'[3] to start the process. Born in Dresden in 1869, Emerson had arrived in the US with his family as a child and went on to graduate from Harvard in 1891 with a BA degree. Reputedly one of Theodore Roosevelt's

Rough Riders during the Spanish-American War, he went on to report on the Russo-Japanese War of 1904–1905 when he was captured by the Japanese. He wrote a number of books including *The Adventures of Theodore Roosevelt*. Later he worked as a journalist at *The Boston Post* and the *New York Evening Post*. During the First World War, he covered the Balkans for *The Washington Post* where he was captured by the Turks and handed over to the Germans. While in captivity, he had been impressed by propaganda denying Germany responsibility for starting the First World War and, under German supervision, began an English language newspaper that was distributed to English PoWs showering them with more pro-German propaganda. It is said that he was personally acquainted with Field Marshal Paul von Hindenburg.

When Emerson returned to the US, he became a vocal critic of the terms the Germans had been forced to accept at Versailles. He moved into 215 East 15th Street with an office at Room 1923 at 17 Battery Place, which was the address of the German consul general. Together with Edmund Fürholzer, he set up a German language newspaper *Deutsche Zeitung* that called itself 'A Fighting Paper for Truth and Right – A Bridge between the United States and Germany'.[4] Deutsche *Zeitung* published articles promoting the new Germany, condemned the 'criminals' who had led Germany to defeat in the war and carried articles railing against the menace of communism. Free copies were distributed to German-American organisations but initially got a mixed reception from them.

Many German-Americans feared reprisals against their communities when an organisation set up by Emerson, the Friends of Germany, started holding meetings attended by uniformed thugs brandishing swastikas and preaching virulent diatribes against Jews and Catholics. Emerson was clearly overstepping the mark and doing more harm than good to the Nazi cause. Goebbels hauled him back to Germany for a swift re-education and reappraisal of his methods. There was a US presidential election coming up and it was thought by the Nazis that it would be in their best interests to see Herbert Hoover returned to office. Emerson was now instructed to join up with the anti-Roosevelt forces and, together, do what they could to influence the election campaign. He teamed up with William Dudley Pelley and offered him $10 for each German he enrolled into his fascist Silver Shirts movement saying that he had sufficient resources to cover 15,000 new members which means, assuming that his offer was genuine, that he had access to significant funds.

Subsequently, there was a change of emphasis and more attention paid to the importation of written propaganda material from Germany using couriers on the North German Lloyd liners and using the same agents to take back to Germany the steadily increasing volume of intelligence being gathered by spies in US industries. The man chosen to organise the distribution of not only propaganda material, but uniforms and flags was an electrical engineer at Raymond Roth Co., 25 West 45th Street called Guenther Orgell who lived at 606 West 115th Street, New York City. The agents Orgell used were mostly from the American branch of the *Stahlhelm* (Steel Helmets), a right-wing German First World War veterans organisation.

In the early days, Nazi movements caused some nervousness in the cities like New York but were seen more as a nuisance than a threat and there were some who were more than happy to take advantage of the disturbed public mood. Harry A. Jung was the Honorary General Manager of the American Vigilant Intelligence Federation, Post Office Box 144, Chicago, an organisation that earned money from terrified employers who paid Jung to spy on communists and socialists. When the threat from these quarters failed to materialise, Jung's revenue stream dwindled, and he looked for new enemies with which to unnerve his customers. The Jewish menace that Emerson and Pelley were warning about was just what he needed and soon his outfit was working hand in hand with the Silver Shirts and the Friends of Germany and others like Edward H. Hunter of the Industrial Defence Association to peddle propaganda for Emerson and earning commission on every book or leaflet they sold.[5]

As well as books and newspapers, leaflets and posters were vital means of spreading the message and the sixth floor of 325 West Ohio Street, Chicago was where much of it came from. This was where the semi-monthly, English-language *American Gentile* was printed by the paper's editor, Captain Victor de Kayville and his financial backer, Charles O'Brien. This newspaper had been started by a man calling himself Prince Peter Kushubue who claimed that the Bolsheviks had confiscated his vast estates and family jewels in Old Russia. He was no prince, however, but a Russian émigré, born in Petrograd (today's St Petersburg) and christened Peter Afanassieff (aka Aphanassieff), who had come to the US seeking his fortune. This, he planned to do by marrying a wealthy heiress but it did not work out that way. Instead he tried forging a United States Treasury cheque, which saw him brought up before Federal Judge F.J. Kerrigan on 19 December 1929 and given eighteen months in prison. When he came out, he changed his name to Peter V. Armstrong and, under that name, turned up in Chicago in 1933 where he teamed up with a group of White (Tsarist)

Russians who were working with Jung to disseminate anti-Semitic propaganda. Jung, in turn, introduced Armstrong to Nazi agents.

Jung, Armstrong and the Nazis set up a small publishing business, the Patriotic Publishing Company, printing a paper called the *Gentile Front* in the basement at 4233 North Kildare. They subsequently changed the company name to the Right Cause Publishing Company and began including literature attacking Roosevelt. Armstrong was far from content to play a supporting role and decided that he could make more money by cutting Jung out of the deal. He started meeting a leading member of *Der Freunde des Neun Deutschland* (Friends of New Germany – FONG), Fritz Gissibl, at Von Thenen's Tavern, 2357 Roscoe Street, Chicago. Griebl's organisation had replaced the defunct Friends of Germany. The two men now formed a secret society, the National Alliance, with de Kayville, J.K. Leibl, Oscar Pfaus, Nick Mueller, Toni Mueller, José Martini, Franz Schaeffer and Gregor Buss. Meetings were held in the private residences of people such as Mrs Emma Schmid, 4710 Winthrop Avenue, Chicago.

The Friends of New Germany held meetings and demonstrations, with security guards dressed in full traditional uniform reminiscent of Nazi storm troopers, and its propaganda denounced minority groups, communists and Catholics at mass meetings. Meetings were often addressed by visiting representatives of fascist movements in Europe. This was starting to strain US-German relations prompting the Department of State to inform the German ambassador to the US, Hans Luther, that the US government was not willing to tolerate 'any spread of the organization of the NSDAP to American soil.'[6]

It was generally accepted by the Nazi propagandists that the tenets of national socialism, as laid out in *Mein Kampf,* would need to be subtly refined for them before it could appeal to an American audience and prepare them for a socially acceptable version of Nazism. The 1935 Nuremberg Laws in particular were too extreme for the US audiences who were more attuned to liberalism and individualism. What was needed was a domestic issue around which to wrap Nazi propaganda in ways that would engage the German-American population in particular. The impending 1936 US presidential elections presented itself as an ideal option given that both Nazis in Germany and their American counterparts saw Roosevelt as essentially anti-fascist and, therefore, anti-Nazi. Resources were channelled into campaigns in support of Roosevelt's presidential opponent, but this did not go unnoticed and came to the attention of the McCormack-Dickstein House Committee on Un-American Activities (HUAC – also known as the Die's Committee) and the House of Representatives Committee on Naturalization and Immigration in 1934. McCormack-Dickstein outlined three objectives of the committe:

1. To ascertain the facts about the role of introduction into [the US] of destructive, subversive propaganda originating from foreign countries.
2. To ascertain facts about organizations in [the US] that seem to be cooperating to spread this alien propaganda to this country.
3. To study and recommend to the House [of Representatives] the appropriate legislation which may correct existing facts and tend to prevent the recurrence of either condition in the future.[7]

Trawling through the vast quantities of Nazi literature, the committee concluded that Emerson's Friends of Germany, which had seemed to submit to foreign directions, represented the US wing of the German Nazi Party.

The RMVP employed a range of strategies including distributing newsreels in the US showing Nazi Party activities in a favourable light and containing 'at least some shots which are of propaganda value for Germany.'[8] Perhaps one of the most important targets of Nazi propaganda, however, were students at American universities. There were German departments and associations on many campuses and extensive exchange programmes in operation. Before leaving Germany, exchange students would spend a week at a camp in Neustrelitz run by the German Academic Exchange Service (DAAD) where they were reminded that their responsibilities were not only to learn about American culture and ideology but also to be active in promoting positive images of Nazism to their hosts. The case of Prince von Lippe at the University of Sothern California illustrates how some were also active in espionage roles. The campus was conveniently located close to the San Diego naval and air bases and von Lippe spent much of his time wandering round photographing installations there.[9]

Some colleges refused to allow German exchange students to spread propaganda, but other university administrations actually played a key role in facilitating the dissemination of Nazi ideology on campus. The US government was not blind to the threat and debated the issue in Congress where John C. Metcalfe, a Federal Bureau of Investigation (FBI) undercover agent who had infiltrated Nazi movements in the US reported that American students were being indoctrinated with fascist ideology and that several university professors were known to have delivered pro-Nazi lectures or invited Nazi sympathisers to address students on campus to validate the Nazi regime. This occurred even at prestigious universities such as Harvard and Columbia.[10]

As early as March 1933, Columbia President Nicholas Murray Butler invited Hans Luther, Germany's ambassador to the US, to speak on campus despite a petition and demonstration organised by the Jewish Students' Society condemning it. The speech went ahead when Luther was introduced to the audience by the international law and diplomacy professor, Charles Hyde. The Dean of Columbia, Thomas Alexander, visited Germany in the following year and came back to announce his support for the Nazi's 'wonderful' program of sterilization and expressed his full support for the practice of 'throwing out the criminals and other undesirables'.[11]

A 'news service' calling itself the Capitol News and Feature Service was set up in 1935 at 209 Kellogg Building, Washington DC. This agency had been set up by Gerald Burton Winrod and the editor, Dan Gilbert, to supply, free of charge, smaller rural newspapers throughout the US with what it termed 'impartial comments' about Nazi Germany in a periodical called *The Revealer*. A regular newspaper, *The Defender*, which regularly reprinted material put out by *Weld-Dienst*, a Nazi propaganda agency set up in 1933 by Ulrich Fleischhauer, claimed a circulation of 110,000 alongside a mailing list that also did a steady trade in in religious tracts.

Up until this time, Winrod had been a poverty-stricken man living at 145 North Green Street, Wichita, Kansas. He had left school as a teenager to become a traveling minister, a calling at which he proved to be particularly adept. In Wichita, this self-educated fundamentalist Protestant preacher had started an organisation called Defenders of the Christian Faith in 1925; one of whose core messages was an absolute rejection of Darwinian evolution in favour of the Biblical creation narrative. He called himself a minister, but he was not associated with any recognised church and lived off collections made from his audience. His brand of puritanical religion denounced Jews whom he accused of plotting to destroy Christian Civilization. When he was exposed to Nazi anti-Semitic propaganda, it naturally fed into his fundamentalist philosophy and led him to see the Nazi regime in Germany as one that was 'cleaning up' Germany.

Judging by the debts he was struggling to pay off at several Wichita department stores, at the end of 1934, Winrod was in dire financial straits but somehow still managed to pay for a three-month trip to Germany where he met the publisher and Nazi propagandist Julius Streicher.[12]

When he returned in February 1935, he had enough money to pay off all his debts and he made no secret of his admiration for Hitler, whom he likened in print to the German theologian Martin Luther calling Hitler 'law-abiding ... a true man's man', and for Germany which he called 'the best country in Europe'.[13] The German press heaped praise on him as someone in the mould of Streicher.

In this period of his new-found prosperity, Winrod established contacts with Nazi agents and fascists like Jung, Emerson, James True and a host of other patrioteers. It was Winrod's strong following in the US' rural heartland that gave him encouragement to run for office on a Republican ticket in the 1938 US Senate elections in Kansas. If successful, he confidently predicted that he would run for the White House in 1940. 'Onward Christian Soldiers' was blasted out from loudspeakers at every one of his rallies. He took a leaf out of Father Charles Coughlin's book and made regular broadcasts across WIBW and KCKN radio networks, sometimes even twice in a single day as the election loomed.

When the press took an interest in Winrod's campaign, it rapidly became a big story with newspapers all across the country. *The Chicago Times* called him an 'arch fascist' and the 'Kansas Nazi'.[14] Winrod threatened to get closer to the levers of power than any fascist before him but when the votes were counted, he had come third making inroads in only a few counties where Ku Klux Klan support was still strong.

Winrod made another trip to Germany and returned with more cash, enough to extend his distribution apparatus. Gilbert was, by now, openly collaborating with Pelley's Silver Shirts movement and became a direct link between the Nazis and American fascist organisations. Now Winrod and his agents canvassed prominent industrialists for donations to support their 'news service' claiming that together they would reinforce the Christian ethic and fight communism. It was also at this time that Winrod began a series of trips to Mexico for meetings with the fascist Gold Shirts movement that had been set up by Hermann Schwinn, director of Nazi activities for the West Coast of the US. The Nazis had also been very active south of the border in Mexico and combined their espionage activities there with Italy and Japan. Germany concentrated on the large Central and South American countries while Italy targeted the small ones with Japan content to give its attention to drawing up charts of coastal areas, harbours and the Panama Canal Zone.

When Goebbels was perfecting his instruments of propaganda to promote National Socialism, he looked to the other side of the world and dreamed of recreating in Germany something as powerful and effective as the Los Angeles motion picture industry. Both he and Hitler, who had alluded to it in *Mein Kampf,* were acutely aware of the power of images compared to the written word. Cinema audiences across the globe flocked to watch Hollywood films and soaked up what Goebbels ruefully perceived to be a worldview that promoted American capitalist values, particularly in a way that served the interests of its Jewish establishment. He was, however, consoled by recognising that the port of Los Angeles was much less regulated than New York, which was the conventional entry point for European immigrants, and would be more convenient for surreptitiously infiltrating spies and couriers into the country. Neither did it escape his attention that southern California, with its white, Anglo-Saxon Protestant traditions and nativist values, had a long history of anti-Semitism and right-wing extremism.

Robert Pape had been a career officer in the German army and had joined the NSDAP in the early days of its existence before he was recruited by the Nazis to go to the US and establish a political presence amongst the German community there. It was to Los Angeles that he went in spring 1927 where he, initially, got by as a door-to-door salesman. He quickly contacted others who had been similarly recruited to further the interests of the Nazi movement in the US. These were Paul Themlitz who ran the Aryan Bookstore selling books, magazines, and pamphlets published in German for a German-American readership, Hans Winterhalder who had been a first lieutenant in the German Imperial Army during the First World War and Herman Schwinn, who had been in the US since 1925 and was a naturalised American. By spring 1933, they had amassed enough support to hold public meetings marshalled by brown-shirted thugs wearing swastika armbands, described as members of the organization's 'sports abteilung', where American and Nazi flags flew side by side. Unemployed Germans in the city were housed in the basement of FONG's Los Angeles headquarters where they were fed and instructed in the virtues of national Socialism. All four men attended a convention in Chicago in July 1933 to take part in the creation of the FONG movement under the leadership of a German national Hans Spanknöbel. The movement was divided into three national zones and Pape was assigned to be leader of FONG on the West Coast. The methods employed on the West Coast mirrored those already operating in New York. Local German-language newspapers were pestered to promote pro-Nazi views, distribution of Nazi literature was widespread, public rallies were organised and there were attempted take-overs of local German-American societies.

The German vice consul in Los Angeles Dr Georg Gyssling, an ambitious and a staunch Nazi, gave the full support of his office to

Pape and Winterhalder and between them, through the *Turn Verein Germania* (the federation of all German-American cultural clubs in Los Angeles) they succeeded in distributing such a volume of Nazi propaganda literature to the German-American community that Los Angeles police Captain William 'Red' Hynes was soon reporting that downtown streets were suddenly littered with 'considerable quantities' of it.[15]

Captain Hynes, 'the most widely hated policemen in the United States', had, for some years, infiltrated police detectives and citizen volunteers into radical political groups.[16] Up to this point they had been spying primarily on communists and labour organisers and Hynes had used the intelligence to prime anti-communist groups such as the American Legion and the Silver Shirts who would come out in force to, pre-emptively and violently, oppose planned strikes and demonstrations. There was a special intelligence unit within the Los Angeles Police Department (LAPD) directed by the business leaders in the city to 'take all measures necessary to protect their political and commercial interests'.[17] This 'Red Squad' quickly earned a reputation for violence when breaking up meetings and the courts rarely questioned how evidence against those accused of political activism was acquired. When more than 40 Jewish organizations called for a citywide anti-Nazi demonstration that was attended by more than 3,000 people, Winterhalder saw his chance to ingratiate himself with the LAPD and told them that they could count on the FONG membership in the fight against communists and Jews. There was clearly a working relationship between the police and Nazi movements.

The impact of this Nazi propaganda tsunami was such that by late summer, Leon Lewis, a local Jewish attorney, complained to Los Angeles Chief of Police, James Davis about 'the most vicious type of class hatred' being preached on the city streets and called for a commitment to monitor Nazi anti-Semitic activity more closely. Davis, however, reflected the prejudices and political priorities of the Protestant majority by dismissing Lewis's criticism as an over-reaction by the Jewish communities and entertained him instead with a lecture on the dangers of communism and the urgent need to protect the city from the subversive forces of organised labour.

Lewis was a lawyer but not at all the stereotypical activist. He was a withdrawn and private person but one fully committed to social justice especially where anti-Semitism was concerned. During the First World War, he had served in France, doing secret intelligence work for the military, and had risen through the ranks to become a major before working for the relief of wounded American soldiers in

British hospitals. He had acquired a reputation as a tireless advocate for veterans' rights and was respected by both the American Legion and the Disabled American Veterans (DAV) in California.

His rebuff by Davis had shown the extent of anti-Semitic prejudice and had made it obvious that any movement to combat Nazi influence in southern California could not rely on official support, so he set about creating an independent organisation, the Jewish Community Committee (LAJCC), to do it. The DAV was by no means a Jewish movement, and neither was it particularly anti-Nazi. It was essentially pro-American and motivated by what its members saw as a threat to American democracy. The circumstances were such that, because of its Jewish membership, the LAJCC could not hope to win public sympathy alone and therefore needed to work under the DAV's leadership whose American-ness was beyond doubt. This demanded great political awareness and strategic skill on Lewis's part to make it work but these he had in abundance.

While he had made little headway with Chief Davis, he had more luck with Hynes who agreed to work with him to infiltrate the local Nazi movement but only on a mercenary basis. Hynes pleaded lack of resources so funding would have to come from the Jewish Federation of Los Angeles and Hynes would take 'a piece of change' along the way.[18] FONG had set out to target American war veterans and members of domestic, right-wing groups so it was natural that Lewis would choose one of these to be his first DAV informant. There were a great many disabled veterans in southern California, many of whom were attracted to the idea of fascism. Unfortunately, at the time, the US government had few resources available to monitor subversive activities. The country was seen by Goebbels as 'east prey' since it had 'neither an espionage system nor a counter-espionage system'.[19]

A naturalised German-American citizen, John Schmidt, was a patriot and a veteran who had fought in France against Germany in 1918 having trained with the German army before emigrating to the US in 1903. He was a man of great integrity, but one who struggled with post-traumatic stress disorder, which had left him almost destitute. Eager to serve and earn a modest stipend, Schmidt was assigned the codename Agent 11 and posed as a Nazi-sympathiser when he presented himself to Pape. He went along with the general flow of FONG ideology, which was to drive Jews and Catholics out of government in the US and replace them with German-Americans.

A man whose father had been a general in the Bavarian Field Artillery, Schmidt exactly fitted the criteria for recruitment to FONG and was quickly assimilated into the organisation. Pape encouraged him to recruit other veterans and Schmidt responded by introducing two more DAV members, Carl Sunderland, whom Lewis labelled Agent 8 and Bert Allen, Agent 7, who agreed with him to attend FONG meetings and report back. Sunderland, in particular, was deeply concerned by the venomous attitude of men like Pape, Winterhalder, Themlitz and Schwinn, whom he claimed would 'massacre you so that your own mother wouldn't know you', if the DAV spying activities were uncovered. Such men he vehemently condemned as having 'no place in the United States'.[20] It soon became clear to Lewis that the threat from the Nazis was much more than just an attack on the Jews, however. By late 1933, FONG had set up what they called a sports abteilung based on the Nazi *Sturmabteilung* (SA) with a membership of around forty. Meetings were held in German and activities included instruction in street-fighting and hand-to-hand combat, as well as live target practice near the Hollywood reservoir. Information showed that SA groups were forming in Chicago, as well as Vancouver and Toronto in Canada. However far-fetched their claims that 'thousands of storm troopers in the US were ready to stand shoulder-to-shoulder with US veterans when the time came ... to help them take back the government from communists and Jews', might have been there was no doubting the seriousness of their intent.[21] Lewis had initially thought that his intervention would last just a few weeks and he certainly never expected to uncover such a huge political conspiracy.

During the following months, Lewis worked hard to secure the financial and political resources to challenge FONG's subversive threat to democracy. Meanwhile Schmidt had become an important member of FONG and continued to introduce more DAV recruits to the movement. Pape too was under pressure from New York to find new sources of income. Spanknöbel ordered him to take control of the local *Deutsche Amerikanische Stadt Verbund* (German-American Alliance), an affiliation of some three dozen German-American social and cultural organizations who owned real estate to the value of £30,000 and whose annual election of officers was imminent. Pape illegally connived with the Nazi president, Max Socha, and others to get a majority of pro-Nazis on the board of directors. Lewis saw his chance and represented the irate non-Nazi members of the Alliance in a civil lawsuit to expose FONG's machinations as a duplicitous, Nazi organization.

Schmidt, Sunderland and Allen appeared as star witnesses for the plaintiffs and told of Nazi spies living in Los Angeles, of money and propaganda smuggled off German ships, of a private army training for revolution and above them all, a complicit German consul. The case made headlines in all Los Angeles' major newspapers. Schmidt received a number of very credible death threats, and he was not the only one. Sunderland testified that Pape had told him he was still an active German officer still in the pay of the German government and had been sent by the German government to US specifically to create a subversive organisation. The judge, Guy Bush, eventually got fed up with what was essentially a petty internal squabble and threw the case out of court, but Lewis had got the publicity he wanted to expose Nazi activities. Dozens of FONG members resigned. Pape was summarily dismissed with a beating and was replaced by Schwinn. Vice Consul Gyssling was forced to deny that FONG had any connection whatsoever with the German government. He and Schwinn shared a mutual dislike and Schwinn consistently looked for ways of undermining Gyssling hoping to see him recalled so that he could take his place, whereas Gyssling thought Schwinn a loose cannon that needed to be tethered. Schwinn liked to present himself in private meetings with *Amerikadeutscher Volksbund* (German-American Bund) members as 'the representative of the Hitler government on the west coast' but in public the two men were forced to disguise the relationship that existed between Germany and the Bund, a relationship that Berlin consistently denied.[22]

In contrast to Pape, Lewis came out of it rather well. He was elected chairman of the DAV's Americanism Committee in Los Angeles and was also chosen to serve as the Deputy Chief of Staff for the DAV in California. Most importantly, he was also selected to serve as executive secretary of a newly created committee formed to combat the rising threat of Nazi-inspired anti-Semitism. This Los Angeles Jewish Community Committee (LAJCC) was created under the chairmanship of Mendel Silberberg when leaders of the Los Angeles Jewish business community met the Jewish moguls of the Hollywood movie industry on 13 March 1934. Up until this point, these two communities had little in common and tended to avoid contact with each other. Hollywood Jews, on the whole, were recent Eastern European immigrants who were seen as a different social class by the well-established city Jews and whose movie industry was seen by them as somewhat *infra dig* and disreputable. It was significant in terms of how seriously the threat was taken that the meeting was held at the Hillcrest Country Club from which the Hollywood Jews had hitherto been barred.

Lewis addressed the meeting and described how his DAV agents had worked inside FONG for the past seven months to expose their subversive activities and how the expense of the recent trial had left the Community Committee flat broke. Right at the start of Lewis's operations, the city Jews had promised much but had come up with very little in the way of hard cash. Lewis had given so much of his time to DAV that his own legal practice had suffered, and his personal financial position was such that if not further funding was forthcoming, he would have to abandon DAV completely simply to concentrate on simply earning a living.

As part of his investigations, Lewis had also been looking into the activities of studio management at the lower levels and had discovered widespread discrimination against Jewish employees which the moguls apparently knew nothing about. What they had been aware of, however, was pressure coming from Gyssling who threatened to have all their films banned in Germany if they did not tone down anti-German sentiment. The Hillcrest meeting had disturbed them to the extent that they agreed to meet Lewis without the city Jews being present and negotiated a deal with him. They would stump up the cash not only to pay agents but also for a monthly stipend of $500 to Lewis personally to continue his wider work against pro-Nazi groups but on two conditions. Lewis must infiltrate his agents into the studios to report on the extent to which FONG was influencing pro-Nazi employment policy at ground level there and it must be done with utmost discretion where involvement of the moguls is kept secret. On no account can it be seen as a crusade against anti-Semitism which would invite a backlash against the Hollywood Jews. While the LAJCC held weekly meetings throughout the rest of the 1930s to review the broader issues of discrimination and prejudice in the city, the Hollywood Committee would work behind the scenes.

In February 1935, the Dies Committee released its findings on Nazi subversive propaganda activity in the US. During their investigations they had been greatly assisted by LAJCC covert operations. Prior to the Hillcrest meeting, Jewish groups had failed to set aside their political differences and bring their considerable resources together in an effective anti-Nazi movement but thanks to Lewis's leadership all that had changed. The report exposed the German government's efforts to bring National Socialism to the US through propaganda and urged Congress to pass legislation to prevent its continuance. Confident that the danger had been everted, Lewis and the LAJCC relaxed their operations, but they were shocked out of their complacency on 29 September 1935 when the *Los Angeles Times* carried an insert sponsored by the American Nationalist Party vehemently condemning Jewish influences in the US. The American Nationalist Party espoused Nazi ideology and echoed its use of political anti-Semitism to rally 'true Americans' against the 'Jewish aliens'.

Lewis quickly responded by engaging two agents, Neil Ness and Charles Slocombe, to infiltrate FONG. Both were eagerly welcomed by Schwinn and soon learned the extent of Nazi influence over the American Nationalist Party and its part in the dissemination of masses of propaganda leaflets. The pro-Nazi German language newspaper, *California Weckruf*, printed a letter in September 1935 from Ingram Hughes, who signed himself as founder of the new American Nationalist Party, calling for a 'solution of the Jewish problem in the United States'.[23] Slocombe discovered that Hughes was in frequent contact with Italian and White Russian fascist groups in Los Angeles, the local Bund leader W.P. Bauer in San Diego and Count Bernhard Ernst von Bülow. His many fascist friends included Pelley, Peter V. Armstrong, publisher of *The American Gentile* in Chicago, James True, publisher of *Industrial Control Reports* in Washington DC, and with Reverend Gerald Winrod of Kansas. This network clearly showed the existence of a national distribution network of extreme right-wing anti-Semitic propaganda. Collectively, they created a hostile and threatening political climate for American Jews and Lewis was determined to expose them. Before long, however, Lewis was to uncover a greater threat than just propaganda.

Schwinn was having frequent meetings with German consuls from other cities, including German Consul Manfred von Killinger in San Francisco who had been assigned by the Reich to organise the Bund in preparation for a coming Nazi sabotage offensive against American shipping and aircraft industries.

He was also socialising with local Silver Shirt leaders Kenneth Alexander and Henry Douglas Allen; the Silver Shirts' most active propagandist in Los Angeles in the late 1930s with connections to the country-wide network of American right-wing organisations.

When Hitler's personal adjutant, Captain Fritz Weidemann, visited Los Angeles he had meetings with Gyssling and Schwinn. Because of the mutual animosity between Gyssling and Schwinn, Berlin planted a Gestapo agent, Hans Diebel, inside the Bund in Los Angeles to muster some control over their activities and report back on Schwinn's activities. When Lewis's spies reported back it was clear that the Bund was not the purely American organisation that it purported to be and was showing its true colours as a threat to American democracy.

Overt Germanophilia in the form of Bund rallies were disturbing enough for the US government but there was a secret and more insidious threat which actually utilised the very engine of democracy to promote the totalitarian doctrine of Nazi Germany. Central to this subterfuge was George Viereck whose pro-German activities during the First World War had nearly cost him his life. That had in no way curbed his devotion to Germany neither had the rise of the Nazis dampened his commitment. In the 1930s, he had met Hitler and joined the Friends of New Germany arguing for a sympathetic approach to the Nazi regime.

Then in 1938, he was given the opportunity to do something constructive. He was recruited into the murky world of espionage in summer 1938 by Hans Dieckhoff, the US ambassador, who was, at the time, on holiday in Germany. Dieckhoff was decidedly unimpressed with the current espionage operation in the US and was on the lookout for someone who could return with him and knock it into shape. He believed that Viereck was just the man to do that and set him up with a cover as the US correspondent of a Munich newspaper the *Münchner Neueste Nachrichten* and periodical *Facts in Review,* a free newspaper which gave him a contract paying $500 per month from the German Library of Information bringing the Nazi version of European affairs to a US readership of some 100,000.

When Dr Hans Thomsen took over from Dieckhoff in November 1938, he inherited Viereck and proceeded to make good use of him by extending his remit. Thomsen was frequently scathing about German espionage operations, or at least he was infuriated by the negative publicity that resulted from them and was damaging US-German relations. His response was to encourage US isolationist policies which he knew was battling against the current of White House sympathies for the British and French cause and it was in a 'behind the scenes' campaign that he was planning now to use the 'cuckoo of propaganda to lay its eggs in every nest'.[24]

Viereck's task would be to collect privileged information and secret intelligence using pro-isolationist paid informants in key strategic positions on Capitol Hill. For this purpose, he persuaded Berlin to allocate a special fund for his own personal use, the expenditure of which would require no receipts. The purpose of this fund would be to oppose Roosevelt's re-election and prevent the US from entering the Second World War by exerting political influence on the democratic process. Berlin duly allocated $50,000 which Thomsen put at Viereck's disposal.

The plan was to reward elected representatives to make speeches at both Republican and Democratic conventions promoting isolationism. For the Republicans, New York Congressman Hamilton Fish, Ernest Lundeen of Minnesota and Karl E. Mundt of South Dakota had all their travelling and accommodation expenses paid by Viereck. A short while later, it was at the Democratic Convention in Chicago where Viereck tried to drive a wedge between Roosevelt and the President of the United Mine Workers' of America and founding president of the Congress of Industrial Organizations, John L. Lewis. This proved to be successful when Lewis broke from the Democrats, attacked Roosevelt by setting up the Peace Party.

The 1940 election was held against a backdrop of German conquest in Europe with Britain under a barrage of nightly bombing raids. Viereck summoned his poetic skills to come up with slogans used by such as Senator Burton Kendall Wheeler who told the American people that Roosevelt's Lend Lease Bill to supply war material to Britain would 'plough under every fourth American boy'.[25] Viereck had a happy knack of coming up with phrases like this and surreptitiously feeding them to sympathetic politicians who would repeat them in speeches giving the impression, and maybe often believing, that they themselves had dreamed them up.

There was a rule that speeches made in the House of Representatives could be reproduced in any quantity and distributed to the people at government expense which meant that significant amounts of free pro-German propaganda was finding its way into American living rooms in the name of as many as twenty-four members of Congress.

Days before the election, Roosevelt was looking the likely winner and all Thomsen and Viereck's efforts seemed to have been in vain but far away in Poland, the Germans had uncovered a document in the Warsaw Foreign Ministry, which seemed to show that Roosevelt had, eighteen months previously, and weeks before the British guarantee, assured the Polish ambassador to the US, Count Jerzy Potocki, that he would give Poland 'all out support in a possible war'.[26] The German Minister of Foreign Affairs Joachim von Ribbentrop, who had been a great admirer of Thomsen and Viereck's campaign, felt sure that this would torpedo Roosevelt's chances of re-election but all efforts Thomsen made to interest the American press in the document failed apart from the *New York Enquirer* that agreed to print it in a greatly enlarged edition of 250,000 copies in return for a payment of $5,000.[27] It was all to no avail. Roosevelt swept to victory with 58 per cent of the votes cast.

A few weeks before Pearl Harbor, Viereck was indicted by a Grand Jury in Washington DC for the alleged act of wilfully concealing activities that should have been listed on his registration form, and when he went to trial a few weeks after Pearl Harbor, Viereck admitted to receiving a salary of $500 per month from Otto Kiep, the Nazi consul general in New York and a further $1,750 per month from the German Tourist Bureau.[28]

A guilty verdict seemed inevitable because of the climate of opinion generated by America's sudden involvement in all-out war against the Axis. He was duly convicted and after spending a year in jail, he was freed on appeal but re-arrested the same year and remained in prison until May 1947. His son, Corporal George Sylvester Viereck Jr was killed in action fighting for the Allies at Anzio on 24 March 1944.

Chapter 3

FBI BACKGROUND

> 'The United States had entered the [First World] war with an MID (Military Intelligence Division) of two officers and two clerks.'[1]

At the start of the twentieth century, as the US experienced rapid industrial and population growth its city and town law-enforcement agencies were fighting a losing battle against the rising tide of criminal and political lawbreakers. Violence on the streets and corruption in government were rampant while big business imposed intolerable employment conditions in the meat packaging plants and factories. Urgent attention was required also to challenge illegal monopolies threatening to control entire industries. In the first decade of the twentieth century there was really no systematic way of enforcing federal law. Local communities and even some states had their own police forces, but these were typically poorly trained, politically appointed and underpaid. Only the Secret Service, admittedly well-trained and dedicated, existed to tackle national crime and security issues and they were also very poorly resourced.

The threat of Anarchist terrorists, whose acolyte, Leon Czolgosz had shot and killed President McKinley in September 1901, galvanised McKinley's successor Theodore Roosevelt to tackle reform. He appointed the grand-nephew of Napoléon Bonaparte, Charles Bonaparte as his second Attorney General in 1906 and tasked him with addressing the problem. Bonaparte, however, soon found out that he had no permanent detective force under his immediate control other than a few examiners trained as accountants and some civil rights investigators. He did, however, have access to Secret Service agents but argued that by using them the DOJ lacked complete control over investigations which meant that he 'had no direct information as to what they did, and [had little] control over the expenses which they might incur.' His own department, he said, 'ought to be clothed with [its own] machinery necessary to conduct prosecutions'.[2]

When he called on Congress to authorise the creation of such a force, he exposed Roosevelt to accusations of making a grab for executive power at the expense of the legislature. Opponents of the president such as Congressmen Sherley, Smith and Fitzpatrick, rallied round James Tawney's Appropriations Committee and supported an amendment to the Fiscal Year 1909 Sundry Civil Appropriation Bill, which would effectively deny Bonaparte any further use of Secret Service agents. They questioned not only whether it was desirable to have a general detective service for the government that was potentially authorised to investigate politicians but also argued that the Secret Service already had too much power. Roosevelt came out fighting and argued that the amendment would 'materially interfere with the administration of justice and will benefit only ... the criminal class.'[3] Despite Roosevelt's intervention, the Bill was approved by Congress. The president was incensed and created an uproar by accusing Congress of putting its own interests before those of the nation by passing the Bill simply to prevent investigation of its own activities.

Within days Bonaparte began to reorganise the DOJ to compensate for the loss of access to the Secret Service operatives. He gathered together the various investigators at his disposal and permanently hired nine Secret Service agents. On 26 July 1908, the Division of Investigation (DOI) was requested to refer most investigative matters to Stanley W. Finch who would now assign his agents to conduct investigations on their behalf. On 5 March 1909, under a new administration, the new Attorney General, George Wickersham, issued a formal order creating the Bureau of Investigation (BOI) and within two years, Congress had tripled the size of this force and greatly broadened its investigative authority.

At first, they investigated mostly civil rights cases, copyright violations, and such like but soon started taking on a few national security issues, including treason and some anarchist activity. It is no surprise that the list of responsibilities Finch was obliged to deal with continued to grow rapidly especially when Congress saw his new organisation as a way to advance its national agenda. In 1910, it was called upon to tackle interstate prostitution and human trafficking. By 1915 the Bureau personnel had ballooned to 360 special agents and support personnel.

It was called on to intervene on the border with Mexico where it opened several offices to investigate smuggling and neutrality violations. Then after the declaration of war on 6 April 1917, it was given the task of investigating subversion and sabotage by foreign agents. The Espionage Act and later the Sabotage Act gave it responsibility as the principal national investigative agency. The BOI was now in the counterespionage business.

At the end of the First World War a new menace, Bolshevism, threatened to exploit widespread labour unrest in the Western world to create economic turmoil and even revolution. Anarchists again came to the fore when the BOI uncovered a plot to assassinate President Wilson when he returned from the Versailles Peace Conference. A group of fourteen Spaniards calling themselves the *Groupa Pro Prenza* were arrested. There was rioting in New York City inspired by communist agitator and some thirty nail bombs were intercepted in parcels addressed to prominent politicians, judges and bankers. Not all were detected however and nine exploded killing two including one of the bombers. Anarchists claimed responsibility for the bombs vowing to 'rid the world of ... tyrannical institutions'.[4]

The BOI head William J. Flynn drew together police chiefs from across the country to devise a strategy for dealing with the violence. A series of bombing attacks against national leaders in 1919, including one against the home of Attorney General A. Mitchell Palmer, prompted Flynn to set up an investigation under the leadership of a young DOJ lawyer named J. Edgar Hoover, who set about collecting information and intelligence on radical movements in the US. His main task of identifying individuals and groups resulted in the discovery of a number of Italian anarchist groups such as the *El Arieto Society* and the *L'era Nuovo Group.* All the information collected about the anarchists along with membership of the Communist Party of America, the Union of Russian Workers and the Industrial Workers of the World was recorded in a burgeoning index system in what became known as the General Intelligence Division (GID) of the DOJ. The alphabetical card index recorded information about individuals, organisations, societies; the publications all separated into geographical regions.

Hoover had been born on New Year's Day 1895 in Washington DC had joined the DOJ in 1917 after attaining his law degree at George Washington University. When the US entered the First World War in 1917, Hoover was appointed head of the DOJ's Alien Enemy Bureau where he was able to arrest and detain allegedly disloyal aliens without trial and by 1921 he had quickly risen to become Assistant Director of the BOI.

Hoover's initial enthusiasm led him to organised raids without formal search or arrest warrants, paying no regard to who was and was not guilty of insurrectionary activity. As a result of mass arrests,

556 people were deported. The fallout from this, bypassed Hoover however and it was Palmer who carried the can and was forced to resign. Hoover actually emerged with his reputation enhanced to the extent that President Calvin Coolidge appointed him as head of BOI on 10 May 1924, with responsibility only to the attorney general and separated from all political oversight. Up until this point, the BOI had been 'riddled with cronyism, nepotism, and overall incompetence, routinely serving the political interests of the Harding administration.'[5]

It was, however, seen as only a temporary appointment for Hoover who was instructed by the new Attorney General Harlan Fiske Stone to reform the organisation under a six-point 'Stone Doctrine'. Five points referred to personnel issues as a result of which Hoover recruited a whole new breed of agent. He collected together an elite group of white, college-educated male agents who would abide by a strict moral code. The organisation effectively became the symbolic guardian of the country's laws, citizens, and its morals. The sixth instruction was to desist from intelligence investigations and restrict all activity to combatting violations of federal law. Under this regulation, no American citizen or alien could be investigated for political reasons or for connections to foreign governments and the BOI was forbidden to share intelligence with other agencies. Crucially, this effectively blocked any potential the BOI might have had to develop into an agency capable of dealing with the challenges that lay ahead in the form of foreign intelligence aggression. The focus of BOI attention was directed away from detection and investigation of foreign espionage, which was traditionally the exclusive responsibility of the Department of State.

The Stone Doctrine was to remain as a guiding light for BOI activities for fifteen years during which the organisation's counterintelligence limitations were exposed. It severely restricted the ability of the FBI to investigate any employee of another government organisation who was suspected of espionage activity without getting Department of State approval. There were no FBI counterespionage squads even in large cities. Any investigations that did come up were handled by the bank robbery squad. The threshold for investigations to be authorised was such that agents would not even bother to follow up leads.

Hoover even went so far as to declare that if he uncovered a foreign plot to overthrow the US government, he would be powerless to act unless some Federal Statute had been violated. This restriction was increasingly frustrating during the 1930s when Nazi Germany began encouraging the formation of German-American movements in the US. Where state security was threatened, such as in the Fritz

Spanknöbel case, Hoover was prevented from acting until the DOJ had issued a warrant for his arrest by which time the Nazi agent had fled the country. It was a huge embarrassment for the government and President Roosevelt called on all key agencies involved to come together in May 1934 to work out a strategy to counter any future threats of foreign states running propaganda or espionage operations on US soil.

Only the Immigration Service had the authority to act against foreign agents. On 10 August 1933, the BOI had been renamed the Division of Investigation and it was this body that now acted as a clearing house for all information collected by the Secret Service, the Immigration Service and the DOJ. The name was changed again on 1 July 1935 when the DOI became the Federal Bureau of Investigation (FBI).

Chapter 4

THE GRIEBL-LONKOWSKI SPY RING

> 'During the Second World War, New York City was the epicenter for war production, ship building, and port facilities. The New York Naval Shipyard, universally known as the Brooklyn Navy Yard, was the largest warship facility in the world, employing more than 100,000 people. Brooklyn was also the headquarters for both the Brewster and Todd shipyards, where workers toiled around the clock building transports and tankers. Just across the East River in Manhattan, where the Norden Company on Lafayette Street was turning out thousands of secret bombsights'.[1]

Article 198 of the Treaty of Versailles had forbidden Germany from having any military or naval air forces but this provision, along with others, was secretly, systematically and unrelentingly undermined at every opportunity as Germany attempted to rearm. By 1926, General Hans von Seeckt had created an illegal special aviation branch, the *Fliegerzentrale* (Flying Centre), with a few squadrons of aircraft converted from civilian use but German industry did not have access to the sort of sophisticated technologies that were being developed in places like the US whose industrial and technological centres were booming. Many of these new developments in aircraft designs such as automatic bombsights, and retractable landing gear were classified as military secrets, of course, but a few were available to buy on the open market. The Abwehr (German military intelligence) chief, Fritz Gempp, had the task of task of acquiring information about these new developments using whatever means possible. The man he chose to send to the US as part of this mission was the 'plain, pale, placid' thin, bespectacled, 34-year-old Wilhelm 'Willi' Lonkowski who arrived in New York from Bremerhaven, under a false passport in the name of

William Schneider, with his wife, Auguste 'Gunny', née Krüger, on the SS *Berlin* on 27 March 1927.[2] A nervous, edgy man, Lonkowski was far from what might be thought of as typical spy material but he was a first class aero engineer, uncomplicated and reserved, which meant that, in fact, he had many of the attributes required in the role.

During the First World War, Lonkowski had flown in the German air force when he had been shot down and badly wounded in a dog-fight with a French aircraft. After the war, he had specialised in the study of aircraft design. His knowledge of aircraft combined with freedom to travel all across Europe, studying foreign aircraft development had led to foreign intelligence assignments and eventually to full-time recruitment in the Abwehr. He had previously worked on an ad hoc basis for them in France where he gained a reputation for being capable and efficient. Now Gempp had given him a shopping list of items that had received some exposure in trade journals before suddenly disappearing from the public gaze indicating that they had been placed on secret development programmes. Of special interest were new engines and propellors under development at the Westinghouse Corporation as well as details of Fairchild Aviation and Douglas aircraft being tested at the US Army's Mitchel and Roosevelt airfields outside New York City.

It was an enormous assignment for one man, but Lonkowski soon discovered that he would be operating in a benign counterintelligence environment. General Friedrich von Boetticher, the German military attaché in Washington DC went so far as to say that,

> It was so easy, the Americans are so broad-minded that they print everything in the newspapers. You don't need an intelligence service[there]. You only have to be industrious and see the papers and what they print.[3]

At that time, the US had no single federal agency charged with counterintelligence and no military intelligence worthy of the name. If he was careful, Lonkowski was very unlikely to become subject to surveillance. The couple settled into the German community of Yorktown where Gunny managed a millinery shop and then a dress shop in Queens Village while Willi worked as a musical instrument repair technician at the Temple of Music store in Hempstead, Long Island.[4] From there he moved on to work as a mechanic at the Ireland Aircraft Corporation at nearby Roosevelt Field, and then at Fairchild Aviation Corporation in Farmingdale, New York and began recruiting agents to provide him with intelligence.

The Yorktown district was heavily populated by German immigrants, many of whom had arrived after the end of the First World War, and who brought with them deep feelings of resentment and indignation at what they saw as the pernicious and unjust terms imposed on Germany in the Treaty of Versailles. Mixing freely within this community, Lonkowski soon identified people who were working in those industries from which important intelligence could be gleaned. By matching personal animosities with sensitive employment roles, it was not difficult for him to find useful contacts and persuade them to do their bit to help Germany regain pride and prestige in world affairs. Quite a number had been in the US for a number of years and were already in positions of some importance. Johannes Karl Steuer was an inspector at the Sperry Gyroscope Company in Brooklyn and he brought Lonkowski information on bombsights. Johann Koechel, a foreman at the Kollmorgan Optical Corporation in Brooklyn, supplied him with data on periscopes.

Others he recruited were later arrivals who had been selected and trained for the roles they would play by *Abteilung III b* before leaving Germany. Elevated to the personnel department where he was responsible for hiring and firing, Lonkowski took on Otto Hermann Voss, a native of Hamburg, Germany, who arrived in October 1928. He had trained as an aircraft mechanic and served with the German Army Corps of Engineers in the First World War. He would soon move on to Baltimore where he worked for a company developing propellors for the US Navy. Werner Georg Gudenberg, a native of Hamburg who arrived at the same time, was another. A trained coppersmith, Gudenberg entered the fuselage and fitting department at Ireland Aircraft Corporation where he was quickly made up to foreman. Between 1932 and 1936, he worked as a foreman in charge of thirty men in the cowling and pattern-making departments at the Curtiss Aeroplane and Motor Company in Buffalo and after that he ran the sheet metal department at the seaplane designers Hall Aluminium Aircraft.[5]

It was one thing for Lonkowski to acquire sensitive information, but it was another to get it safely and secretly back to Berlin. The arrangements for that were established through couriers, such as Karl Eitel and Karl Schlütter, who worked as stewards on the German liners that regularly crossed the Atlantic. For his services, Lonkowski was paid a generous $500 a month and also had a sizeable budget to pay his informants. Soon, he was so involved with his espionage activities that he gave up regular employment but he maintained cover by passing himself off as the US correspondent for *Luftreise*, a popular

German aircraft magazine. With this cloak of respectability, he was given access to a number of aircraft factories to interview important engineers supposedly for articles that would appear in Germany.

By 1935, German intelligence had established two significant espionage networks and several minor ones inside the US. Their objectives were fivefold. Firstly, to ascertain the political mood and make judgements about the strength of the isolationist lobby and the likelihood of the country becoming involved in any future European war. Secondly, to acquire information about scientific and technological developments in the US military. Thirdly, to gauge production levels especially in the armament industry. Fourthly, to monitor maritime activity and last but by no means least, to carry out sabotage operations that might slow down production of war material that could be sold to potential enemies of the Reich.

The first inkling the US had that the Germans were carrying out espionage operations on their patch was when Colonel Vernon Kell, the head of British domestic counterintelligence (MI5), called on Colonel Raymond E. Lee, the US military attaché in London at the end of 1937, and showed him a copy of a letter the British postal authorities had intercepted while monitoring an address in Dundee, Scotland. Unlikely as it seemed at first, this letter referred to a plot to kidnap a US colonel in New York with a view to acquiring from him sensitive military intelligence about US coastal defences. The letter was from someone in New York codenamed 'Crown' and was part of a package being sent from the Dundee address to a person called Sanders at Post Office Box 629 in Hamburg when MI5 intercepted it.

Responsible for the identification of foreign agents, Kell worked with only a small staff, but had the full weight of Special Branch of the Metropolitan Police at his disposal, if required. Post Office Box 629 had been known to MI5 as an Abwehr mailbox since early 1936 and all mail going to it from the United Kingdom was routinely intercepted and examined. Prior to the discovery of the 'Crown' letter, in late summer 1937, one package addressed to Post Office Box 629 had been found to contain a letter sent from the mysterious Sanders postmarked Amsterdam, the Netherlands containing instructions for the recipient to travel to The Hague 'for the purpose of discussion in detail all your business affairs which are still pending in Germany'.[6] Inside, also, was an envelope with an address in Perth, Scotland – 16 Breadalbane Terrace – which proved to be that of William Haddow, who had his half-sister, Jessie Jordan, living with him temporarily. Authorisation was established for extensive surveillance of all mail to and from this address and when Jordan moved to 1 Kinloch Street in

Dundee the monitoring operation expanded to cover both addresses. She had purchased a hairdressing business, Jolly's salon, a few doors away from her residence in the same street.

Investigations by MI5's Colonel William Edward Hinchley Cooke revealed that Jordan had been born in Glasgow in 1887 to a single mother, and had been given her mother's maiden name of Wallace before changing it to Haddow when her mother married John Haddow five years later. Having left home to avoid her violent stepfather, Jordan took up employment as a chambermaid in the Royal Hotel in Dundee where she met a German waiter, Karl Friedrich 'Fritz' Jordan. The couple moved to Germany in 1912. Now, twenty-five years later, she had returned with enough money to buy and completely refurbish her new business. Jordan's assistant in the salon, Mary Curran, whom she had inherited from the previous proprietor, was seemingly not well disposed towards her new employer and, in conversation with the previous owner Patrick Robbins, complained about being left to run the salon alone while Jordan went off on frequent trips to Germany from one of which she returned with her 23-year-old daughter Marga Wilhelmina. When Jordan had bought the business, Robbins had been amazed that Jordan had paid him about three times what it was worth and paid for it in Bank of England £5 notes. Furthermore, Jordan had expensive hairdressing equipment brought in from Germany for her business and large amounts of money were spent on the refurbishment, again paid for with £5 notes. Curran found all this suspicious because in such an impoverished area of the city, there was little likelihood of ever getting a return on such an investment. Robbins had a word with the Dundee police who thought it worth making further inquiries and informing MI5.

When Jordan's movements were monitored, it became clear that, as well as trips to Germany, she was making frequent journeys to local sites of military importance. Then there was the issue of mail arriving at the salon. By this time, Hinchley Cooke was already aware of the large quantities of letters and packages coming from the US, France, the Netherlands, Canada and South America, and similar quantities of outgoing mail consisting of 'bulging envelopes [going] to all sorts of faraway places'.[7] It was clear to the surveillance team that she was acting as a mail relay station, or in the terminology of intelligence, a 'live letter box' receiving and re-sending mail to various parts of the world.

What MI5 didn't know, at the time, was that when Jordan and her husband went to Hanover before the First World War, they had married and had a daughter, Marga, named after Jordan's mother. She had taken German citizenship and set up a small chain of three hairdressers' shops in the prosperous Hoheluftstaßequarter of Hamburg, but Fritz Jordan died in 1918 from war wounds and her fortunes took a turn for the worse. She quickly re-married another Jewish German, her first husband's cousin, Baur Baumgarten, but the marriage failed and a family member, to whom she had made substantial loans, went bankrupt. Furthermore, most of her clientele were Jewish and the Nazi persecutions of Jews was rapidly depleting her customer base.

Forced to sell up her business in 1937, she planned to return to Scotland leaving her two children with relatives but, according to her own account, which cannot be corroborated, on her way to the harbour in Hamburg on 2 February 1937 she was delayed having been intercepted by a Gestapo agent, Herr Ostjes, and taken to Harvestehude.[8] Ostjes evidently knew enough about Jordan to see beyond the quiet, demure hairdresser to the 'voracious reader of crime stories and spy thrillers' who craved 'excitement and change'.[9] He also knew that Jordan was in dire financial straits, and he used these two pieces of information to persuade her to work for the Abwehr in return for sufficient funds for her to establish a business in Scotland as well as a modest income. For eight days, she was taught basic espionage skill and trained in how to collect basic information about British military facilities without arousing suspicion. It was barely adequate preparation, but her role would not be onerous and would require no great skill. It was also recognised by the Abwehr that MI5 had no confidence in female agents and did not employ them and so were less likely to suspect a woman of being involved in espionage activity.

Two other persons to whom Jordan addressed mail were significant. The first was someone called Spielman in Bremen, who was also already on the MI5 radar, and another identified only by the codename 'Crown' who was operating in the US. Initially MI5 was content to allow Jordan to carry on with her secret work while they continued to intercept her mail and collect as much information as possible before interceding and gaining control by 'doctoring' the communications. They were forced to re-think their strategy, however, when one of the letters sent by 'Crown' for redirecting to Germany contained references to a plan for stealing details regarding the US coast defence operations and bases on the Atlantic coast. These records, 'Crown' explained, were kept in the office of Colonel Henry Eglin, the commander of Fort Totten in New York. It was planned to trick Eglin into bringing the plans to what he would be told was an emergency staff meeting at the McAlpin Hotel in Manhattan at the end of January 1938. There he would be kidnapped, possibly killed, and relieved of the documents.

It was assumed that 'Crown' was a German agent working for Spielman and, although crude, the plan to ensnare Eglin might well pose a threat to his life. Analysis of other references to 'Crown' in Jordan's correspondence showed that he was probably an educated, married man living in the Bronx in New York, a fluent German speaker who understood the technicalities of photography but who was perpetually short of money. Initially, MI5 was reluctant to pass on this intelligence to the Americans fearing that they would not be sufficiently secure and might risk exposing their surveillance of Jordan. They were hoping to use Jordan to reveal the identities of other Nazi spies in Britain and did not want any details of their operation against her to be leaked; but if a German spy network was active inside the US and posing a threatening to Eglin's life, then MI5 felt obliged to warn them.

When Lee passed on Kell's intelligence to Lieutenant Colonel C.M. Busbee of the US Department of War in Washington DC, he, in turn, passed it on to Major Joseph N. Dalton, Assistant Chief of Staff of G-2, United States Military Intelligence, at Governor's Island. Dalton ran a small department and had very few resources that would allow him to follow up on it, so he took Busbee to the United States Court House in Foley Square where, on 30 January 1938, they dropped it onto Hoover's desk at the FBI. When Hoover looked at the Elgin report, he had no hesitation in assigning his star agent, Leon Turrou to follow it up. He had a high opinion of Turrou and as far back as 1921, Hoover had wanted to recruit him to his office in the DOJ but had faced opposition due to Turrou not having a law degree.

Turrou, born Leon Turovsky in 1895 in Kobryn, Belarus had, by his own account led a colourful early life in Europe before arriving as an immigrant at Ellis Island on 12 March 1913. He had fought with the French Foreign Legion in the First World War. Recovering from wounds in a hospital in Paris, France, Turrou had met Teresa Zakrewski, whose family lived in China. The two then travelled to China to be married and had two children there, Edward and Victor. Afterwards, they moved to live in Siberia at the Russian terminus of Turrou's employer, the Chinese Eastern Railway. During the Russian Civil War, Teresa and the children were caught in the fighting while Turrou was on business in China. All the evidence suggested that they had died at the hands of communist revolutionaries and Turrou returned to the US where he joined the Marines. In 1922, he travelled to Russia as an interpreter with the American Relief Administration and amazingly discovered that his family was still alive. He found them and took them back with him when he returned to the US. Turrou eventually joined the FBI on 1 April 1928 as a special agent in Chicago where his language skills were very much in demand. He rapidly gained a reputation as the 'best investigator of criminal violations in the Bureau'.[10]

With little to go on, Turrou settled for maintaining surveillance on the McAlpin Hotel and waited for 'Crown' to reveal himself. By 15 February 1938, he had made no progress, but he got lucky when John S. Murray and Arthur J. Silk of the New York Police Department (NYPD) arrested Günther Gustav Maria Rumrich for attempting to illegally obtain thirty-five blank US passports. Rumrich was a chancer working for Dr Erich Pheiffer, the head of the Abwehr US section but it is indicative of Rumrich's singular ineffectiveness as an agent that when he posed as Undersecretary of State Edward Weston, and called the New York branch of the passport division he asked for passport blanks, which were application forms for passports, instead of blank passports. Why such an official should request thirty-five application forms, that were freely available, prompted an investigation which showed that Edward Weston was a fiction. A handover was arranged with a fake parcel when Rumrich was arrested by the NYPD.

He was interviewed by Major Dalton at G-2 and a search of his property revealed another operation that Rumrich had been plotting. A rough note was found which turned out to be a script of a telephone message Rumrich had been planning to deliver to one Colonel Henry W.T. Eglin. He planned to pose as a military official and request that Eglin attend a secret emergency staff meeting at the McAlpin Hotel, New York. Dalton immediately saw the significance of this intelligence and put pressure on Rumrich to cooperate. Confronted with this, Rumrich feared that he would be deported to Germany, an eventuality that he was anxious to avoid, and so offered to cooperate with the investigation in return for an amnesty. Holding a strong hand, Dalton would not agree but, on the other hand, he was not over eager to prosecute.

Rumrich, a former US Army sergeant had been born on 8 December 1911, in Chicago but his father, who was secretary to the imperial Austrian consul general, was transferred to Bremen in 1913 and from there moved around to Hungary, Italy and Russia spending ten years in Czechoslovakia. It was in Prague, that Günther applied for and received a US passport and American citizenship. He arrived in New York on 28 September 1929 and a year later joined the US Army. Despite running up large debts, stealing and absconding then being imprisoned by a court martial, the boastful but smart Rumrich studied for and passed his sergeant's exams and became a sergeant at the age of 21 before being discharged on 27 April 1933.[11]

He re-enlisted the very next day and spent two years working at the station hospital in Fort Clayton in the Panama Canal Zone. In 1935, he found himself at Fort Missoula, Montana where, despite having married the 16-year-old Guiri Blomquist, he faced more accusations of embezzlement which sent him on the road again as a fugitive. He arrived in New York penniless and was able to get work as a teacher of German but his taste for high living drove him to look for extra income. Drinking with crewmen of German ships and listening to their stories, he got the idea of offering his services to German intelligence as a spy. He wrote a letter to Colonel Walter Nicolai, who had been a director of German intelligence during the First World War, described himself as a 'high official in the United States Army' with access to important military information and offering himself as a spy. Since he did not know the colonel's address, he sent his application to the *Volkischer Beobachter* newspaper offices in Berlin. At the time Rumrich was, in fact, working as a translator for the Denver Chemical Manufacturing Company on Varick Street in Lower Manhattan. Nicolai had long since retired but the letter found its way to the Abwehr offices in Hamburg and since they were quite keen to take on new recruits, they sent two officers to check him out; Kapitänleutnant (line officer) Hermann Menzel, and his deputy Kapitänleutnant Udo Wilhelm Bogislav von Bonin both of whom worked with Pheiffer who was in charge of all Nazi spying activities in North and South America. Menzel and von Bonin contacted Rumrich and gave him a few simple tasks to perform. After providing information about his deployment to Panama, he sent further data on troop dispositions and other military matters that he obtained from open army and navy sources, and from newspapers. Having completed his initial tasks satisfactorily, he was summoned to a meeting at the Café Hindenburg in New York with Karl Schlütter, ostensibly a steward on the German liner SS *Europa* but, in reality, one of Pheiffer's New York representatives. It was Schlütter who would later set up the passport scam to facilitate the infiltration of German secret agents, posing as American sailors, into the Soviet Union, for which Rumrich was promised a £300 fee and for which he was subsequently arrested.

Schlütter had done his homework and knew all about Rumrich and his penchant for high-living. It was suggested that Rumrich establish himself as a *bon-viveur* throwing drinking parties to which he would bring young girls and for which he would send invitations to young naval officers from local military shipyards on forged official stationery. Rumrich was to sift through the officers and try to determine who, if any, had German sympathies and others who might be drawn into espionage with the promise of financial reward.

On his own initiative he used his knowledge of the US Army Medical Corps to get statistical information about the level of venereal disease among US troops worldwide and this he passed on to Schlütter. This proved to be valuable for the Germans when assessing the readiness of US troops for combat but it was the plot to acquire thirty-five blank US passports by posing as a US Department of State official that was his undoing.

Unfortunately, although impersonating an official was an indictable offence, trying to get blank passports evidently was not and the case against Rumrich might require high-status Department of State officials to testify. Dalton saw that the involvement of four US agencies, not to mention British intelligence, would make any prosecution a messy business with low probability of a conviction for espionage and he was keen to divest himself of the case especially after details of it had been leaked to the press. The War Office, however, was strongly opposed to letting Rumrich walk free and handed Rumrich over to Turrou to see what he could make of him.

Turrou had been involved in a number of high-profile cases including the Lindbergh kidnapping and the Kansas City Massacre where the gangster Frank Nash, two police officers and an FBI agent were killed outside the Kansas City train station on the morning of 17 June 1933. In a book he wrote later, Turrou described Rumrich as

> a well-set-up young man of about twenty-seven, just under six feet, with black hair combed back in a long pompadour from an oddly high forehead. He had piercing, intelligent black eyes and a small, pointed chin, small, self-indulgent mouth. I'd call it a good-looking face, proud but weak.[12]

Turrou adopted a soft approach. He allowed Rumrich a visit from his wife and child and had little trouble persuading him to talk with promises of amnesty in exchange for information. Rumrich began talking and hardly stopped for two days but it was not always easy to separate fact from fiction. He recounted his life story and gave up details of his recruitment through Otto Maurer, an official of the Hamburg-America Line and his boss Kapitänleutnant William Dreschel, assigned to the office of the marine superintendent of Hamburg-America Line. Above Dreschel was Captain Heinrich Lorentz, chief officer of the German cruise ship SS *Europa*, which made weekly crossings of the Atlantic Ocean between Europe and the United States. All of these men, said Rumrich, answered to Pheiffer in Bremen.

Under Turrou's questioning, Rumrich admitted to frequenting bars along the New York docks casually chatting to unsuspecting sailors, merchant seamen, longshoremen and stevedores over a few drinks. Snippets of information he picked up were combined with his own observations to get a picture of ship destinations and descriptions, warship movement and construction, and the volumes, types and destinations of cargoes moving in and out of the port. He also admitted to having stolen copies of ship-to-shore communication codes and detailed plans of a new anti-aircraft gun developed at Fort Monmouth, New Jersey. He gave Turrou details of how he had planned the Elgin operation along with a newly recruited agent Erich Glaser.

Glaser was 'a strapping six-footer of about twenty-nine, rather handsome, with dark brown hair and dark, stupid eyes.'[13] Born in 1909 in Leipzig, Glaser had arrived in New York in 1931 and, despite speaking very poor English, was taken into the Second Field Artillery as a private and promptly shipped to Fort Clayton in the Panama Canal Zone where he had met Rumrich. Later when Rumrich was looking for agents, he remembered Glaser and when Glaser was discharged, he brought him to New York. After agreeing to work for Rumrich, Glaser re-enlisted this time in the 18th Reconnaissance Squadron of the Air Corps at Mitchell Field where he copied code books which were sent, via Jordan in Scotland, to Germany.

At first the Germans considered a 'honey trap' where Eglin might be lured into a liaison with a woman and then be susceptible to blackmail but they decided that he was not the type of man who would fall for that. Instead, Rumrich would impersonate the Adjutant to General Craig and make the telephone call to invite Eglin to the meeting. Once inside the hotel room, the unsuspecting colonel would be overpowered and, if necessary, killed and his document case stolen. It was all highly speculative and quite unlike any other operation either man had hitherto been involved in. The prospects of it ever coming off were extremely remote. When he was arrested and charged with supplying highly sensitive cypher and code data to the Germans, Glaser made a full confession.

Rumrich also said that Schlütter was due to arrive in New York on 24 February 1938 at Pier 86 on the SS *Europa* with his assistant, Jeni Hofmann (aka Ruth Hofmann, or Johanna Hofmann), who was posing as the ship's assistant purser and hairdresser. When Turrou apprehended Hofmann, he was clearly impressed, describing her later as 'a trim young woman in a crisp white uniform, with … a wealth of wavy, auburn hair [framing] a delicate, fair skin [setting off] her clear, deep-blue eyes.'[14] He exaggerated her importance in the German espionage operation somewhat and the press jumped on the story with much elaboration especially when Hoover chimed in as well telling them that he had unearthed a widespread plot and anticipated further arrests. However, Schlütter would not be one of them. He had evidently been tipped off about Rumrich's arrest and had not even boarded the ship in Bremerhaven.

Back at FBI headquarters, Turrou confronted Hofmann with what he knew of Rumrich and Schlütter, but she denied knowing either man. He went back to the ship and searched her cabin, coming up with a brown suitcase which he brought back to his office and opened in front of Hofmann. It contained letters written in code of which she denied all knowledge. Playing his trump card, Turrou now brought Rumrich into the room at which point Hofmann broke down and confessed to her relationship with Schlütter, and her role as his assistant. From that point she became an important source of information revealing much about Nazi methods of recruiting and running of agents, especially those on the transatlantic passenger liners. She decoded the letters, all written by Schlütter, and addressed to three more agents; Katherine 'Kate' Moog Busch, Martin Schade and Dr Ignatz Theodor Griebl. On the following day, Rumrich, Glaser and Hofmann all appeared in court, charged with espionage and, since none could pay the $25,000 bail, they were all remanded in custody pending the convening of a Federal Grand Jury.[15]

In London, Kell was anxious to avoid Jessie Jordan's name being made public, but he had little doubt that, given half a chance, the American press would have her on their front pages before too long. For him it turned into a damage limitation operation. To forestall the US from naming her as a witness in any future trial of Rumrich and his associates, Kell dispatched Hinchley Cooke to detain Jordan and make a thorough search of the three Scottish premises associated with her looking for evidence of any espionage activity she had undertaken against exclusively British interests. It transpired that she had indeed been visiting sites of military interest, but it was quite low-level surveillance, much of which would not normally be deemed illegal. There was a danger of allowing the investigation to receive sensational press coverage with little of substance to back up any charges of espionage. MI5 not only came under significant political pressure to avoid letting the investigation explode into a diplomatic row with Germany, but also did not want to alert the Abwehr to the fact that the 'Crown' connection had been uncovered.

Their solution was to create a web of disinformation from which nobody could divine the truth. Jordan was brought before a court on

3 March 1938 to face charges under the Official Secrets Act but MI5 were determined to keep it low key. To hide MI5's surveillance of Post Box 629, Jordan's exposure was attributed to the curiosity of her local postman who, it was claimed, raised his concerns about the volume of mail she was receiving and sending. Another story put out was that MI5 had actually been tipped off about Jordan by the FBI. All this would be to no avail, however, if two other developments were to come to fruition. Jordan's assistant, Mary Curran, had sold her story to the *Daily Record* claiming to have been central to the exposure of Jordan, and Jordan, herself, having pleaded not guilty to all charges, was now requesting permission from the Secretary of State for Scotland to sign a publishing contact to tell her account of the matter. With Jordan's arrest now public knowledge, and MI5 unable to find sufficient grounds to prevent publication, they agreed to it on condition that they would be allowed to edit the manuscript before publication.

Jordan was then gently interviewed by Hinchley Cooke who recognised her vulnerability and concern for her daughter, Marga, and granddaughter, Jessie, both of whom had joined her from Germany. When the case came to court, it was held in camera with no press allowed. The alterations to the indictment removed all references to Jordan's activities as a forwarder of spy mail. The case against her would focus on her well-documented personal espionage activities.[16] She pleaded guilty and hoped for leniency. The charges were serious but the evidence of serious harm having been dealt to British security was weak. Hoping to keep Jordan out of the clutches of US prosecutors, she was handed down a four-year sentence, but the FBI did not give up hope of extradition.

Following up the leads uncovered by the Rumrich and Hofmann interviews, the FBI focussed on the most intriguing one: Griebl. When questioned further about Griebl, Hofmann spoke quietly, 'Oh, he is a very important man,' she said, 'probably the most important Nazi secret-service agent in all America.'[17] Turrou went to interview Griebl in his offices on East 87th Street in Yorkville. He found 'a pudgy man, of medium height, about thirty-nine [wearing] gold-rimmed glasses' who meekly agreed to accompany Turrou to FBI headquarters.[18]

Under questioning, Griebl denied knowing either Schlütter or Hofmann but when Turrou confronted him with Hofmann in person his mild countenance fell away and he erupted in a stream of invective threatening to have her shot. A search of his offices turned up large quantities of anti-Semitic materials. There were files on many prominent Jewish Americans such as Treasury Secretary Henry Morgenthau and New York City's Mayor Fiorello LaGuardia all containing defamatory and obscene remarks, but these were certainly not actionable under the law. There seemed to be no actual incriminating evidence of espionage at all until an innocent-looking book of matches revealed, on opening, a set of symbols similar to those discovered in the documents from Hofmann's suitcase. Faced with this evidence and after further questioning, Griebl made a full confession which led Turrou to another two agent, Eleanor Böhme, a 'strikingly pretty girl of twenty-two: blonde, with blue eyes, fair skin, a dimple in the centre of her chin and an oddly deep, mature voice', and Kate Moog.[19] Böhme had been born in the US to German parents. She had gained a Batchelor of Arts degree from Hunter College and spent much of her leisure time socialising with German sailors and officers whose ships were docked in New York which is where she had met Schlütter. At Schlütter's behest, she had a meeting with Moog on a bitterly cold January day in 1938, where discussions hedged around the possibility of Böhme taking on work of national interest to Germany but nothing specific was proposed and there are no details of any espionage work actually ever having been carried out by her. Moog was a different case altogether, though, and it became clear that Griebl was having an affair with this 'tall, handsome woman, with flashing eyes.'

Turrou was now able to assemble a background file on Griebl. He was born in Würzberg and had served as an artillery officer during the First World War. His brother was reputed to have been a close friend of Joseph Goebbels. After studying medicine in Munich, Griebl had arrived in the US in 1925 to continue his studies at Long Island Medical College where he graduated with a degree in medicine. After a spell in the US Army Medical Reserve Corps, he obtained a licence to practice as a gynaecologist in Bangor, Maine before moving to the Yorkville community, known as Little Berlin, in New York where a German-speaking physician was highly valued. There he established himself as the official doctor of a number of German-American societies and he joined the US Army Reserve.

The 'pudgy, dimple-cheeked, bespectacled' Griebl had never hidden his intense loyalty to Nazism and it was no surprise when, in 1933, he had come to the attention of the Dies Committee. He was found to be in frequent contact with German-American organisations such as FONG and had personal relationships with prominent individuals in Nazi Germany's government, including Hans Borchers, the German consul in New York.

He was also a member of the German cultural organisation, the Steuben Society, and was popular within the German-American community but had an unfortunate reputation with the American press as a man not slow to use his fists in an argument and was a fiery speaker at Nazi rallies. In 1934, he had given a speech to 20,000 German-Americans at a swastika-clad Madison Square Garden on German Day where his blazing rhetoric had been rapturously received. At one time, Griebl had ambitions to lead FONG but it was the NSDAP candidate Fritz Gissibl who was chosen in his place. Counting on a hard core of Spanknöbel supporters, Griebl threatening to split the movement, but Gissibl went into action in the best Nazi traditions by initiating a smear campaign against Griebl that proven sufficiently venomous to see his rival ousted in short order. His undisclosed association with Nazi officials suggested an intelligence role but with little evidence to go on he was just marked down in the FBI files as a fascist sympathiser and no action was taken at the time. It did, however, result in his forced unceremonious resignation as assistant clinical surgeon at Harlem Hospital in New York.

In March 1934, he offered his services to the Abwehr by writing to Goebbels but Goebbels, believing that the intelligence service had no interest in the US, forwarded his letter to the Gestapo instead. This ended up on the desk of Paul Kraus who was engaged in setting up a clandestine courier operation on transatlantic liners. He invited Griebl to come to Hamburg where they discussed ways in which Griebl could contribute. In his medical practice, inevitably, many of Griebl's patients were Jews and he built up an extensive file of their personal details. Of others, he was able to find out their occupations, place of employment, incomes, capacity to pay medical bills, and, most important, attitudes, feelings and loyalties toward Germany and the new Nazi leadership. This allowed him to identify any who might be prevailed upon to become Abwehr espionage agents. One of his first recruits which clearly shows the efficacity of this approach was Christian F. Danielsen, a one-armed marine engineer working at the Bath Iron Works in Bangor. Although a forty-year resident of the US, Danielsen had three daughters living in Germany and strong ties to the old country. He agreed to work as an agent by copying secret blueprints of destroyers that his employer was designing and building for the navy. He would travel to New York on a monthly basis and deliver his drawings to Griebl personally.

With his wide range of active agents, Griebl was the recipient of valuable technical intelligence from

> a Swiss-born captain in the United States Army who supplied details of new infantry weapons, a draftsman in a firm of naval architects in New York, a designer of guns in Montreal, an engineer in the metallurgical

> laboratory of the Federal Shipbuilding and dry Dock Company at Kearny, New Jersey, contacts in the navy yards in Boston and Newport News, Virginia.

All was sent directly to Germany using couriers on German liners.[20]

Nazi spies had been operating in the US since 1933 under the control of Wilhelm Lonkowski, Griebl told Turrou. A search of FBI files came up with a report entitled 'William [Wilhelm] Lonkowski. Suspected spy. Reported 9/25/35 [25 September 1935] by US Customs and United States Military Intelligence.' Wilhelm Lonkowski, aliases William Schneider, Willie Meller, William Sex, William Sexton and William Lonkis, had slipped through the fingers of US customs officials on 25 September 1935 as he tried to pass US military secrets to an agent on board the Bremen-bound SS *Europa* in New York Harbor. This was the very first inclination anyone in the US had that Lonkowski was 'a person of interest' but by this time he had been operating inside the country running a nation-wide network of spies for five years. Compromised but still free, he fled to Canada and from there to Germany.

Griebl and Lonkowski had met by accident when Lonkowski had visit Griebl's premises as a patient suffering from a troublesome duodenal ulcer. They had worked together briefly in 1922 on assignments in Paris when they both worked for Abwehr Chief Gempp. The two men now merged their networks with Griebl using Lonkowski's couriers and Lonkowski tapping into Greibl's list of potential agents. Their first joint venture was in June 1934 when they both went to Montreal to meet a Nazi agent working at a company doing work for the US Navy. From him, they obtained details of a new anti-aircraft gun that used electromagnetism to vastly increase its rate of fire. As the months passed, Lonkowski and Griebl harvested a bountiful crop of secret including army maps and troop strength tables, drawings of devices that the Lear Radio Corporation was building for the army and navy; detailed reports of experiments with chromium; an army critique on tactical air exercises at Mitchel Field; and specifications of every aircraft being built at Seversky.[21]

The Griebl-Lonkowski ring had grown into a formidable web of infiltration and espionage but it was operating in something of a vacuum with little interest being shown by the Abwehr, still under the control of Patzig, Kraus's desk was piling up with reports brought in by Eitel and Schlütter his transatlantic couriers but the Gestapo really had no use for them until, that is, Erich Pheiffer had arrived at Wilhelmshaven *Reichsmarineamt* (Imperial German Naval Office) with orders to establish a US network of intelligence agents. With little to work with,

Pheiffer was pleased to take them off Kraus's hands. Variously known as Dr Erdhoff or N. Spielman, the tall, lean bespectacled Pheiffer would remain a 'faceless, shadowy figure' whose fingerprints would be all over many of the Abwehr's US espionage operations, but he would later be indicted by several US Grand Juries for conspiracy.[22] He quickly made effective use of the courier operations and changed the whole complexion of US espionage operations. Eitel was established as the senior courier (Agent R.2307) and Griebl was designated 'Ilberg' (Agent A.2339). All agents in 'Operation Sex' were allocated numbers within the 2300 series, where 'R' signified a travelling agent and 'A' signified one who was producing intelligence.

Soon 'Sex' had become the most productive operation within the Abwehr. Pheiffer was summoned to Berlin to meet Colonel Hans Piekenbrock, head of *Amstgruppe I,* and von Bonin with the new diminutive Abwehr chief, Canaris, who had replaced Patzig.

This was, at a time, when the Nazi High Command was expressing particular displeasure at the 'intolerable and perceptibly high levels of inactivity' in the US. Despite not having much idea of what was going on across the Atlantic, they complained of inadequate supervision of undercover operatives and low levels of penetration in in government and military circles.[23]

Pheiffer told Canaris that he was keen to inject some life into the US operations and convert the presently nondescript groups into formidable intelligence-gathering units. New headquarters were set up in Bremerhaven. Lonkowski, too, became more established with a new house in Hempstead, Long Island.

With Washington DC and New York as the central hubs, a web of semi-independent informants was established in Montreal, Newport News, Boston, Buffalo, Bristol, Philadelphia, San Diego and Bath. For security, spy network cells would be compartmentalised meaning that none would know much about any of the others. By 1936, German military intelligence had several hundred local-level employees and part-time informants providing a steady stream of intelligence ranging from information readily available in newspapers and periodicals to specialised data on industrial production. At the European end of the link, the Abwehr had *Umleitungstelle* (transfer agents) at all principal European sea ports with letter boxes in Portugal, the Netherlands and Scotland, Brazil and China.

Now renamed Operation Ilberg, the spy ring was extraordinarily productive. In the period between January and July 1938, German agents sent to Germany details of every aircraft built at the Sikorsky plant in Farmingdale, blueprints for the FLG-2 and the SBU-1 carrier-based scout bomber at the Vought Company, specifications of a bomber in production at Boeing and another aircraft made by the Douglas Aircraft Corporation and blueprints for three new navy destroyers, DD-397, DD-398 and DD-399.[24] Pheiffer was even able to scrutinise finished drawings of a new gunsight weeks before the US Navy did. By now Griebl was enjoying a monthly retainer of $500.

Another target was an employee of the Sperry Gyroscope Company specialising in automatic pilot devices. Irwin Backhaus was an expert in his field. He had been offered a very lucrative two-year contract in Germany on the understanding that he would divulge to his new employers all he knew about developments in Sperry. It was an example of the way that the Lonkowski and Griebl were inveigling Germans working in sensitive military industries to work for the Abwehr, but Backhaus, for one turned down the offer and reported the approach to the police, but no laws had been broken and the matter was taken no further.

Senta de Wanger was born Senta Dirlewanger in Ulm but had grown bored with the austerity of Weimar Germany and craved excitement. She had changed her name to Dirwa and at the age of 22 sailed for the US. Turrou, who interrogated her in connection with the Lonkowski case described her as 'a good-looking woman ... strong-minded ... rather tall ... with dark hair and blue eyes'. She had a strong but well-modulated voice with a guttural accent that Turrou found charming.[25] When she opened a liquor store at 330 Clinton Street on Long Island, she became acquainted with Lonkowski's wife who was a regular customer finding solace in gin while her husband was absent on 'business'. The friendship grew and de Wanger took the couple in as boarders at her home, 83 Lincoln Boulevard in Hempstead believing Lonkowski to be a piano tuner with only a meagre income. It was with some surprise, therefore, when he started throwing parties in her apartment to which he invited men from the nearby airfield together with some of his German acquaintances including Voss and Griebl, whom she recognised from his association with FONG. De Wanger had been further puzzled when Lonkowski set up a photographic dark room in the house. She challenged Lonkowski's wife one day when her husband was off travelling, and she had consumed a fair amount of gin. Out came a confession that Lonkowski was not a piano tuner at all but an important man who was getting large amounts of money from Germany. When he returned, Lonkowski decided to tell de Wanger the whole truth and coerced her to work for him as a courier.

In August 1935, Lonkowski and his wife went on a trip to Buffalo to visit Gudenberg. From there they sent a package to de Wanger which she was instructed to take to Pier 86, North River, New York and hand it over to Schlütter on the SS *Europa*. She did as she was asked but could not find Schlütter and so instead left the package with a purser and asked him to pass on the package when Schlütter turned up. When Lonkowski heard this, he was furious and became extremely agitated until he got word from Schlütter that the package had been successfully passed on to him.

Lonkowski decided that the next time he would go himself. On 27 September 1935, he had another package for Schlütter but when he took it to the SS *Europa* he was detained by customs officer Morris Josephs and as he was talking to Schlütter. Josephs, who had observed him furtively passing a parcel to the steward, later testified at Lonkowski's trial saying that he had suspected it of being contraband. Some versions of this story refer to the documents being contained in a violin case but Turrou, who was the FBI investigating officer, wrote about the incident in a book and makes no reference to any violin case. When Josephs opened the package, he found letters and photographs. Lonkowski told Josephs that he was a journalist, and the material was merely information for an article he was writing for the *Luftreise* magazine in Germany. Josephs took it to his boss, Lieutenant Morgan, who handed it over to Major Stanley Grogan of G-2 Military Intelligence.

Grogan looked at the confiscated documents one of which referred to a machine gun sight with automatic compensation for speed and wind velocity, a device used on navy fighting aircraft.

Other letters, written in German, contained the following,

> As regards your query reference report of July 18, 1935: reference to construction bulkheads, etc., of Seversky [aeroplane] floats. I expect sketches shortly. On Seversky aeroplanes not the running wheels but the floats are pulled in or extended. This is done by means of a small oil- pump, hydraulic. The running wheel opening in the floats has no effect whatsoever on the start. The floats are lowered so far that the wheel quickly disappears therein through the thoroughgoing opening in the float. The quick running off of the water is assured. I attach to this letter several enlargements of the type. At present not received. It will, of course, require some time to get the desired information about the water-tank at Langley Field. As soon as I receive same I will again refer to your query.

And

> I have just been informed that FLGZ aeroplanes, which for more than a year were used in the Army and Marine Corps, were authorised for foreign delivery. On your list also appears the NR BF2-C1, which was built by Curtiss. Please inform me at once if still interested. [This referred to an experimental army plane for night-bombing flights.]

Photograph of blueprints for the Curtiss XO3C-1, Prototype SOC-1 aircraft confiscated from Rumrich were later shown to have been stolen a full six months before they were due to be delivered to the US Navy. A note attached to them said,

> Of interest are the single strut, fully streamlined landing-gear, full enclosure for pilot and crew, short span, deep chord ailerons, slots and flaps fitted to the upper wing, trailing edge-flaps for controlled engine cooling on the NACA cowl. 'Planes of this type are fitted with landing-gear as shown for carrier operations, but floats may be substituted for catapulting from battleships and cruisers.

There were detailed instructions of how to put the various photographs together to show a complete blueprint of the navy's secret, experimental new light bomber, the Curtiss X2.[26] It has never been satisfactorily explained why Lonkowski was allowed to go home after only a few hours of questioning with a promise to make himself available for recall if necessary. Grogan's boss, Major Dalton, later told Turrou that the bulk of the material was in the public domain and Lonkowski's explanation had seemed reasonable at the time. Lonkowski was spooked, however, and was not going to wait for a knock on his door. By the following morning he was frantically packing a bag and contacting Griebl. For three days he hid in Griebl's country house in Larchmont, Westchester County. From there he was driven across the border into Canada at Rock Island, Vermont by Ulrich Hausmann. Going through Montreal, Lonkowski arrived at Rivière-de-Loup on the St Lawrence river where he boarded a freighter bound for Germany and once there took up a job in the Ministry of Aviation.[27]

Griebl had known Lonkowski since 1933 but it was only in 1935 that he had decided to offer his services to the Abwehr. Despite his operational naivety and minimal knowledge of security measures, he would become a valuable asset for the by Abwehr. Through Lonkowski he contacted Pheiffer in Bremen. Erich Pheiffer had begun his espionage career in 1933 after being recruited by Kapitänleutnant von Hohnhorst, who asked him to a form of a Customs Security Service along the coastal area controlled by the Nordsee command. In spring

1935 Canaris suggested that he establish a *Stelle Bremen* where he could concentrate on the collection of worldwide shipping intelligence using the codenames 'Spielman' and 'Sanders', it was he who had recruited Jessie Jordan and set up the North German Lloyd courier system that included Schlütter and Eitel. Pheiffer had served in the German navy and had seen action at the Battle of Jutland as a junior officer on the *König*. After the First World War he gained a doctorate in economics at the University of Freiburg and later joined German intelligence in Hamburg from where Canaris recruited to concentrate on shipping intelligence and obtain the fullest information on local and worldwide industrial traffic by sea. On 1 October 1935, *Nest Bremen* opened its offices in the Kriegsmarine Dienststelle (German navy department) building. Pheiffer launched his espionage career with a major coup in 1935 when a French naval officer, Marc Aubert, offered his services as an agent to the German naval attaché in Paris. When Aubert met Pheiffer in the Hotel Century in Antwerp he brought with him two large suitcases full of important secret documents stolen from the Brest training establishment. They included full details of French naval vessels; with blueprints and papers describing the latest type of remote-control mines and torpedoes of which the Germans previously had neither knowledge nor suspicion.

Griebl decided to take advantage of his new connections in Germany to expedite a swindle he was plotting to illegally acquire the Giessen property of a Jewish couple Isidore and Heln Berliner, both of whom later died in Auschwitz concentration camp. When he asked for Pheiffer's help he was told that he would have to come to Germany and sort it out. On 1 June 1937, Griebl and his 'travelling companion' Kate Moog left New York on the SS *Europa* bound for Bremerhaven. The twice married and twice divorced Kate Moog had been born to wealthy parents in Germany and had arrived in the US as a young girl. A trained nurse, she worked in Washington DC where she married into a political family and became acquainted with a number of high-ranking members of the US administration. Later she ran a nursing home in New York enjoying a comfortable lifestyle with a large fourteen-room apartment on Riverside Drive and half a dozen servants. At this stage, Moog was just one of Griebl's many girlfriends but one that he seemed particularly well disposed towards since he was taking her with him on his trip to Germany.

On board the *Europa,* Schlütter introduced Griebl to Menzel and von Bonin and upon arrival in Bremerhaven, all four were met by Pheiffer with some ceremony. Griebl and Pheiffer held private meetings in which Pheiffer suggested that Moog, with her Washington connections might be useful as an agent but it was little more than a passing thought since he was not particularly interested in political espionage. The US Navy was his target. Already, he told Griebl, Eitel had brought him details of two aircraft carriers under construction, the *Yorktown* and the *Enterprise* and he wanted Griebl to get more information about their flight deck arrester mechanisms. In return, the property scam in Giessen would be arranged to Griebl's satisfaction.

Joining an express train, Griebl and Moog took a specially reserved compartment for their journey to Berlin where they were put up at the luxurious Hotel Adlon. With hardly enough time to settled down, they were visited by von Bonin and Menzel, who escorted them to 76–78 Tirpitzufer, the offices of Canaris, himself. Canaris was effusive with his praise for Griebl's work and assured him of a comfortable retirement when the next war was over. Later over lunch von Bonin and Menzel went to work on persuading Moog to make use of her American contacts that included a number of senators and senior officers in the military. The Germans told her what they knew of the dire financial circumstances of many of the military men who lived above their means and suggested that she invite them to parties, paid for by Berlin, where they might meet young women. She should then explain to them how such a lifestyle might become a more regular feature of their lives if they had a little extra cash, which she would provide in return for a little cooperation. It was later in the absence of Moog that Pheiffer opened up and told Griebl about the extent of Abwehr penetration in the US 'In every strategic point in the United States we have an operative.' He said, 'In every armament factory in America we have a spy. In every shipyard we have an agent in every key position. The country cannot plan a warship, design a fighting 'plane, develop a new instrument or device, that we do not know of at once!'[28] After a three-week holiday, Griebl and Moog sailed back to New York, but their affair soon came to an end. When Moog expressed doubts about Griebl's promise that he and his wife were divorcing, Griebl 'became very excited, slammed the door and left the apartment'.[29]

The Griebl-Lonkowski ring had been a diverse and highly effective group of spies operating in an open environment so different from the political and social atmosphere in their home country. Griebl was now working with Lonkowski's successor, the Munich-born depressive, Gustav Guellich (agent number A.2338) who worked as a metallurgist in the laboratories of the Federal Shipbuilding Company. His position and the extremely lax security employed by US companies allowed him to carry out his clandestine work with little stress or subterfuge. He simply copied documents that came across his desk. These included underwater 'sonar' devices, blueprints of new ships, and samples of new cabling for ships. In January 1936, he had been privy to a four-page report about work being done by Professor Robert H. Goddard on rocket-propelled missiles. He was even invited to watch test firings of the Nell missile at Roswell in the New Mexico desert.[30] The German army's rocket program had been started late in 1929 when Dr Karl Becker, head of the ballistics and munitions section of the *Heereswaffenamt* (German Army Ordnance Office) weapons testing division. This programme eventually produced the V-1 and V-2 flying bombs in the Second World War and beyond that, the rockets that took Americans to the Moon in 1969. Guellich sent Berlin a memorandum 'Experiments with High-Altitude Rockets in the United States', followed by other reports but their value to the Germans is disputed.

Turrou was having a lot of success with Griebl. The doctor had obviously decided that the best way out of his predicament was to cooperate and hope for clemency in return. 'Self-preservation has always been my god' he told his FBI interrogators.[31]

While Griebl was delivering in terms of his own network, he was oblivious of others in operation all across the continent. Nazi spy rings were strictly compartmentalised for security and ranged in effectiveness from the simple accumulation of open source material from periodicals and newspapers to high-level research intelligence from inside military industries. By 1936, there were hundreds of local-level employees and part-time informants at work funnelling information back to Pheiffer who was constantly under pressure from the German navy in particular for intelligence on the latest developments in naval information and technology.

One notable revelation Griebl came up with was the extent of information exchange with Japanese intelligence services. Any information the Germans came up with that they thought might be of interest to Japan was sold to them. The Japanese saw the US as a potential enemy and were always most anxious for any US naval intelligence. Because of their appearance, Japanese agents found it almost impossible to carry out espionage inside the US themselves.

Griebl pointed the FBI to the apartment of Margaret Simpson at 75 West 89th Street where they found the 'thin, dapper' and surprisingly meek and mild-mannered Karl Friedrich Wilhelm 'Willi' Herrmann who worked as a waiter at the Longchamps Restaurant on 59th Street at Madison Avenue and in the Brooklyn Club. It was hard to believe that this was the man that Griebl had told them was the Gestapo chief in New York responsible for pressurising and intimidating German-Americans, with violence, if necessary, to cooperate in espionage activity. Having worked on German transatlantic liners for a number of years, Herrmann settled in New York in August 1937. He had been allowed to enter the country having been sponsored by Herman Umbreidt, the owner of the Café Hindenburg, on East 86th Street, in Yorkville and it was there that he had met Rumrich. Herrmann's second-in-command was Ewald Fritz Rossberg, Griebl said, but when questioned Rossberg refused to admit to anything, and he was released. Rossberg did not return to his wife and child, however, he went straight to Pier 86 and boarded the SS *St Louis* that sailed before dawn. He later wrote to a friend in America that he had 'received a hero's welcome in Germany'.[32]

When Griebl gave up Voss, he was told to invite him to his apartment where FBI agents would take a surreptitious look at him. They saw a tall, thin, gaunt-looking man of about 40 and set up twenty-four-hour surveillance on him. His bank account showed a balance of $8,000 which was pretty good for a man earning $45 a week. When he was arrested, he denied everything and, at first, a search of his flat proved fruitless but when Turrou found a note Voss's diary mentioning Lonkowski, Voss confessed to having worked for the Abwehr for about the ten years. Bail for Voss was set at $10,000 and, incredibly, the next day his wife turned up with the money. No witnesses could be found to implicate Voss and so, fearing that he would abscond, his bail was re-set to $25,000 which was not forthcoming, so he was jailed.

As was often the case, one arrest led to another. This time it was Karl Eitel who was offered up by Voss, confident that Eitel was no longer in the country. Eitel was chief wine steward on the SS *Bremen* and had at first been approached to simply collect certain readily available magazines and periodicals such as *Popular Mechanics, Popular Science,* and the *Army and Navy Journal,* when he was in New York. Having been quietly initiated into the gentle art of espionage, Eitel's handlers next asked him to report back on certain dockside facilities and shipping movements in the ports of Southampton, Cherbourg and New York which were the *Bremen's* regular stops. It was clear to Eitel that he was now being drawn deeper into espionage work and might become dangerous, but security was lax around the ports and there seemed little risk. Eventually he was invited to meet Pheiffer who flattered him for his work and took him on the next step which was to establish some contact with individuals either serving in the US Navy or having some indirect connection with it. This proved to be beyond his capabilities, but he continued to act as a courier between Pheiffer and his American spy ring.

Another of Lonkowski's recruits, the 'squarely proportioned man with close-cropped hair,[33] Gudenberg was named but when agents searched for him at the Curtiss plant in Buffalo, he had already moved on to the Hall Aluminium Aircraft Company in Bristol, Pennsylvania which was developing bombing aircraft for the US Navy. When challenged, Gudenberg readily and apparently remorsefully admitted that he had passed on plans of aircraft to Lonkowski but denied that any of them were actual military secrets. Again, the FBI chose to leave a suspect in circulation hoping that he would lead them to other contacts and not abscond like Rossberg had done. It was another mistake. Having already testified to a Grand Jury, Gudenberg was scheduled to appear again on 27 May 1938, but stowed away on the SS *Hamburg* and made it safely back to Germany avoiding arrest in Cherbourg and Southampton by feigning sickness.

It was Rumrich who put the FBI onto Karl Weigand who spent a lot of time crossing the Atlantic on various ships of the Hamburg-America Line but Weigand could not be traced. Then Griebl told them that Weigand was an alias of Theodor Schütz, a 'middle-aged man, of medium height, with strong, lined face and very clever eyes'[34] who worked as a steward on the SS *New York*. When the vessel boarded the next time it docked in New York, Schütz was found to have left the ship when it had made an unscheduled stop in Havana. Faced with being hauled in as a suspect in a criminal investigation, the skipper of the *New York* admitted that he had received an urgent signal from Germany telling him to make the diversion. From Havana, Schütz had taken a tramp steamer to Vera Cruz in Mexico and boarded a ship there back to Germany. Pressed for further explanation of why the SS *New York* had been diverted, The Hamburg-America Line replied that Schütz had been suspected of currency smuggling and had been repatriated to face charges.

The FBI was seemingly having great success and increasing its knowledge of German espionage operations almost daily. More than a dozen spies had been identified and details of secrets lost to the Nazis were becoming compendious, but Schütz's evasion alerted them to the fact that the Germans were aware of the dangers to their agents and were now taking steps to protect them. Griebl, however, was still a free man continuing his medical work but would be called into Foley Square from time to time for questioning. He was quite forthcoming about his activities sprinkling his discourse with easily verifiable details but his overall involvement in the espionage ring was still unclear. He seemed to be cooperating just enough to stay out of prison but giving up the bare minimum necessary. He was open about his involvement in the German-American political movements and visits to the US by people such as Hitler's personal adjutant Fritz Wiedermann. Griebl knew that some of his acquaintances were involved in espionage, he told Turrou, but he claimed never to have had anything to do with that sort of thing himself.

It was obvious to Turrou from his interviews with Rumrich and others that this was not the case and armed with this information his endless questioning led Griebl to begin admitting that he might have had certain knowledge of certain activities He was caught between a rock and a hard place Turrou was sure that Griebl was a central figure around whom much espionage was planned and carried out. He kept putting bits of evidence before Griebl and it was becoming clear to the German that a case was building against him, one that would see him serving many years in an American prison. On the other hand, if he cooperated beyond a certain point, he would become the target of Nazi retribution and he was all too well aware of what that would mean.

He chose a path that he hoped would keep him somewhere between by acknowledged his assistance to German intelligence but claiming that it only started after his trip to Germany with Moog in 1937. It was on board ship, he said, that Schlütter had introduced him to Menzel and von Bonin. On 30 April, Turrou's boss FBI Special agent Reed Vetterli wrote to Hoover requesting that Griebl, Moog, Dreschel, von Bonin and Herrmann be subjected to polygraph tests. This would be the first documented instance of polygraph tests being employed in espionage cases.

The polygraph used by the FBI in this case was one that had been developed by Professor Leonard Keeler in the North-Western University Scientific Crime Detection Laboratory. He called it 'a diagnostic method for detecting deceptions.'[35] The polygraph recorded a number of different bodily reactions which were then used to determine whether the subject was telling the truth or not. Usually it measured blood pressure, changes in breathing and sweating of the skin. Lying can increase stress and lying detection techniques can measure the behavioural and physiological changes that occur when a subject is stressed.

Under test conditions, the subject was seated in a chair close to the apparatus, which looked something like an old-fashioned table radio. One tube led from the machine to a blood pressure cuff which was wrapped round his upper arm and the other to a bigger one wrapped around his chest. Connected to the machine was a continuous paper feed on which two pens marked out a graph. For a few minutes the machine ran with no questioning to settle him down then a few irrelevant questions were asked. More pertinent ones were then intermingled, and his bodily responses recorded on the graph which showed any sudden increase in blood pressure or breathing.

First up was Dreschel who showed no adverse reactions to questioning. The report showed that 'the attitude of this subject was that of unusual frankness and the Polygraph does not reflect any reactions which are particularly inconsistent with this attitude.' Herrmann, however, showed 'pronounced reactions [that] were obvious whenever we gave him a question which would involve him directly in the spy ring.' The results of tests on von Bonin were inconclusive.[36] Moog brought a dash of glamour to proceedings and smiled flirtatiously throughout her test. When questioned her about her own connection with the spy ring, the Polygraph showed reactions but her response seemed genuine when she blandly replied 'no' to a question about Griebl's involvement. The experts reported she was not telling the truth, but that there was no point continuing with further tests on her.

As for Griebl, the report of his questioning stated that he was 'unusually responsive' meaning that his answers could be taken to be essentially 'reliable'. It was noted that 'his present cooperation with the FBI agents was sincere up to a certain point but that he is still withholding much information concerning his own complicity in the espionage work.'[37]

The FBI was having mixed success with Griebl but worse was to follow. He had been called up to appear before a Grand Jury on 12 May but a week before that, Moog called Turrou saying that she feared Griebl had been kidnapped and taken back to Germany to be executed. In fact, he had slipped aboard the SS *Bremen* during the previous night abandoning both his wife and mistress. Agent E.A. Tamm could not be absolutely sure that Griebl was on the ship but wrote a memo for Hoover saying he thought 'the odds very heavy in that direction'. Vetterli had requested permission to send an agent to apprehend Griebl when the ship docked at Cherbourg but was told that the Bureau did not have funds or manpower for such an assignment. The memo clearly shows that the FBI was frantically making a case to show that 'the Bureau is not at fault'. They wanted to hand it all over to the State department since 'this matter may develop into an international incident and … the Bureau should not be in the foreground … and the Bureau cannot be left holding the bag'.[38]

The FBI demanded that when the ship made its scheduled stop in Cherbourg Captain Adolph Ahrens hand Griebl over to the French police but on instructions, from Bremen, when the ship docked at

Cherbourg, he refused to allow the French authorities to remove Griebl who, he said, was being taken back to Germany to face unspecified criminal changes. When he landed in Bremen, Griebl was indeed arrested by the Gestapo but that was interpreted as a crude device to disguise his true status.

When the Grand Jury issued indictments on 20 June, they named eighteen defendants but eleven of them, Griebl, Menzel, von Bonin, Mueller, Pheiffer, Lonkowski, Eitel, Schlütter, Schütz, Gudenberg and another ship's steward Karl Herbert Jänichen were no longer in the US. Two others named, Spielman and Sanders, were not even real people but aliases that had been used at one time or another by Schlütter and Rumrich. Only five were in custody. In the US, Hofmann, Glaser and Rumrich were charged with stealing military codes and Voss with the transmission of secret information about army aircraft designs while Jessie Jordan was under armed guard in the Edinburgh Royal Infirmary having a fibroid operation. Potential witnesses absconded and two ship's captains, Heinrich Lorentz and Franz Friske, who were arrested as material witnesses, posted bail of $2,500 each, then promptly disappeared also.

The whole investigation collapsed into a huge publicity disaster. Methods that had proved successful against homegrown criminals whose motivation was financial gain had proved to be less than efficacious against foreign agents whose prize was information. The FBI had been building their case purely on what the accused were telling them with little corroborating evidence to back it up. They were just taking the word of one against the other with no clear idea of whose version was closest to the truth and now they had apparently allowed the majority of the accused to escape. Vetterli went as far as to publicly declare that the German Intelligence agencies were probably laughing at them, but the German press did not exploit the debacle and printed not one single word about it.

Not so in the US however, where a scandal erupted on the front pages of newspapers across the country. Politicians scurried to deflect criticism from the FBI. To say that Hoover was angry is the understatement of the year. He issued a statement blaming US Attorney General Lamar Hardy, who angrily replied that the disappearance of so many accused was not 'in any way the result of negligence in the slightest degree on the part of my office.'[39] Defending his department against incompetence, Hardy had actually singled out FBI agent Turrou for praise saying that he had 'worked unceasingly since the beginning of the investigation and [had] done an extraordinary piece of investigative work.'[40]

Turrou was either a villain or hero depending on which side of the blame game he was viewed from but it was on the very day that the Grand Jury issued the indictments that he chose to resign from the Bureau. He somewhat disingenuously claimed that it was because his health had suffered during the spy investigations. The real reason was evident when the *New York Post* devoted two whole pages to announce that it had agreed a $40,000 deal with Turrou to publish his account of the whole affair. An unholy row broke out at FBI headquarters. Vetterli, apparently had, for some weeks, been working with Turrou to get a book and film contract, claiming that Hoover, himself, was planning to do the same. Tamm jealously complained to Hoover that Turrou was 'getting his picture in the paper too often' which was never likely to please Hoover who usually reserved celebrity for himself.[41] Hardy called for and got an injunction to prevent the *New York Post* from publish Turrou's story saying that it would prejudice the trial. 'Suppression of press freedom' cried Turrou's lawyer, Simon Rifkind. What Turrou was doing, he said, was little more than Hoover, himself, had done many times over the years by leaking stories about the Bureau's cases to publications such as the *American Magazine*. Judge Murray Hulbert compromised and allowed a temporary injunction but only until such time as the trial had been concluded. The issue of press freedom that had been raised by the injunction was a sensitive matter that sent ripples through the political landscape all the way up to the White House. It was a relief for President Roosevelt to see that the matter would lie dormant until after the forthcoming presidential election especially as he did not want to have his campaign sidetracked by sensational stories about German spies. He publicly criticised Turrou for his 'questionable patriotism' and sided with Hoover but was sufficiently concerned by the Bureau's obvious failings during the investigation to authorise a substantial increase in its budget.

Hoover fumed as Turrou continued to take all the press attention that he craved for himself and plotted his downfall. If Turrou was allowed to get away with his high-profile and lucrative publishing deal it would set a precedent for other top agents to follow and in no time at all the whole workings of the FBI would be splashed over every front page in the country. The Bureau could not survive such a calamity. His first move was to prevent Turrou giving evidence at the forthcoming trial of the spies. His second was to find a way of discrediting Turrou without prejudicing the trial. In 1935, Turrou had signed a statement acknowledging the confidential nature of his work at the FBI and agreeing not to divulge any information about this to anyone who lacked official entitlement to it. On this basis, Turrou was dismissed from the Bureau 'with prejudice' on 25 June 1935. Clearly, Hoover had refused to accept Turrou's 20 June 1935 resignation which meant that Turrou lost all holiday entitlement and also his pension. Vetterli resigned days later and took employment as a private detective.

The FBI issued a flurry of arrest warrants for all other people who had been implicated in the spy network only to find that they had all disappeared presumably on board transatlantic liners. Frustrated and under huge political pressure, the FBI arrested Maria Griebl hoping to force her husband to return to face trial but they failed again. From her prison cell she told reporters that her husband was an innocent man and that she had been falsely accused by his enemies. Seward Collins, editor of the *American Review* accused the government of holding Maria Griebl as a hostage and put up her $50,000 bail hoping to get an exclusive story. He lost his money when the lady also quickly disappeared only to reappear in Germany.

The trial opened on 14 October 1938 before Judge John Clark Knox at the United States Court House on Foley Square, New York. It was front page news in both Britain, where the *Daily Express* called it the 'biggest show in town in twenty years', and Moscow where both *Pravda* and *Izvestia* gave it extensive coverage. Unsurprisingly, in Germany the *Völkischer Beobachter* ignored it. In Washington DC, however, the German ambassador, Hans Heinrich Dieckhoff was lobbying the defence team to lodge guilty pleas all round so that the matter would go away as quickly as possible. He told Undersecretary of State Benjamin Sumner Welles that he accepted the guilt of the accused but claimed that they had been acting on the order of 'persons of lesser authority' with no official authority. Unfortunately for him, the defence lawyers, especially George C. Dix, were out to make names for themselves and wanted as much publicity as possible.

US Attorney Lamar Hardy led the team of prosecutors assisted by John W. Burke Jr, Lester C. Dunigan and Robert Werner with FBI Special Agent John T. McLoughlin. Defended by Charles W. Phillipbar Jr, Voss faced the most serious charges of sketching and supplying information on the construction of aircraft wings, fuel and gasoline compartments, and bomb racks built at the Sikorsky Aircraft Corp in Farmingdale, New York.

Hofmann's charges were almost as serious. Accused of serving as a courier, transmitting restricted code used for communication between military aircraft and its station, she faced twenty years in prison if found guilty. Lawyer, Dix, planned her defence by attacking Turrou's evidence as coming from a discredited witness. Glaser was charged with providing army and navy radio telephone-telegraph procedure manuals to the Abwehr and was represented by Benjamin Matthews. Rumrich hoped to avoid a conviction by pleading guilty and cooperating fully with the prosecution.

Hardy opened by accusing Hofmann, Voss and Glaser of enabling the German government to infiltrate strategically important US military research and production facilities. He told the court that Pheiffer was reputed to have said that 'he had a Nazi spy in every aircraft factory in America.' Calling Rumrich to the stand, he was able to show that the accused had undertaken many assignments on behalf of the Abwehr including attempting to acquire White House stationery for the purpose of forging presidential orders. Rumrich explained also how documents were smuggled out of the country by couriers working on German liners and how they also opened transatlantic mail bags during the crossing. Rumrich's failed attempt to obtain the blank passports was described as were details of Nazi espionage objectives according to information gleaned from correspondence between Rumrich and Pheiffer.

1. The secret code used between the United States fleet and shore defence batteries to coordinate firing in the event of defensive action against an invading power.
2. The strength of the United States Army on the Eastern seaboard.
3. The numbers of the regiments stationed in the Canal Zone and the general strength of the troops there.
4. United States fleet movements in Atlantic waters.
5. The names of all army officers in the metropolitan New York area.
6. Army mobilization and coast defence plans for the Eastern seaboard.
7. Passports for the use of German agents seeking entry into the Soviet Union.
8. Construction plans of the aircraft carriers Enterprise and Yorktown.
9. Anti-aircraft gun emplacements around New York City.
10. Information about experiments at Fort Monmouth, N. J., as to detection of approaching enemy aircraft.

Rumrich told the court that his first payment of $40 had been for a list of troops stationed in the Panama Canal Zone. He went on to give details of the plot to kidnap Eglin and about the close cooperation between the German Embassy in Washington DC and Pheiffer's spy network.

Hofmann also pleaded guilty to acting as a courier between New York and Bremen. Griebl's house, she said was the 'clearing house' for information. Pleading for leniency for his client, Dix called Rumrich a communist and accused him of conspiring with his Moscow handlers to tell a pack of lies. Dix also had a 17,000-word deposition taken from Griebl in Germany saying that Turrou was a liar and had taken a $5,000 bribe to help get him out of the country on the *Bremen*. Everything he had told Turrou under questioning had been a lie. Griebl called Turrou 'ridiculous' for inventing what was no more than a spy fiction and, referring to his prospective publishing deal, Dix derided him as a man who was interested only in fame and money. Turrou, Dix claimed, had been corrupted by the 'arrogance of office' and suggested that he had coached Griebl to provide false evidence.[42] In defence of his reputation, and maybe with one eye on publicity, Turrou wanted to put Hoover on the stand to give him a character reference. One is left to imagine Hoover's private reaction to that. Publicly he declared that if the prosecution case was flawed it was because of 'the dishonest viewpoint of former Special Agent in Charge Vetterli and former Special Agent Turrou'.[43] Dix now called for Turrou's FBI file to be admitted as evidence. He was aware that it had been modified to show Turrou in an unfavourable light despite his impressive record with the Bureau and his former status as Hoover's 'blue-eyed boy'. Release of the file required Hoover's personal approval but when it was requested approval was not forthcoming as he was 'out of the city for a few days'.

Having failed in that regard, Dix now stunned the courtroom by introducing a witness who identified Turrou as a man he had known before the First World War as Leon Petrov, who he claimed had been a patient in the psychiatric ward of the King's County Hospital in New York. Judge Knox permitted the relevant hospital file into evidence allowing Dix to read from it the final diagnosis of Turrou's condition at the time which was 'undifferentiated depression'.[44] Dix's next target was Hardy, who, he said, had not even interviewed any of the accused and had failed to push for Griebl's extradition from Germany. His attack on government officers was so virulent that the judge held Dix to be in contempt of court.

When Hofmann took the stand, she appeared contrite, shedding tears as she told how she had done no more than what she believed to be her duty to her country. When she was confronted by the evidence found in the case in her cabin on the SS *Europa,* Dix called it a violation of her rights to privacy under the Fourth Amendment and was not admissible, but he was overruled and it was allowed to stand. Neither Griebl nor any of the other accused made any effort to mitigate Hofmann's jeopardy. When Rumrich was recalled to the stand he gave details of a 'Winter Aid Fund' set up by Henry Ford, the Woolworth empire and General Motors which, he was told by Schlütter, was diverted to finance German espionage operations in the US.

At the end of a 'theatrical farce, played out daily for the entire world to witness',[45] Turrou's evidence carried the day for the prosecution. Guilty verdicts were handed down. Hofmann wept as she received a four-year sentence in the Federal Prison for Women at Alderson, West Virginia. Glaser and Rumrich each received two years, while Voss got six.

The whole investigation and trial had given Hoover and the FBI a great deal of unwanted publicity. With large numbers of special agents having been assigned over a six-month period, it had also taken up much of their time and efforts. It was exceedingly disappointing, therefore, that it failed to deliver up more than a handful of rather pathetic suspects and even fewer convictions. On the other hand, much had been learned about German espionage activity and the extent to which US military and industrial establishment was vulnerable to what had been relatively unsophisticated spying operations. The Griebl-Lonkowski affair encapsulated what was wrong with the FBI in 1938 but that was because of how it had developed since its inception in 1908.

On the surface, the creation of the *Bund,* in March 1936 offered up a pool of potential agents inside the US to be recruited by Ernst Wilhelm Bohle's *Abteilung für Deutsche im Ausland* (Nazi organisation for Germans abroad). In cooperation with the Abwehr, Bohle had built up an efficient network of spies, especially across northern Europe and South America but there was a great reluctance on the part of the A*uswärtiges Amt* (Federal Foreign Office) to take any risks with German-US relations. Neither was the leader of the Bund, Fritz Kuhn, enthusiastic about having German spies in his ranks declaring on one occasion that spies should be shot.[46]

After April 1933, much of what Bohle learned about US military capabilities came from the Washington military attaché, von Boetticher. Upon his arrival in New York, both the American flag and the swastika were paraded on the dockside indicating exactly how official German representation in America was to proceed under the new regime in Berlin. Very soon, by displaying his acumen as an American Civil War historian, von Boetticher, 'an amiable extrovert with easy manners'[47] began establishing good relations with members of the American military establishment in his attempt to be a 'bridge' between the US and Germany.[48] His success in this endeavour is clearly illustrated by his close friendship with three successive Chiefs of Staff, General Douglas MacArthur, General Malin Craig and General George C. Marshall as well as the Secretary of War Harry Hines Woodring.[49] One of his, somewhat over-ambitious, objectives was to establish German military tradition as a criteria among Americans for interpreting world affairs. He refrained from any illegal espionage activity but his reports, covering shipping movements in and out of New York Harbor and details of diplomatic visits to Washington DC, were easily compiled from newspapers and official publications, but were often replete with anti-Semitic remarks. On the whole they were well received by Hitler who placed great store by them which is unfortunate for him since they generally repeated von Boetticher's misconceptions and those of US General Staff officers whose views coincided with his own. While he recognised the vast military potential of the US, he told Berlin that American aid to the Allies would not and could not be a decisive factor before 1941, and failed to realise that through the late 1930s, American public opinion was slowly moving away from a non-interventionist position. In his opinion, the US was also preoccupied with the threat from Japan and was focusing its military priorities on the Pacific theatre.

Chapter 5

NAZIS ON THE WEST COAST

'Nazis are a German political party and are not present anywhere in America. We are purely an American organization.'

Hermann Schwinn,
Western Region Commander of the German-American Bund[1]

Because of its extensive oil reserves, Mexico played an important part in Nazi military strategy. They made considerable efforts to undermine the anti-fascist Lázaro Cárdenas government and tighten up contracts for much needed oil supplies that would be crucial for their economy in the event of war. The Mexican government, however, was far from stable and there had been two failed military coups – one in 1935 and another in 1938 – and arms caches were being stored in the Sonora region of north-west Mexico by General Ramón Yocupicio in preparation for a third.

As early as 1933, the Nazis had targeted Mexico as a country that might be ripe for conversion to their style of fascism. With this as a strategic aim, Schwinn had been instrumental in organising the Mexican Gold Shirts under the direction of General Nicholás Rodriguez. On 20 November 1935, Rodriguez staged a military demonstration in Mexico City, and marched on the presidential palace where a pitched battle broke out when the Gold Shirts were confronted by a left-wing coalition of trade-unionists, liberals and communists. The Gold Shirts were made illegal, and Rodriguez was exiled to El Paso, Texas, US where he plotted the amalgamation of all Mexican fascist groups. Schwinn and Rodriguez continued to keep in touch with each other through San Diego-based Henry Douglas Allen, a native American and fluent Spanish speaker. Despite being 'a physically unimposing figure', the middle-aged Allen was a brawler who was described as small, thin and wiry but pugnacious.[2] Allen was encouraged by Schwinn to join the Silver Shirt movement and set up a recruiting headquarters in Room 693 at 730 South Grand Avenue, Los Angeles which was a fertile ground for right-wing extremist groups. There were large numbers of newly arrived lower-middle-class people in the state who were uncertain and insecure who could very easily take to the streets as populist vigilantes if they were persuaded that their values and social structures were being threatened. Other local groups like the American Nationalist Party were competing for the same support but lacked funds and effective leadership unlike the Silver Shirts, which appeared to have the resources and leadership needed to become a viable political organisation.

Between them, Allen and Schwinn smuggled arms into Mexico along the border between Laredo and Brownsville and hid them in Monterrey. Along with the arms came large quantities of Nazi propaganda in Spanish, which had come into the country and was stored at 634 West 15th Street in Los Angeles and turned over to Schwinn, who forwarded the batches to Rodriguez.

Towards the end of June 1935, Dr Heinrich Northe, a low-grade civilian attaché to the German legation had arrived from Berlin, set himself up at a somewhat luxurious house at 64 Tokyo Street and bought a private aircraft for 'pleasure trips'. He went on to spend much of his time in Acapulco and the Sonora region. Before coming to Mexico, Northe had working for the Gestapo as one of the first secret agents sent, under diplomatic cover, to the German Embassy in Moscow. One of Northe's accomplices was another German spy, Baron Hans Heinrich von Holleuffer whose chequered past had seen him fleeing to Guatemala then Mexico under the name of Hans Helbing, to avoid charges in Germany. Now his brother-in-law was head of the Berlin police and he was no longer *persona non grata* in Germany. Much like Northe, he now lived in high style at 36 Danubio Street in Mexico City and between the two of them they organised the regular unloading of weapons and munitions from ships onto small boats off the deserted coastline of Campeche.

On 30 June 1937, the SS *Panuco* a ship of the New York and Cuba Mail Steamship Company entered Tampico harbour in Mexico with a cargo consigned to Armeria Estrada. This cargo was transferred to the Atchison, Topeka and Santa Fe Railroad freight car number 45169 for shipment to the state of San Luis Potosí. The shipper of this consignment was the Winchester Repeating Arms Company of New Haven, Connecticut and the cargo was a large quantity of rifles, pistols and 140 cases of cartridges for various calibre guns. An elderly German, Baron Ernst von Merck, received the shipment and delivered it to General Saturnino Cedillo, a former governor of the state, who was known to oppose the Mexican government. Von Merck had been a German spy stationed in Brussels during the First World War but was now Cedillo's right-hand man. Von Merck was also active in Guatemala, where President Jorge Ubico was also receiving shipments of German arms alongside 280 portable machine guns, 60 anti-aircraft machine guns and 70 small calibre cannon all Italian arms manufactured by Bredda. Guiseppe Sotanis sent Ubico.[3]

Allen did not restrict his activities to plotting to overthrow the Cárdenas government south of the border, however. He promoted himself as the liaison between Nazi agents and plotters conspiring to raise a secret army in the US capable of starting sporadic outbreaks tantamount to civil war, a procedure which, if successful, would effectively deflect the country's energies in wartime. Despite his anathema for spies, Kuhn was more than willing offer the resources of his Bund organisation in support of the idea. He supplied Schwinn with a complete list of all Bund members from which Schwinn selected all American nationals and allocated to each a code number. If they were going to participate in revolutionary activity it was essential to keep their identities secret. The leaders were given codenames. Allen, for instance was given the name Rosenthal to go along with several aliases, including H.O. Moffet and Howard Leighton Allen, he had accumulated over a long and not so salubrious career that included time spent as an inmate of San Quentin and Folsom prisons.

His criminal record is of interest. On 17 May 1910, he was arrested in Los Angeles charged with forging cheques (Los Angeles Police Department file number 7613) for which he was sentenced to three years' imprisonment, suspended. Two years later he was arrested in Philadelphia, charged with violating his parole and brought back to Los Angeles where he was committed to San Quentin as prisoner number 25835. After serving his sentence, he was immediately committed to Folsom, prisoner number 9542, on more forgery charges. Then on 1 February 1919 he was arrested again in Los Angeles County, this time charged with suspicion of a felony. His penchant for issuing forged cheques got him into trouble again in June 1924 in San Francisco and in the following year back in Los Angeles.

Two people associated with Allen at this time were C.F. Ingalls and George Deatherage, a Southern rabble rouser who had promoted himself as leader of the fascist movement, Knights of the White Camelia. Using then codename 'Laura', Schwinn wrote to Deatherage saying,

> We must get busy organizing grid-lattice-work or skeleton for a military staff throughout the nation, and in this we need representatives of fascist groups … After we do all this, now then we shall have the national military framework all steamed up and oiled and coupled to the multiplicity of working parts ready to appear on all fronts.[4]

Allen went to meet Kuhn in New York in January 1938 with a note from Schwinn saying, 'The bearer of this letter is my old friend and comrade-in-arms, Henry Allen [in whom you can have] absolute confidence.'[5] Allen was going east to meet Deatherage and to contact the Italian Embassy, the Hungarian Legation, and James True of the James True Associates. True subsequently wrote to Allen saying,

> If your friends want some pea shooters, I have connections now for any quantity and at the right price. They are United States standard surplus.

Things began to unravel for Allen on 22 April 1938 when he, Schwinn, Leon Lewis's Hollywood spy Slocombe and a few other men were arrested by Naval Intelligence for 'snowstorming' at an outdoor public meeting in San Diego where Superior Court Judge, Harry Hollzer, was addressing an audience of mostly Jews at the busy intersection of Hollywood and Vine. This was a particularly effective method of propaganda distribution often used by the Bund and the Silver Legion whereby a few men would stand on rooftops, in this case the Broadway Department Store, a bank building, and two other tall buildings, and releases pamphlets onto the wind.

While the others were fined and released, Allen was detained for carrying an illegal weapon kept in a leather sheath on the side of the front door of his car, described by Slocombe as

> an oak club about 19" long with a leather thong to wrap around his wrist. The club is about an inch thick, and two and a half inches wide. The back of it is rounded and its face is quite sharp. He calls it a 'kike killer' and showed me how to use it. 'You wrap it around your wrist and then poke it in the man's stomach, and when he bends over come down on top of his head with the flat side.'[6]

A search of his briefcase uncovered

> a large mass of correspondence and other data covering the past six months, exposing widespread fascist conspiracies, numerous representatives and agents throughout the country and close affiliation with Nazi leaders and Nazi organizations. It further contained a

> blue-print of a set up [*sic*] of military and civil organisations with the objective of over-throwing the American government after the 1940 elections.[7]

Documents included a list of almost 100 Nazi, Japanese and Italian secret agents working in the US and Mexico along with their contacts in their home countries. Only three months earlier, Cordell Hull at the Department of State had confidently declared that Nazis had no connection with the Gold Shirt movement in Mexico but here in Allen's briefcase was clear proof to the contrary. There were also maps, diaries and reports of meetings Allen had held with some of these spies, but most disquieting were letters between Allen and the American Nationalist Confederation, a coalition of militant Christian groups, describing a plot to overthrow the US government. This treasure trove of damning evidence even included the names and addresses of hundreds of activists all across the country who were assigned to take leading roles during the insurrection. Weapons would be acquired through the National Rifle Association in Washington DC. There were instructions to the effect that anyone who resisted the coup must be shot 'on the spot [and] to hell with public opinion'[8]

Allen was released on bail and allowed to take his briefcase with him but not before its contents had been photographed. These contents would later form the basis for the Dies Committee's most celebrated revelation of Nazi activity in the US. The authorities hoped to bring charges against Allen who, if convicted of a third felony, would find himself incarcerated for a considerable time under the Habitual Criminals Act. In any event, they had made sure that Allen knew they were on to him and he couldn't afford to take any chance of being hauled up again. They had also been alerted to a wider network that included a woman calling herself Leslie Fry.

Fry's real name was Louise A. Chandor who had been born in Paris to American parents in 1882 and later met and married an officer in the Russian Imperial Army, Colonel Feodor Ivanovich Shishmarev. When he was killed in the Russian Revolution, she and her sons Kyrill and Misha, fled to Vladivostok but by August 1920 they were in San Francisco. It is believed that it was Chandor who first introduced the industrialist Henry Ford to the infamous anti-Semitic forgery, *The Protocols of the Elders of Zion*. By 1936, the fiercely intelligent Chandor had moved to San Diego where she founded the Militant Christian Patriots movement and edited the *Christian Free Press*, a newspaper modelled on the German *Der Stürmer* but she assiduously maintained a low profile. When she wrote and published two anti-Semitic books she adopted the pseudonym Leslie Fry. Working with a small band of trusted collaborators including Deatherage, Allen and Schwinn she became 'the shrewdest and most calculating of all the Nazi agents operating in Los Angles'.[9]

Fry was funding a number of fascist groups in and around San Diego either from her own personal wealth or using funds donated by the heiress Mrs W.K. Jewett. She had recently paid for Allen to go on a six-week trip across the continent to drum up political and financial support for the West Coast fascist movements. In Atlanta he met the Ku Klux Klan Grand Wizard Hiram Evans and then in Washington DC, his letters of introduction got him an audience with officials from the Austrian, Egyptian, Italian, Rumanian and Iraqi embassies to update them on the progress of the fascist movement in the United States. It is a measure of Fry's status as a German agent that Allen was also granted a private meeting with the American and German consuls held at the German Embassy to welcome Hitler's visiting private adjutant, Fritz Weidemann.

Only now, with the revelation of the briefcase contents, was US intelligence becoming aware of the significance of this particular meeting. Some of the documents had revealed clear evidence of Allen's Nazi connections with correspondence between Deatherage, Fry, and a White Russian Vladimir Kositsin that discussed payments to Allen and instructions concerning the recruitment of retired US Army General George van Horn Moseley to lead the coup against the US government. There was even a hand-drawn plan outlining the paramilitary structure of the US government under Moseley's new fascist regime.

With Allen effectively prevented from carrying out any further activities that might render him liable to arrest, it was the moment for Schwinn to step up to claim a leadership role and further his ambitions to take over the leadership of the Bund from Kuhn. He organised the first Western Conference of the Anti-Communist Federation in August 1938 but he was restrained by the knowledge that Fry had the backing from Berlin and it was still she who called the shots. He would only get the top job if Berlin gave its backing. He knew that it was Fry who had most to lose if Allen was ever called to testify and forced to incriminate her in the conspiracy as a paid Nazi agent and if that happened they would all suffer for it. Schwinn would fail to unseat Kuhn at the Bund convention, but he was now well placed to succeed him if the leader faltered.

Clearly rattled by the danger posed by the exposure of Allen's document case, Fry went on the offensive by issuing none-too-veiled threats against Hollzer and Leon Lewis reminding them that Allen was 'not alone'. She plotted with Allen to kidnap Lewis's children and, at the same time, took steps to distance herself from the plotters. Writing anonymously in the *Christian Free Press*, she broke from Deathridge by denouncing the American Nationalist Confederation as un-American for its use of the swastika. Up until this point she had privately continued to maintain a close relationship with both Allen and Schwinn but this turnaround had alienated Allen. Suddenly the Fry-Allen relationship began to fracture. When Slocombe bumped into Allen in September, Allen looked drawn and haggard and said he was 'through with her'.[10] He was even trying to turn the movement away from Fry claiming that she had changed sides. Fry responded by printing an article denouncing Allen as a fool. Allen saw a chance to gain some traction with the police by informing them of Fry's illegal activities and denounced her as a Soviet spy.

The West Coast Nazi leadership had been gearing up for action by recruiting men from the police and sheriff's departments, the National Guard, and army and naval personnel but seizure of Allen's briefcase had changed the landscape. Out in the open and undermined by Allen's attack, there was nothing Fry could do to protect herself and when the Dies Committee opened its hearings on subversive activities, she fled the country to Rome.

Chapter 6

FINANCIAL ESPIONAGE

'Following the Money'[1]

Not all German espionage in the US was carried out by shadowy figures, secret radio operators and industrial spies. Diplomats, of course, were heavily implicated although embassies went to great lengths to deny it and even discourage it. It was also men in suits in offices deep inside Manhattan's financial district that were also active agents working to undermine the US willingness to become involved in the European war.

US Secretary of the Treasury Henry Morgenthau was a loyal Roosevelt supporter and an advocate of asserting US power to slow the remorseless slide to war in Europe. His deep mistrust of Germany had only been heightened by investigations in the 1930s into the Black Tom explosion of 1916 which concluded that Germany had actively recruited secret agents from ethnic groups in the US at the time and that the disaster had been the result of sabotage. There was no reason to think that they would not do it again. His position in the Treasury gave him insight into the way in which secret funds had been fed to the German agents during the First World War in such a way as to disguise the involvement of the German government. In an effort to get one step ahead of the Germans this time round, he took steps to monitor the movement of all foreign money passing through US banks with the help of Hoover at the FBI.

Hoover was well placed to offer assistance due to FBI involvement in the investigation of widespread fraud committed during the stock market collapse of 1929 when thousands of banks collapsed. His agents had gained much experience in exposing falsification of bank records and tracing the flow of money through the banking system. By 1939,

Hoover was routinely providing Morgenthau with information on the movement of foreign money through US banks.

One of the main concerns was the level of collusion between Nazi Germany and Soviet Russia over the trade in goods vital to the armament industry. The danger was that material such as Molybdenum, essential for tank and aircraft production was being bought by the Soviets and then being sold on to Germany. Attention was focused on the Amtorg Trading Corporation, established in New York in 1924 to handle most of the Soviet exports and all imports of raw materials and machinery. It facilitated trade and exchange of news and information between US and Soviet companies but was also suspected of channelling funds for the American Communist Party.

After almost a decade in which the US government had encouraged US industry to enter into partnership agreements with European companies to expand their markets and encourage foreign investment in the US, the country realised that this was now its Achilles' Heel with many of the foreign departments of these companies under German control and involved to a greater or lesser extent in the German war effort. These arrangements were seriously threatening US access to vital resources and preparations for national defence that had been accelerated after the German occupation of northern Europe. It was also a loophole whereby German and Italian companies could evade the government freeze on assets. For too many years, the US Treasury had ignored the potential threat posed by both German and Soviet intelligence agencies who had been taking advantage of business partnerships to move money across the Atlantic. The distinction between business and espionage was blurred.

When Hitler's forces swarmed over northern Europe in May 1940, Roosevelt froze all US-held assets of the occupied countries and allowed Morgenthau to request Hoover's assistance to monitor the sources, routes and destinations of funds passing through US banks, especially from France, the Netherlands and Belgium. The measure was taken not only to prevent Germany using those funds to finance its war effort but also to track the movement of money that might be used to fund espionage activities. When the Marine Midland Trust Company told Hoover that a $9 million transfer was due from an Italian bank, ostensibly the contents of a family trust, Roosevelt authorised him to use the Treasury to prevent any of those funds moving out of the country again. In a move that clearly illustrated the extent of collusion between US banks and the FBI, the Chase National Bank held a fund of $1 million in notes with recorded serial numbers and whenever the German Consulate made withdrawals, as was the case of $50,000 going to the Women's Foreign Missionary Society of the Methodist Episcopal Church, it was tracked to see exactly where it ended up.

As early as autumn 1939, the US Treasury had become aware of a £6 million fund put at the disposal of Hans Borchers at the German Embassy in New York exclusively to fund espionage. Much of this went through Chase and was tracked and some of it led to Robert C. Mayer and Company of Chicago whose company president, August T. Gauseback was observed to be making donations in small denomination notes to Father Charles Coughlin's anti-Semitic movement. Other money was going to Hautz and Company.

By the end of the year money was coming into US banks at an accelerated rate not only to protect it from the ravages of war but to finance espionage. The FBI was stretched to its limits trying to monitor the more than 3,000 accounts that were suspected of being connected to subversive activities. All this came to a halt on 14 June 1941 when Roosevelt ordered the freezing of all Axis assets in the US.

Chapter 7

TORKILD RIEBER

> Rieber always thought it was much better to deal with autocrats than democracies. He said 'with an autocrat you really only have to bribe him once. With democracies you have to keep doing it over and over.'[1]

Torkild Rieber was no Nazi but he admired authoritarian regimes. As chairman of the Texaco, the fourth largest oil company in the US, he was first and foremost a businessman and a very important businessman at that. His devotion to profit had seen him supply the Franco regime, which was financially broke, with 3.5 million tons of oil during the Spanish Civil War in return for which the Spanish leader had awarded him the Knight of the Grand Cross of the Order of Isabella the Catholic. This had been done despite the January 1937 Neutrality Act having made it illegal to provide credit to either side in the conflict. Texaco oil tankers sailing from Galveston with manifests recording Antwerp. Rotterdam and Amsterdam as destinations were diverted in mid-Atlantic to Spanish ports. When Roosevelt stepped in to stop the practice, Rieber simply sent the oil to Italy instead where it was reloaded and transhipped to Southern Spain.

Rieber had been born in Voss, Norway in 1882 and, as a boy, had gone to sea as a cabin boy. At the age of 16, he found himself in the US and stayed there become naturalised in 1904. Working his way through the ranks on oil tankers he ended up as chairman of Texaco in 1935 and became something of a legend among oilmen.

While dealing with Franco, Rieber had been approached by Dr Friedrich Fetzer, of the German navy who suggested that there was plenty of profitable business to be done with the Nazis also. Arrangements were made for oil to be shipped from Colombian ports and the payments held in Reichsmark accounts in Hamburg. The process continued after the outbreak of the Second World War despite the British embargo, but Rieber started to worry about getting his money out of Germany. To get round it he proposed a deal whereby the Nazis would hand over three new oil tankers to Texaco in lieu of the cash held in Hamburg. On behalf of the regime, Hermann Göring suggested that such a deal might be envisaged if Rieber agreed to act as a peace emissary to the White House. Having no diplomatic or political finesse, Riber completely failed to influence Roosevelt's policy but he got a second chance to persuade Göring to agree the deal by financing a visit to the US of the German lawyer Dr Gerhard Alois Westrick. As acting commercial counsellor of the German Embassy, Westrick proceeded to wine and dine the biggest names in the US business world: Colonel Sosthenes Behn of the International Telephone and Telegraph Company, Ralph Beaver Strassburger the millionaire financier, James D. Mooney of General Motors, Edsel Ford and executives of Eastman Kodak, the Underwood Faber Company and the International Milk Corporation.[2] This group of men agreed to 'put pressure' on Roosevelt to suspend arms deliveries to Britain.

While in Germany negotiating the oil tanker deal, Rieber had made the acquaintance of Dr Nikolas 'Niko' Bensmann, a partner in the Bremen form of Hermann Bensmann and Co. that handled Texaco patents in Germany. Bensmann had initiated the contact not for business reason but in his role as a *Sonderführer* (special leader) (F.2531) of the Bremen Abwehr, something that he was careful to hide from Rieber. He intimated that he had contacts with the Nazi regime that would facilitate the proposed tanker deal which had run into difficulties when the first ship that the Germans had released to him was impounded by the Royal Navy.

As his part of the deal, Rieber was to keep Bensmann informed about oil shipments leaving US ports bound for Britain. He agreed but saw it as a short-term measure that would last only until his third tanker was released. He later claimed that 'under no circumstances could I be identified with, or sympathetic to, any un-American activity'.[3] Special offices were set up in Bremen where mail addressed to 'Dr. Bremer' would be sent. An Abwehr agent was installed in Texaco's New York offices and a new code was devised for communications. This code was based upon patent numbers, which were commonly quoted in everyday correspondence.

Over the course of the latter part of 1940, this high-grade intelligence proved to be of immense value to the Nazis when estimating the Allied oil-producing potential. Not only that but information concerning the production of aircraft fuel and lubricants could be extrapolated to give an estimate of proposed aircraft manufacture, a figure which, when it was calculated, was so high that Canaris refused to believe it and was certainly not going to incur Hitler's wrath by passing it higher up the line. The industrial manufacturing potential of the US was clear, however, which was a sobering thought for Canaris already less than totally committed to the Nazis.

Neither the British nor the FBI ever caught on to what Bensmann and Rieber were up to. Their communication code was never broken but the Achilles Heel in the whole operation was Westrick. He was put under intense scrutiny by a man who had just arrived on the scene, William Stephenson, the chief of MI6 operations in the Western hemisphere. Rieber was already on the MI6 watch list for suspected blockade running but it was only when Stephenson realised that Westrick had set himself up with an office at Texaco headquarters to mastermind his propaganda blitz that another potentially serious link was suspected between Rieber and the Nazis. Further investigations revealed that Westrick's accommodation, transport was paid for by Texaco and even his hospitality that included entertaining the leaders of US business was going on Texaco's tab. This had included a party to celebrate the fall of France at the Manhattan Waldorf Astorial Hotel on 26 June 1940, attended by senior executives of IT&T, General Motors and Ford. None of this was actually illegal but Stephenson put a stop to it by simply passing all this information on to the *New York Herald Tribume* who gave it maximum publicity. The resulting public outcry saw Westrick expelled from the country and Rieber fired from the Texaco board of directors in August 1940.

Chapter 8

RITTER, DUQUESNE AND SEBOLD

'Intelligence agencies in Germany indiscriminately trained totally unqualified persons and sent them to the United States. The operations of the German agencies were marked by naivete, carelessness and lack of coordination.'

Dr Hans Thomsen,
Chargé of the German Embassy[1]

Nickolaus Ritter had been born in Rheydt, Germany and served in the 162nd Infantry Regiment during the First World War when he was twice wounded and ended up as a lieutenant. After the war, he had become a textile engineer and, hoping for a better life than the fractured Weimar economy could offer him, emigrated to the US in 1924 to work at the Mallinson Silk Company on Long Island. From there he moved to the Manhattan Textile Works in New York where he worked his way up to general manager but like many in the US at this time, he found some residual post-war hostility towards Germans. When he met and married Mary Aurora Evans, an Irish-American teacher from Clayton, Alabama in 1926, he hoped that life with her and the two children, Klaus Haveland and Katharina Francis, would settle him but it was not to be. In his business life he was, for a time, rather more successful. After working intermittently as an importer, factory operator and textile worker, he found commercial success by establishing a number of profitable business ventures. The Great Depression, however, saw his businesses collapse and he found himself in dire financial difficulties.

All German emigrants were registered at the German Consulate, who gave assistance in finding accommodation and employment and

Ritter had some contact with them over the years, so it was not a great surprise when the German consul general in New York contacted him. It was not a routine check, however. It turned out to be von Boetticher, the German military attaché in Washington DC asking Ritter if he would consider returning to Germany where employment might be found for him in an economy that was slowly dragging itself out of the depression years. His ten years living and working in the US would, von Boetticher said, be of considerable use to German firms looking for export markets in the US. Ritter jumped at the chance but his wife was less enthusiastic and did not want to uproot the children but Ritter won the argument and the family moved to Europe.

Arriving back in Germany, however, it was not the textile industry that had sought his return, but the Abwehr who were busy building up a network of agents to provide information about potential enemies if Europe descended into war. Although Ritter had no previous experience in aviation or intelligence of any sort, he had been identified as a potential agent by virtue of his time spent in the US where he had numerous business contacts. He was signed up to the Abwehr and was assigned to the Wehrmacht High Command on 1 September 1936.

Canaris found a niche for him in air intelligence with X Army Corps in Hamburg where Ritter's new boss, the tall, friendly, open and frank Hans Piekenbrock was quite the opposite of Canaris.[2] Initially, Ritter's job would be to acquire as much information as he could about the Royal Air Force but then around the middle of 1937, he received a note signed by Canaris himself saying 'Effective immediately, the intelligence service is also to cover the United States [with emphasis on] the United States Army Air Corps armament industry'.[3] He discussed it with his manager Lieutenant Commander Joachim Burghardt, someone who had lost all enthusiasm for espionage and had allowed what contacts he previously had in the US to lie dormant. It was not difficult for Ritter to convince him that such an assignment could only be carried out by someone on the spot in the US, preferably Ritter himself, but others would take more persuading. It was not without some misgivings that Piekenbrock and Canaris considered the idea but eventually agreed to Ritter appointing himself as chief of field operations inside the US but they insisted that under no circumstances was he to contact friends and acquaintances from his former life when he returned to America. Furthermore, he was instructed to avoid contact with any German military and diplomatic personnel in New York, especially von Boetticher who had 'no understanding of our work'. It was an important aspect of Abwehr strategy that espionage cells should remain independent of one another to avoid widespread disruption if one should be discovered.[4] It should also be remembered that von Boetticher had long been a vocal critic of Abwehr operations in the US whose agents he called 'a sorry lot'.[5]

Arrangements were made for Ritter to return to the US, but the nature of his work meant that his family could not accompany him despite Evans pleading to be allowed to take the children back home. She would soon file for divorce on the grounds of Ritter's infidelity, but Ritter contested custody of the children and she would not return to the US without them. The divorce was completed but Evans and the children would not be able to leave Germany until after the Second World War by which time Ritter was in prison. A strategy was worked out for Ritter to trawl for agents in the US who might have access to valuable information. He had only a single Abwehr contact from his previous life there whom he planned to reactivate. Frédéric 'Fritz' Joubert Duquesne had been a German agent in the US during the First World War and had remained in the country albeit as a 'sleeper' agent for the previous fifteen years. Next, Ritter would need couriers and more than one reliable communications network to get the information back to Germany. Then just days before he was due to sail, he was told about documents that had been couriered in by a steward of the Hamburg-American liner SS *Reliance*. They were crude blueprints of a new device that experts were having difficulty in deciphering. Finding out more about them would be a top priority.

On his passage across the Atlantic, Ritter contacted the ship's steward who had couriered the documents from the US. Many stewards working on ships of the Hapag-Lloyd Shipping Lines worked for various German agencies including the Abwehr. The steward gave Ritter instructions how to locate the man who had provided him with the blueprints. When he landed in New York on 17 October 1937, Ritter became Dr Hans Rankin, the managing director of an export-import firm in Hamburg, visiting the US on a business trip, but by the time he got to the Taft Hotel he had changed his name again and booked in under the name of Alfred Landing and the first thing he did was to send a postcard to a Mr Landing c/o the Taft. He also sent a letter addressed to Mr Landing to be called for at the main Post Office. When the postcard arrived, he took it to the Post Office to identify himself and claimed the letter. He now used the franked letter as identification allowing him to go to a branch of the City National Bank and cash a letter of credit. He also rented a safety deposit box into which he placed his Ritter passport and all papers in that name. Now he went to 262 Monitor Street and introduced himself to the occupant who turned out to be a stocky middle-aged man whom Ritter recognised from the description the steward had given him. He gave a pre-arranged greeting from 'Roland in Bremen' and was admitted to the apartment of the man who called himself Mr Sohn. Sohn was also a German immigrant and, like Ritter, had fought in the German army during the First World War and now wanted to do something to help the fatherland. He had established himself as a low-level operative whose home served as a letter box where agents would deposit their 'deliveries' to be forwarded to Germany.[6]

Sohn told Ritter that it was he who had sent the documents but he, in turn had been given them by a friend of his whom he called Paul. Two days later Ritter returned to Sohn's apartment where Paul was waiting for him. Paul introduced himself as Herman Lang and told Ritter he worked at the Norden factory at 80 Lafayette Street in Manhattan where they were developing a new revolutionary bombsight.

Carl Lucas Norden had been born in Semarang in Dutch Java in 1880 and had moved to Dresden where he graduated as a mechanical engineer and then emigrated to the US in 1904. He worked for two years for the Worthington Pump and Machine Company in Brooklyn and from 1906 to 1911 at the J.H. Lidgerwood Manufacturing Company before moving to the Sperry Gyroscope Company in New York. In 1915, Norden left the Sperry Gyroscope Company to set up his own business. He won several patents on control systems for launching aerial torpedoes from ships, robot flying bombs, radio-controlled target planes, and the catapults and arresting gear used on aircraft carriers. Since 1930, Norden had been developing his high-altitude bombsight for use by the US Navy, but he was causing ripples through military intelligence agencies for his eccentric behaviour. The navy called him a 'self-centred, driven, impatient, and abrasive [man] who had little tolerance for anyone unfortunate enough to possess a lesser mind'.[7] Norden's family lived in Switzerland and he visited them often which was seen as a security risk given the nature of his work and when drawings of the bombsight were found in the offices of the Sperry Gyroscope Company, the navy felt obliged to issue an official warning 'to prevent information regarding [the bombsight] from becoming available to any person who might utilise it in any manner contrary to the best interests of the United States'.[8] These admonitions seemed to have no effect on Norden, however and Lang had little difficulty in breaching such security measures as were in place.

His job was as an inspector in the assembly department of the bombsight. It was a complicated mechanism that required detailed drawings of each stage of the manufacturing process. Sometimes Lang would keep the drawings for several days and was supposed to lock them into a safe each night, but he spirited them out of the factory and traced them in his apartment at night. He had brought with him more tracings and Ritter arranged to have them couriered back to Germany. They were hidden inside the hollow stem of an umbrella and taken on board the SS *Reliance* by a steward called Jänischen (codename Oskar). In return Lang received his $1,500. However, not all the blueprints could be copied, and in order to complete the model Ritter had to invite Lang to Germany, where he was greeted by Hermann Göring himself. Eventually, German technicians were able to a construct a device calling it the *Nordensches ZieJ-geraet*. Later in the Second World War, Luftwaffe bombers used the Carl Zeiss Rotfernrohr 7 (or Rotfe 7), which had an advanced mechanical system similar to the Norden bombsight but was much easier to operate and maintain.

Ritter now looked up Duquesne who was a lecturer and journalist working for technical magazines. He had been born in 1877 in South Africa and had fought against the British during the Second Anglo-Boer War. When he discovered that the British had burned his family farm to the ground, raped and murdered his sister and sent his mother to a concentration camp, along with twenty other men, he plotted to kill Lord Herbert Kitchener. When the plot was exposed all, except Duquesne, were executed. He survived by promising to reveal secrets about the Boers to the British but later claimed that all the information he gave was false. He escaped from imprisonment on the island of Bermuda and found his way to New York where he established himself as a journalist and lecturer on the subject of his own adventurous life. He was even taken along as a hunting guide for President Roosevelt on one of his big-game hunting trips. When the First World War broke out, he adopted the name, Frederick Fredericks posing as a scientist doing research on rubber plants and went to Brazil. There, using two more aliases, George Fordam and Piet Nicaud, he took an active part in the war by bombing and sinking ships.

Duquesne had been implicated in fraudulent insurance claims, including one that resulted from a fire aboard the British steamship SS *Tennyson*, which caused the vessel to sink on 18 February 1916. When he was arrested on 17 November 1917, he was carrying a large file of news clippings concerning bomb explosions on ships, as well as a letter from the German assistant vice consul at Managua, Nicaragua. The letter indicated that 'Captain Duquesne' was 'one who has rendered considerable service to the German cause'.[9] Brought to trial, Duquesne avoided imprisonment by faking paralysis and pleading mental incompetence. Confined to the prison ward of Bellvue psychiatric hospital, he easily escaped by disguising himself as a woman and evaded further arrest. After his escape, Duquesne travelled to Europe and Mexico then returned to New York in 1926 where he used the alias Frank de Trafford Craven.

Ritter had known Duquesne since 1931 and met up with him again at the home of Evelyn Clayton Lewis on 57th Street West. In his autobiography, Ritter described Duquesne as 'thin and agile, in his early thirties, with a narrow intelligent face and an aristocratic nose, wavy, salt and pepper hair, and gray [*sic*] eyes'.[10] It is hardly surprising to find that Ritter is cavalier with truth given his profession but Duquesne must have been approaching 60 years old at the time. Ritter gave him $100 and arranged to assimilate Duquesne into a new espionage cell. His couriers would be Ritter's own brother Hans, who lived in New York, and Karl Keitel, a steward on the SS *Bremen*. From now on, any and all information Duquesne gathered would be handed to one or other of these two men.

His mission now would be to contact manufacturers of military hardware on the pretext of being a journalist writing articles about various of their products. Duquesne was a wily and experienced old hand at this game and during interviews he would often tease out information, which was supposed to be strictly secret and whilst he was careful never to put any of that into his published articles, it would very quickly find its way onto a desk in Berlin. Often he got the information he wanted by writing to manufacturers in which he described himself as a student or a 'well-known, responsible, and reputable writer and lecturer [and] good citizen' or even a manufacturer. Usually, he got positive replies claiming at one time to have got photographs of a new navy speedboat simply by writing and requesting it from the Department of the Navy in Washington DC.[11] On one occasion, much later in December 1940, he had written to the Department of State purporting to be from the Securities Service Company of 60 Wall Tower, New York City and suggesting that his company was interested in the possible financing of 'a chemical war device' the government had recently published an article about for distribution 'to those interested in the subject'. He politely requested a copy giving assurances that he 'would not allow anything of a confidential nature to get out of [his] hands.' It duly arrived.[12]

This new network, set up by Ritter personally, would eventually cover prominent sections of the northern and eastern US with a large number of active agents who acquired information through a variety of hard and soft techniques. Agents were embedded within industries and occupations of high intelligence value to access lucrative sources of strategic and sensitive information. In January 1940, the Duquesne network was given significant extra funding to pursue active penetration. It was just at this time however, that the tightly knit operation that had been working so well and effectively started to unravel.

The agent of this disruption was Wilhelm Georg Debrowski. Born in Mulheim, Germany in 1899, Debrowski had served with the German Army Corps of Engineers during the First World War and, after discharge in 1919, had escaped from the revolutionary upheaval that was tearing Germany apart and joined the merchant marine sailing mostly on the Atlantic routes. He eventually settled in California in 1922, changed his name to William Gotlieb Sebold, married an American woman and got a job with the Consolidated Aircraft Company in San Diego. Very soon afterwards he moved to New York and was granted US citizenship in 1936.

Sebold obtained extended leave of absence to visit his family in Mūlheim, Germany and travelled there on the SS *Deutschland* in spring 1939. All German transatlantic liners at the time carried Gestapo agents and many of the stewards were informers or couriers acting on their behalf. Part of their remit was to find out as much as possible about the passengers while at sea and so, by the time the *Deutschland* docked in Hamburg, the local Gestapo had been alerted to the fact that a US aircraft company employee was on board. Sebold was put under immediate surveillance and apprehended at the customs desk.

He was taken to Gestapo headquarters in Hamburg, where Colonel Paul Kraus briefly questioned him about his work in the US and made no bones about suggesting that Sebold consent to enlisting as an informant. When he declined, the Gestapo reminded him of a temporary period of incarceration in Germany on smuggling charges before he had emigrated to the US. If this became known to the US Immigration Service it could have serious implications when he tried to return home. His passport and identification papers were withheld and he was told to remain in Hamburg and await further contact and under no circumstances attempt to travel on to his family home in Mūlheim. Failure to comply might have serious consequences for his family in Germany. Sebold felt the net closing in on him.

For his second interview, Sebold was instructed to go to the Duisburgerhoff Hotel in Duisburg where he would be contacted by a man identifying himself as Dr Gassner.[13] At that meeting with Gassner, he was interrogated about his knowledge of military aircraft and technology in the US and received assurances that his circumstances would markedly improve, and his family would no longer have to fear reprisals, if he cooperated. Given time to consider, Sebold was allowed to visit the American Consulate in Cologne to arrange for his wife's welfare while he was in Germany. Once inside, Sebold had a secret meeting with Vice Consul Dale Mahler and confided in him that he was being coerced into working for the Abwehr. Mahler told him to return in a few days and in the meantime, asked Washington what to do about him. When he came back, Sebold was told that his case had been handed over to the DOJ and the FBI. He was advised to comply with Gestapo demands and hope that his passport might be returned at which point he could return to the US but once there would have to submit to a debriefing by the FBI. It was only marginally reassuring but Sebold had little choice. He went back to Kraus and told him that he agreed to cooperate.

Complying with the communications protocols, Kraus had forwarded details of his latest acquisition to his opposite numbers in the Abwehr so, when Sebold returned to the Dusseldorf Gestapo office, he was interviewed there by someone calling himself Dr Renken. This turned out to be none other than Nickolaus Ritter, the man who had got the Norden bombsight documents calling himself Dr Rankin at that time. Ritter was now considered to be the Abwehr's senior expert on the US and was the senior Abwehr commander of espionage against the US and Britain. He was unimpressed by Sebold and described him as 'quite ordinary ... of average intelligence, and obviously [of] modest means' but agreed to take him on.[14]

Sebold was housed in the Klopstock boarding house in Hamburg, a place where Abwehr trainees were billeted. He was allocated the agent number A.3559 and given the codename 'Tramp'.[15] There he stayed there for several months learning about microphotography, Morse Code, radio transmission, coding, disguise and personal security after which he was given a new US passport under the name of Harry Sawyer. Both Piekenbrock and Ritter are recorded as showing 'remarkable enthusiasm for the observable progress [and significant potential] demonstrated by William Sebold at the Hamburg spy school' where he was instructed by Ritter personally.[16] He was now instructed to return to the US with a new passport and set up a shortwave radio station with which to send back information on a prearranged frequency using a special code.

Canaris had become increasingly frustrated by the amount of time that it took intelligence to find its way back to Germany from the US. Sending messages direct through the post risked interception and where mail was sent by circuitous routes the time delay often meant that the intelligence was out of date by the time it arrived. This was especially true of sailing times of military transports across the Atlantic. Courier delivery was quicker and safer but still relied upon sailing schedules, which were often disrupted or cancelled. The answer was radio, and it became a top priority for the Abwehr to develop shortwave radio stations across the globe.

The problems with this, however, were many and seemingly insurmountable. They had portable *Afu* apparatus but, with a maximum power of twenty watts, its signals were too weak to cross the Atlantic. At first the Germans tried smuggling fully assembled large transmitters to places such as Argentina but they were discovered at the ports of entry and confiscated.

The task of developing a simple, compact radio with a wide frequency range and a loop antenna that could be built in situ wherever the need arose was given to Abwehr Lieutenant Colonel Trautmann, chief of the signals service at Wohldorf and SS-Sturmbannführer (SS assault leader) Siepen, director of the Havelinstitut, the radio centre of *Amt VI* at Wansee. They would be able to call on the expertise and resources of the German radio and electronics company Telefunken. When the first radios were tested in the US by Dr Josef Jacob Johannes Starziczny, it was clear that the quality of signal was subjected to severe disruption because of natural atmospheric disturbances such as sunspots but eventually the problems were overcome sufficiently to have a working communications system but one that was still vulnerable to weather and geomagnetic forces.

The two men appointed to run the US radio operation, called 'Operation Jimmy' were Felix Jahnke, a trained radio man who had been naturalised in the US in 1930 and the diligent but somewhat dim Russian-born Axel Wheeler-Hill who proved to be much less proficient. Both men had been trained in Germany when it had become clear that Wheeler-Hill was not up to the job but pressure from Canaris to expedite the operation had not left enough time to replace him. When they got back to New York in January 1940 they built a radio set in an apartment on Cauldwell Avenue with the intention of moving it from place to place to avoid detection, but Wheeler-Hill was confident that the 'stupid Americans will never find us'.[17] Soon the whole East Coast intelligence-gathering operation was proving to be enormously successful and overloading both the radio link and the courier system. It was 'Tramp' who would now ease the burden on Jahnke and Wheeler-Hill as far as the radio operation was concerned.

When he was put on board the SS *Washington* in Genoa on 1 February 1940, Sebold was also carrying $500 in cash that he was to give to a man called Everett Minster Roeder in Long Island, along with microphotographed instructions. The Abwehr had perfected techniques of reducing a document to a size smaller than a human fingernail. Other instructions were to be given to Duquesne c/o Air Terminals, 17 East 42nd Street and Lilly Stein at 127 East 54th Street. Financial and other material necessities would all be available after he established himself back in New York.

When he landed back on home ground in New York on 8 February 1940 eager to remove himself from the bizarre circumstances he found himself in, Sebold went to Yorktown where he was debriefed by FBI agents hoping that it would be the end of his involvement. He showed them how the back of his wristwatch unscrewed to reveal five photomicrographs. This was a vast improvement on smuggling techniques that had been previously employed by such as Lonkowski and threatened to herald a new age of espionage beyond the means of the FBI to counter. When Sebold gave up the names of those for whom the secret material was destined, a whole new Nazi espionage operation was uncovered. Sebold told how he had been instructed to use the name Harry Sawyer with cover as a diesel engineering consultant and contact someone called Herman Lang in Ridgewood, Queens using the phrase 'Hamburg Berlin greeting from Rantzau'.

The FBI wanted Sebold to act as a double agent and carry on working for Ritter as if they knew nothing about it, but he was, quite naturally, concerned that if he was discovered acting for the FBI, he would be in serious danger of being killed by the Nazis. Eventually he was persuaded to continue following the orders that Ritter had given him and, under instructions from the FBI, Sebold began sending reports back via courier to Ritter who initially described them as 'nothing to get excited about'[18]

It is doubtful if the FBI realised at first exactly what they had stumbled upon. It was clear to them that Sebold was a valuable asset for the Abwehr given the amount of time and effort they had expended in his training but just how important his role was to become in their East Coast espionage operations emerged only gradually. Over the next weeks the FBI found themselves confronted by a complex and multi-faceted espionage operation involving diplomatic officials, secret agents, secret radio transmitters and a flow of German money to finance it all. Hoover had to sharpen up his game very quickly to counter it and got authorisation for widespread radio and telephone communications surveillance to monitor the activities of known agents and discover the identities of their contacts. The old ways that had served the FBI so poorly during the Griebl-Lonkowski years were ditched in favour of a more aggressive but much more covert approach. The arrest of any suspect would alarm the others and see the German operation closed down very quickly. The last thing Hoover wanted was to see a whole bunch of suspects suddenly disappearing from view and turning up in Hamburg.

It was clear from the efforts put in by Ritter when coaching Sebold that there were many more agents undercover in the US than the four identified by Sebold. At FBI headquarters a special unit was set up especially to manage the Duquesne case and in New York, a special squad under Inspector Earl Connelly was established to handle the operational side. Hoover demanded absolute secrecy from all agents directly involved. He was still not sure about Sebold, however, and planned to check him out and make sure that the FBI was not being taken for a ride.

A German-speaking agent, James C. Ellsworth, was called up from Laguna Beach, California to come to New York for special duties. Once there, he was given a new identity and ordered to make friends with Sebold and spend a lot of time with him. Both he and Sebold were placed under twenty-four-hour surveillance for weeks until Hoover was sufficiently satisfied that Sebold had not been planted on him by the Nazis that he was now officially put on the FBI payroll at $50 a week and allowed to be reunited with his wife.[19]

When the FBI looked closely at the agents that Sebold had identified they found Roeder to be an engineer working at the Sperry Gyroscope Company in Brooklyn having previously worked at the Airplane and Marine Direction Finder Corporation and the Arma Engineering Company. He had recently borrowed money from a bank pending receipt of royalties from Germany for unspecified work. It was Lang, however, who, as a senior inspector at the Norden Corporation, raised the most concern. Both men were put under FBI surveillance. Notwithstanding the importance of these two agents it was still Duquesne who was at the heart of Ritter's US espionage operation.

Using his Sawyer pseudonym, Sebold now contacted Duquesne, initially by letter, according to Ritter's instructions but then personally when he found Duquesne, a past master of intrigue to be extremely apprehensive about security insisting that all discussions be conducted while they walked in the street or as they sat in a local laundromat. It was only after detailed questioning of Sebold that Duquesne was willing to accept his credentials and opened up to him about his operation. He boasted to Sebold that he was an expert saboteur and had furnished explosive devices to Nazi espionage teams throughout the US. He told Sebold that he had made plans to bomb the General Electric plant in Schenectady, New York, and sabotage the DuPont powder works at

Wilmington, Delaware. He had even worked out how to plant a bomb in Franklin Roosevelt's church at Hyde Park.

He warned Sebold to avoid contact with any other German nationals who, he said, could not be trusted. All paper communications must be burned after their contents had been digested. Rather than surveillance of Roeder, Lang and Duquesne leading to other agents, it came as a brutal shock for Hoover to discover that none of the three men knew any of the others personally. All communications between them were handled by cut-outs.

Ritter now began demanding a return on his investment. A vital part of Ritter's plans for Sebold was the establishment of a shortwave radio station as a vital means of communication between Hamburg and Duquesne's operation. Material for constructing the transmitter and receiver were not exactly freely available at the time and it took a while for Sebold and Connelly to find all the necessary components but by April the equipment was up and running and installed in an empty house at Centrepoint, Long Island.

The idea, of course, was that Sebold would transmit only such information as the FBI authorised him to do but there was an outside chance that he might still be holding out and working for both sides. If that was the case he could easily use the transmitter, which the FBI had so carefully and surreptitiously helped him to construct, to send messages that were decidedly against the interests of the US. Rather than risk that, an FBI agent, Morris H. Price, was assigned to study Sebold's unique style of tapping out Morse Code, known as fisting, which was known to the Abwehr and it would be he who would transmit all the messages. These were received and transmitted on an almost daily basis but it never occurred to Ritter to question how Sebold could do this and perform all his other duties at the same time.

A complex operation was now put in place to handle communications with the Nazi Hamburg station, known as AOR. When a message was received, Price handed it over to Ellsworth and Sebold who decoded it using a system based on the novel *All This and Heaven Too* by Rachel Young. After decoding the messages were translated from German into English. The process was reversed to send messages. Sebold was instructed by the FBI to ensure that all written communications from Nazi agents were typewritten so that they could later be identified with particular typewriters. This meant that they could be presented as evidence in any future prosecution case against them.

One of the most significant developments in the case was insight gained into the way that the Nazis handled communications with their agents spread across the world. A courier on the SS *Manhattan*, the ship's butcher Erwin Siegler, gave Sebold a list of addresses in China, Brazil and Portugal that he was to use when sending written communications. These instructions were amended in the early spring when the German invasion of France was being prepared. Letters were now to be sent to Dr Schmid-Gyula, Irány utca 25, Budapest.

Once Sebold's radio was up and running, he made almost daily reports about weather and shipping movements in and out of New York Harbor using the call letters CQDXVW-2. The speed with which this information was received in Hamburg allowed shipping movements to be tracked across the Atlantic for the benefit if U-boats that were active there. So efficient was Sebold's radio operation that Ritter expanded the group for which Sebold transmitted and he became acquainted with a number of German agents operating independently or in conjunction with groups in the New York area other than those in the Duquesne spy ring.

The White House was kept up to date with all demands for intelligence that Hamburg was making of Sebold. It is a measure of the levels of penetration of Duquesne's espionage ring that these included monthly figures of aircraft production at various factories, export of equipment and munitions to Britain and France, methods of shipment and details of payment structure for all military exports. The difficulty was that in order for Sebold to continue to be a valuable agent in place he would have to continue to have the confidence of Ritter and there must be no hint that he was in any way under FBI control. This inevitably meant that the information he was sending back to Hamburg would be compared to other German intelligence and had to be essentially accurate. This required Sebold's US handlers to maintain a delicate balance between maintain his credibility and sending sensitive information that might prove to be damaging to US interests. Every piece of intelligence that Sebold was allowed to transmit was weighed on this basis. As an example of the extreme sensitivity of the intelligence that flowed through Duquesne and hence through Sebold was the contents of a letter sent by Duquesne to Sebold at the end of May 1940 that shook the US security forces. It accurately assessed the strength of the US military at that time stating that it had 303 warships, 2,665 aircraft, and 227,000 soldiers. Sebold did not forward this information to Hamburg.[20]

Over the next eighteen months, the nature of Ritter's demands and the contents of messages Sebold was required to send gave the FBI clear indications of exactly what positions the Nazi agents held within the US industrial and banking systems. Duquesne continued to send a wide variety of reports on new weapons and military technology but

The devastating aftermath of the Black Tom Island explosion on 30 July 1916

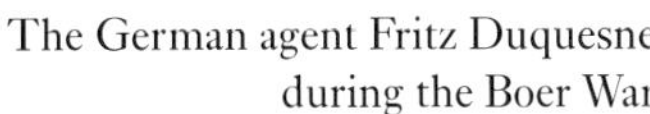

The German agent Fritz Duquesne during the Boer War

Colonel Erwin von Lahousen, commander of *Abteilung II*, German counterintelligence and security

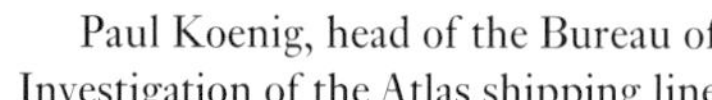

Paul Koenig, head of the Bureau of Investigation of the Atlas shipping line

The German spy, Ignatz Theodor Griebl

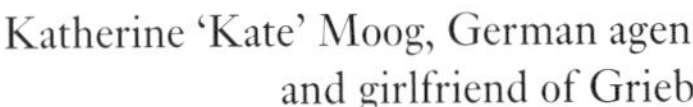

Katherine 'Kate' Moog, German agent and girlfriend of Griebl

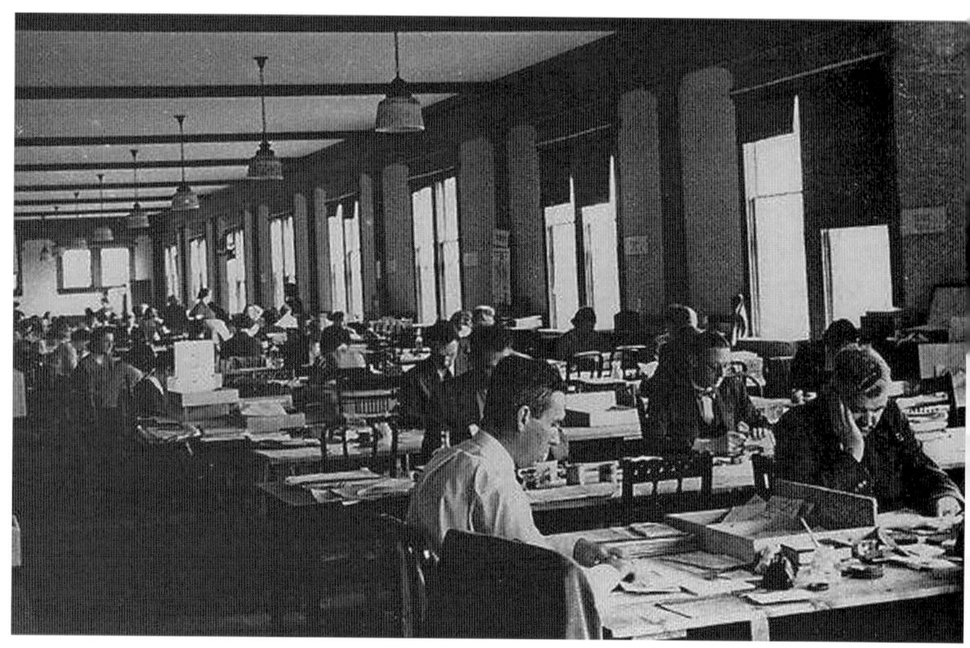

British censors working at the Princess Hotel in Bermuda

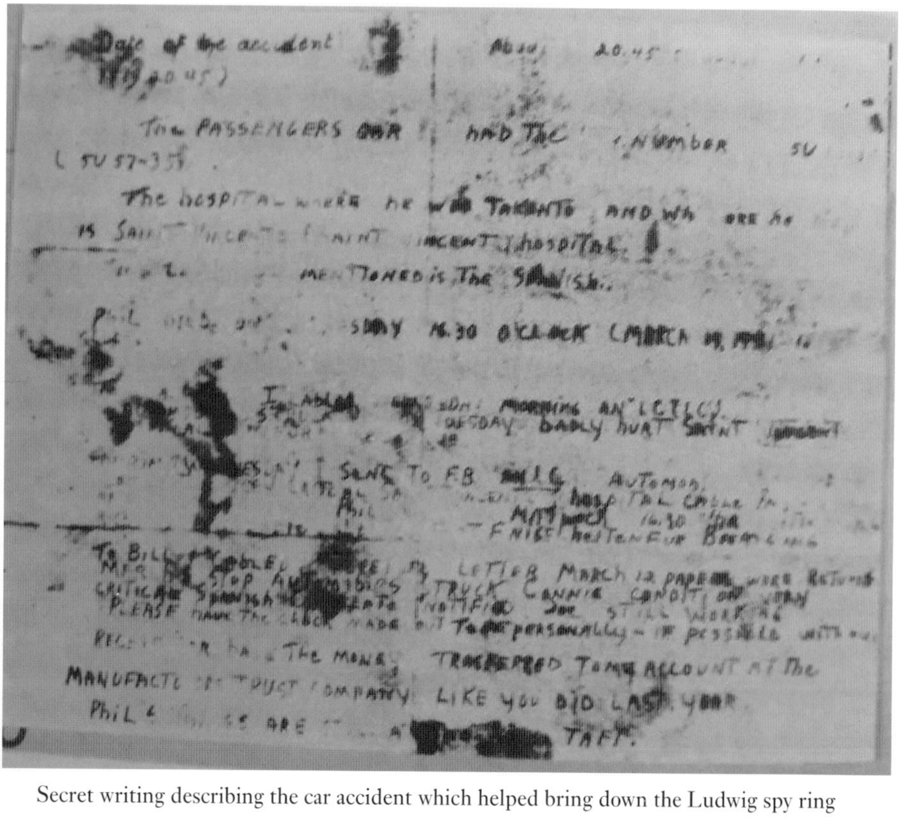

Date of the accident
20.45

The PASSENGERS ... AND THE ... NUMBER

The hospital where he was taken to and where he is Saint Vincent ... Saint Vincent hospital.

... MENTIONED IS THE SPANISH.

... 16.30 O'CLOCK (MARCH ...

... MORNING ...
... BADLY HURT SAINT ...
... SENT TO FB ... AUTOMOB...
... HOSPITAL ...

To Bill ... LETTER MARCH 12 PAPER ... RETURNED
... TRUCK ...
PLEASE HAVE THE CHECK MADE OUT TO ME PERSONALLY – IF POSSIBLE WITH...
... THE MONEY TRANSFERRED TO MY ACCOUNT AT THE
MANUFACTURERS TRUST COMPANY LIKE YOU DID LAST YEAR
Phil ... TAFT.

Secret writing describing the car accident which helped bring down the Ludwig spy ring

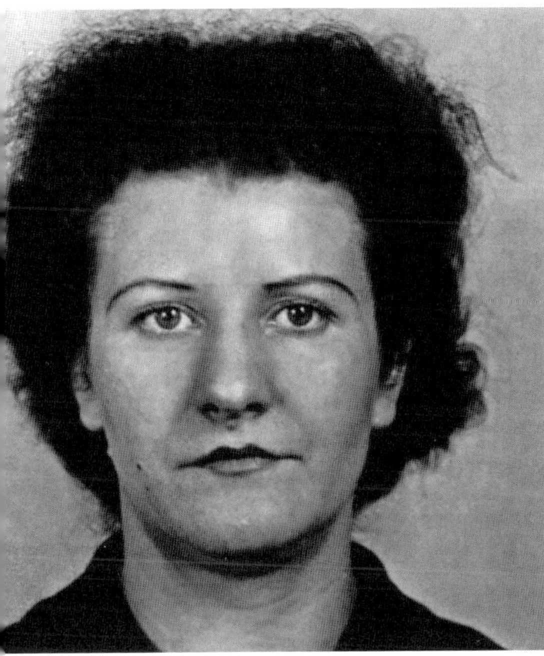

Johanna Hofmann, German courier who worked as a hairdresser of the SS *Europa*

Eight times married heiress, film star and German spy Mary Fahrney

US aviator and Nazi sympathiser Laura Ingalls

Hellmuth Siegfried Goldschmidt,
adventurer and German spy

Kurt Frederick Ludwig, sentenced to twenty years, imprisonment for spying in the US

Benson House in Wading River where the FBI set up a fake radio link with German intelligence

Hotel Mayflower in Jacksonville, Florida where German saboteurs stayed after arriving by U-boat

US cryptanalyst Elizebeth Smith Friedman who helped to break the German codes

constantly berated Hamburg for providing insufficient funds to allow him the freedom of movement across the country that he required. As well as these reports, Duquesne was an inveterate gossip and told Sebold much more than he needed to about the operation he was conducting.

The FBI net widened to investigate all known contacts of Duquesne. Of the three names Sebold had been given at the start of his life as a double agent, the attractive Austrian-born Lilly Barbara Carola Stein, living quietly in an apartment on East 54th Street and running a ladies clothing shop, seemed the one least likely to be a spy. Described as a 'willowy person of about 30 years of age, she might have been pretty had it not been for a sneer that constantly played about her lips'.[21] Alongside her retail business, she also worked as a somewhat demure fashion model developing ties to influential people in New York and Washington DC, which allowed her to pick up information simply by listening to their conversations. Her outwardly innocuous appearance was soon exposed as a sham, however, when analysis of her mail showed that she was receiving regular payments from Dutch and South American banks, much of which she passed on to Duquesne along with letters she received from Germany. Further surveillance revealed her relationship with Else Weustenfeld, an employee of the Topken and Farley law firm who acted for the German Consulate in New York. It transpired that Weustenfeld had once lived with Nickolaus Ritter's brother, Hans, and she was observed handing over money to various German agents. It was clear from this that the consulate had an important part to play in German espionage operations. Sebold visited Stein on a number of occasions and was given letters Stein had received from Detroit that he was to forward to Hamburg. These referred to stratosphere aircraft, particularly the Boeing Stratoliner type 307.[22]

When the FBI traced the source of the letters they came upon Edmund Carl Heine who ran a small advertising company Display-Rite in Detroit that appeared to be doing absolutely no business at all. His lack of income was in stark contrast to the affluent lifestyle enjoyed by Heine. Investigations revealed that he had been born in 1891 in Zeulen Roda in Saxony. He had arrived in the US before the outbreak of the First World War becoming a citizen in 1920 and taking up employment as a travelling salesman for the Ford Motor Company ending up in Berlin in the mid-1930s as Ford's representative there. He was recruited by the Abwehr and sent back to the US in May 1940 where he set up his business. When he was later questioned by the FBI he said that he had been ordered to acquire information about the development of aviation in the US but ruefully admitted that he had no knowledge of the industry and was able to glean no more information than what was available through mainstream newspapers and industry publications. He was clearly not one of Ritter's better agents and perhaps illustrates how the placement of spies was somewhat hit and miss at times.

Roeder, like Stein, had been recruited by Ritter when he visited the US in 1937. Although working at the Long Island Sperry industrial plant at the time of Lang's theft of the Norden bombsight, Ritter had not called upon his services at the time and allowed him to remain inactive as a 'sleeper' agent. Now, however, he was a senior Abwehr agent with a considerable reputation within German intelligence circles and 'probably the Abwehr's greatest producer of detailed technical data in America'.[23] His professional competencies allowed him to make complete technical drawings of aeronautic and industrial technology blueprints but his relationship with Hamburg was threatened by his constant demands for more money. Intelligence supplied by Roeder included specifications of the radio instrumentation on the Glenn Martin bomber. He also had a secondary income derived from his work inventing firearm-related devices, some of which he supplied to the Abwehr. At the end of October 1940, Sebold received instructions from Germany to send Roeder to a rendezvous at the Nippon Club at 161 West 93rd Street. This would reveal yet another method that the Abwehr were employing to have stolen documents transported safely back to Germany. At the restaurant, Roeder was to contact an elderly Japanese man who would identify himself as E. Satotsu after which he would give the man his 'Kind regards from the Steamer' and hand over a sealed letter. This man was Lieutenant Colonel Takeo Ejima of the Imperial Japanese Navy (codename KATO) who was operating in New York as an engineer inspector. He had arrived at Heian Maru in Seattle, Washington (state), US in 1938. Ejima was filmed by the FBI meeting Siebold in New York. He was also filmed meeting with Kengoro Koike, the chief budget commander of the Imperial Japanese Navy.

In May 1938, Sebold and Roeder made contact again with the mysterious Mr Sato this time at the Miyako restaurant at 20 East 56th Street. All three went to an apartment in Lower Manhattan where Sato identified himself as Takeo Ejima of the Imperial Japanese Navy. Sebold handed over a number of documents according to his instructions from Germany. Further meetings took place at a different Japanese restaurant at 41 East 19th Street when more documents were handed over including microfilmed copies of a drawing of a hydraulic unit with pressure switch A-5 of the Sperry Gyroscope and an original drawing from the Lawrence Engineering and Research Corporation. The material handed over would now be sent to Germany via Japan. Investigations led the FBI to reveal further collaboration between

German and Japanese secret agents whereby German and Japanese re-insurance companies were acting as underwriters to national defence industries. In 1941, Ejima would be tried and sentenced to fifteen years' imprisonment but US naval intelligence documents state that at the request of the Department of State, he was released and deported to Japan.

The radio communications were a goldmine of intelligence for the FBI as more and more names were revealed. Clearly, the Abwehr had made a serious mistake by linking far too many of its agents to Sebold's communications hub. Among them was Paul Fehse, a US citizen of German birth, referred to in radio messages as head of the marine division of the German espionage network. He proved to be a pivotal figure around whom much organisation was enacted. He arranged meetings, directed members' activities, correlated information that had been developed, and arranged for its transmittal to Germany, chiefly through Sebold. It was through Fehse that Carl Alfred Reuper came to the FBI's attention.

Reuper had first arrived in the US in 1929 and had acquired US citizenship in 1936. He then spent some time in Germany where he underwent training with the Abwehr before returning to the US again just before Christmas 1939. Within a year he had become 'one of the busiest agents the Abwehr had in America'.[24] By this time he was employed as an inspector at the Westinghouse Electric Corporation in New Jersey where he worked on development programmes for state-of-the-art military technology. Josef Klein, a photographer and lithographer, had been recruited by Jahnke and Wheeler-Hill to set up and operate a second shortwave radio station in a Bronx apartment but the involvement of all three with Sebold allowed the FBI to monitor all transmissions and eventually break the code. Reuper made use of Klein's radio facilities and both were peripherally involved with another spy ring separate from Duquesne's.

Paul Bante, another German First World War veteran, had been a supporter of the German-American Bund and had been active stirring up trouble among union workers. He had a passing but unimportant connection to the Lonkowski spy ring but had essentially stayed away from espionage until contacted by Sebold according to instructions from Hamburg. Making contact through the Little Casino restaurant on 206 East 85th Street, a favourite haunt of Duquesne's agents, Bante was now called upon to begin the monitoring of shipping in and out of New York Harbor.

Maintaining surveillance on Duquesne and his spy ring without being detected was going to be far from easy for an organisation like the FBI that was really just finding its feet in the murky world of espionage.

Duquesne, especially, was an old hand at the game and, over the years, had developed an acute sense of danger. Sebold warned Connelly that Duquesne had told him he thought he was being followed. With Duquesne on high alert it meant that the FBI had to back off for a while and risk losing control of the operation. They were thrown a lifeline, however, when Hamburg told Sebold they were making a large deposit with a New York bank that would be used to make faster and more secure payments to Duquesne's agents. Money would be withdrawn by couriers and handed over to the agents in person as required. Connelly told Sebold to suggest an alternative arrangement whereby he would set up a dummy company and arrange for all payments to be made through there so that he could personally oversee all transactions and exert proper control over the funds. Ritter agreed and signalled agreement to 'open office immediately [and] advise highest amount possible for you to handle without suspicion'.[25] Connelly wasted no time in establishing the Diesel Research Corporation in early December 1940 on the sixth floor of the *Newsweek* building at 152 West 42nd Street with its business account at Chase National Bank. The idea was that Sebold would now conduct many of his meetings with ring members at these premises and make payments to them there.

It might have seemed an extravagance to completely redecorate the offices with bright colours and install special lighting but the expense was justified by the installation also of a two-way mirror between the office and an adjoining sound-proof room. In this second room recording equipment was set up connected to hidden microphones and a 16-millimetre film camera was able to record everything that went on. Whenever Sebold held meetings with agents in his office, two FBI men, William G. Friedmann and John G. Fellner, would observe from the secret room, sometimes separately and sometimes together.

Money flowed into the Diesel account from a bank in Mexico usually $5,000 at a time and distributed throughout the spy network. Hoover knew that no information he got from the operation would be admissible as evidence in any trial but it proved to be a most valuable means of collecting information.

At the beginning of 1941, surveillance of the Little Casino restaurant brought Heinrich Clausen to the FBI's attention. He quickly formed a friendship with Sebold and proved to be something of a security risk given the copious amounts of information he gave Sebold about couriers operating on ships between New York and South America. Information they carried there, said Clausen, was sent on to Germany using Italian airlines. Nor was Clausen slow to point out the shortcomings of several of his fellow spies. Bante in particular came in for special criticism, ironically, as 'a vociferous braggart with minimal comprehension of operational security'.[26] Sebold no doubt observed that it takes one to know one.

Fehse was giving Hoover a headache. He had told Sebold that he was growing tired of espionage. There was no doubt that by spring 1941, security was being ratcheted up all across the US military and industrial landscape making exposure ever more likely. One agent, René-Emmanuel Mezenen, a steward on the Pan Am Clipper flying between the US and Portugal had been arrested at LaGuardia Airport while carrying 158 ounces of platinum. He wanted to return to Germany and asked Sebold to get permission from Hamburg to leave. They agreed but when Sebold passed on this information to the FBI, Hoover was adamant that he was not going to let any of this batch of spies to slip through his fingers. The problem was, how to pull Fehse in without alerting Duquesne that they were onto them.

That particular problem was solved when a routine inspection of undelivered mail lying in an international mail depot in New York threw up a letter that had been held up because of inadequate postage. The address alerted the agency and when it was opened it was found to have been sent by Fehse a couple of years earlier, long before his connection with Duquesne, and had contained information about ships and cargoes. It was possible, therefore, to charge Fehse with violating the Foreign Agents Registration Act and put him on trial without any reference to his more recent activities. Nevertheless, Duquesne, ever alert to danger, took it as a warning. Hoover, too, saw that time was running out and if he didn't act quickly, he risked finding himself at the centre of another farcical situation and one that could not be so easily shrugged off with the US now moving ever closer to war.

Roosevelt was just as anxious as Hoover to avoid embarrassment and ordered more than sixty German and Italian ships in US ports to be prevented from sailing. All the crews were arrested and taken in for questioning about smuggling and espionage. The Italian naval attaché was expelled and in its next move, all German and Italian financial assets in the US were frozen on 14 June 1941 cutting off all money to the spies. Two couriers, Franz Stigler and Erwin Siegler, were not going to wait for a tap on the shoulder and signed on to a ship bound for Portugal. Their arrest was authorised by the White House but legislation was still not in place to charge them with any offence. Nevertheless, they could not be allowed to go free and alert the others so they were held illegally for ten days to give Hoover time to organise a sweep to pick up all the other known members of the ring.

Undersecretary of State Sumner Welles went public and condemned the German diplomatic mission of engaging in illegal activity and ordered all German consulates in the country to be closed. Thirty-three arrest warrants were issued, and Connelly organised a team of ninety-six agents to round up the suspects. Duquesne was arrested on 28 June 1941 at 24 West 76th Street, and at the same time, a second group of agents detained Evelyn Clayton Lewis, a woman with whom he had been living. The others were quickly rounded up. Amazingly, Hamburg continued to communicate with Sebold whom they assumed had avoided detection and it was only when he appeared in court on behalf of the prosecution that the penny dropped. For sentences handed down to the accused – see Appendix 2.

The arrest of Fehse had alerted German intelligence to the possibility that the FBI was closing in on Duquesne's spy ring but it did little to change protocols and operational parameters. Both Canaris and Piekenbrock were pleased with the way things were going and saw no reason to make any changes. They might have been a little more cautious had they been aware of the general laxity of security many of the agents inside the US were exhibiting. Sebold's radio transmitter had become a central element in not only Duquesne's operation but a number of others also that used it to send and receive messages to Hamburg. Too little scrutiny was given to the way in which the Long Island station had become a link to far too many spy rings that should have remained separate and unaware of each other.

The pressure to come up with results had overridden sound security procedures and agents were co-opted with insufficient background checks being made. Even Sebold's background had not been investigated in the way that it should have been which was a serious mistake given the way that, over the year and a half of his association with Duquesne, he had become one of, if not the, central figure in the whole East Coast operation.

Chapter 9

SLEEPERS

> 'Never in the history of espionage was a secret service serviced directly by the victim it was spying on.'[1]

When Simon Emil Koedel was denied entry to the Chemical Warfare Centre at Edgewood Arsenal, Maryland, in high dudgeon, he called the American Ordnance Association (AOA) offices in Washington DC. Within hours he returned to the facility and was given a guided tour. Two weeks later, in mid-November 1939, his report detailing everything he had seen on the visit was on the desk of Johannes Bischoff at Abwehr headquarters in Bremen. The major supplier of the Arsenal, the report stated, were Baker in Philipsburg, the General Chemical Company, a factory in Lodi and, most important of all, Eimer and Amend on Third Avenue, New York, a business part owner by German interests.[2]

Just how Koedel was given access to the site where the US Army tested many of its new weapons was hard to believe given that he had already been revealed as a German spy operating on US soil as early as 1915. Born in Würzburg, Bavaria, in 1881, Koedel had arrived in the US in 1904 when he enlisted in the US Army and gained US citizenship. When the First World War broke out, he began spying for Germany on shipping leaving US ports and then doing the same work when he went to Britain. After he was deported to the US, he went to Germany where he had enlisted in the German army.

In 1936, Bischoff was laying the foundations of a worldwide spy network and chose Koedel to be his man in the US. This 'lean, sinewy … man with thin lips and piggish little eyes'[3] was designated agent A.2011, given an exhaustive course on espionage in Hamburg, then returned as a 'sleeper' to the US in 1937 with a salary of $200 a month plus a generous expense allowance that would allow him to set up in Riverside Drive, Manhattan, and create a persona able to impress the local dignitaries.

Posing as a chemical engineer, he applied for and gained membership of the AOA, a semi-official trade organisation for armament and munitions manufacturers, such as Sperry Gyroscope and Curtiss-Wright, with close connections to the US Department of War. This was despite scrutiny of all new members by the FBI who completely failed to register any details of Koedel's life beyond his army discharge in 1909. As an AOA member he was placed on the Department of War confidential mailing list and given unrestricted access to private meetings and lectures about new weapons systems.

Koedel now began writing to members of the military and naval affairs committees in Congress passing himself off as 'an investor with considerable stake in the American defence industry'.[4] His credentials were further enhanced when he began writing letters and making personal representations to the AOA complaining that it was revealing too much information about the US armaments industry that should remain top secret. He offered to visit industrial plants to see for himself how security might be tightened up.

When the call came from Bischoff on 5 September 1939 to 'wake up', Koedel was well placed to begin his espionage mission.

His first recruit was his 20-year-old 'willowy brunette'[5] foster daughter, Marie Hedwig Koeler, who now also began playing an active role in his operation. Young and flighty, she was ruled with iron discipline and Koedel would beat her for insubordination. She would wander daily across the New York waterfront attracting admiring looks from the seamen and dock workers. In the bars she would cast flirtatious glances that quickly brought the company of men eager to impress her. Tongues loosened by drink and her presence told her all she needed to know about departure dates of convoys, their routes, ship armaments, cargoes and other maritime secrets. Daily reports flowed to Hamburg from where the information was relayed to U-boat commanders out in the Atlantic sea-lanes.[6]

In March 1940, Koedel wrote to his friend, Senator Robert Rice Reynolds, an isolationist, Nazi sympathiser and supporter of US fascist movements, saying that he was planning to send supplies to France but needed details of port facilities in Nantes and La Rochelle. As a result of the information he received back, Koedel was able to inform Dr Bensmann in Bremen just weeks before the German attack against France, that 'according to the US Maritime Commission, these ports ... are capable of handling ships loading oil and coal as well as general cargo'.[7] From Reynolds also he got a copy of weekly reports of permits issued for the export of war materials to Britain.

Koedel had two main communication methods. He had been given access to the facilities of the German Consulate in New York and was allowed to use their codes but also had his own highly effective method of sending written reports. As a member of AOA he would often receive mail stamped with 'War Department Washington DC. Official Business'. He simply steamed open the letters, inserted his own reports and resealed them. He then scored out his own address and wrote next to it his maildrop address in Milan, Italy hoping that official mail would not be intercepted by the censors.

Koedel was rapidly turning into the best all-round spy the Abwehr would have in the US in the period 1939–1941. In September 1940, he was able to report on his visit to the US Arsenal in Waterfleet. Weeks later he was sending photographs of installations in the explosives factory in Radford, Virginia, Charlestown, Indiana and Childersburg, Alabama. The volume of intelligence he and Koedel furnished their employers was vast but his enduring triumphs were undoubtedly two reports 'Report Concerning American Ships Inspected by England on Suspicion of Contraband' and 'Report on the Conduct of Enemy Ships in Convoy at Sea in the Atlantic. Based on conversations with British Seamen.' For much of the intelligence included in the latter report, Koedel had befriended an English sailor, Duncan Alexander Croall Scott-Ford, who later went on to spy for the Abwehr against the British and was subsequently hanged by the British as a traitor in November 1942.

Someone who was active at the same time under the same Bremen controllers as Koedel was 'a thin man with wire-rimmed glasses and a very small moustache' called Maximilian Gerhard Waldemar Othmer. Born in Saxony, he had moved to the US in 1929 becoming an American citizen in 1935. He had earlier joined up with the pro-Nazi group Friends of New Germany and later became leader of the German-American Bund in Trenton, New Jersey. On a trip to Germany in 1936, as part of a 300-strong Bund presence at the Olympic Games, Othmer had quietly slipped away to meet Bischoff and Bensmann to volunteer his services as a spy. He was trained and returned to the US as a 'sleeper' agent, A.2018, just like Koedel but was not allocated nearly as much money and had to make do with his earnings as an electrician at Briscoe Electrics while living at the local YMCA in Norfolk. From here he was able to keep a close eye on shipping moving in and out of the harbour there.

Othmer certainly lacked Koedel's connections but was prolific nonetheless and his voluminous reports allowed the Abwehr to build up a good understanding of the level of aid the US was providing to Britain in 1940. Both he and the Koedel's managed to avoid being swept up the mass arrests of 1941 when the Duquesne ring was rolled up, but both were put on FBI watch lists soon afterwards.

Koedel and his daughter were arrested in 1944 and appeared before Brooklyn Federal Court on 24 October 1941 charged with conspiracy to commit espionage. Charge with them *in absentia* were Carl Hermann Nicholas Bensmann, R.A. Homburg, Fred Textor, Johannes Bischoff, Herman Heinrich Rullhausen Spalthoff, Hans Alberts, Hans Grimm and Waldemar Othmer. In spring 1945, the father pleaded guilty and was sentenced to fifteen years' imprisonment but his daughter claimed that she had been coerced and forced to become a spy by a violent stepfather. Nevertheless she was found guilty and given a sentence of seven and a half years. Both avoided possible death sentences since their known spying activities happened before the US entered the Second World War. The father served only one year before being deported to Germany where he died homeless and penniless in 1949.

Chapter 10

THE LUDWIG SPY RING

'Most and apparently all of the people involved in this affair were completely unadapted for such activity. It is to be assumed that the American authorities knew of the entire network, which certainly was no work of art in view of the naive and stupid way these people carried on.'

Dr Hans Thomsen,
German charge d'affaires[1]

Major Ulrich von der Osten had become a favourite of Canaris almost from the moment he took command of the Abwehr in 1935. Intelligence was a family tradition for the von der Osten family and he had known how to keep a low profile during the many years he had worked for the Abwehr. It was he who had gone to Spain at the start of the Spanish Civil War and helped General José Sanjurjo to organise the attack on Burgos, the first city to fall to the Nationalists. He remained in Spain for the duration of the Spanish Civil War ending up as head of the Abwehr in Castile. He got to know many German agents such as Walter von Hausberger and Kurt Frederick Ludwig who passed through Spain on their way to the US and Mexico. In March 1941, Canaris decided that it was time to send someone to the US to pull together all the disparate strands of the espionage web into a cohesive, dynamic force. He chose von der Osten who entered the US through Los Angeles. By the 16 March 1941, he was in New York staying at that luxurious outpost of the Abwehr known as the Taft Hotel on the corner of 50th and 51st streets.

A traffic accident in Times Square, New York, at around 10.00 pm on the evening of 18 March 1941 resulted in the death of a tall, swarthy 50-year-old man with black hair and horn-rimmed glasses. Another man who had been with him as they tried to cross against the constant flow of traffic, grabbed a briefcase that the fallen man had dropped and fled the scene before the police arrived. The injured man was taken to St Vincent's Hospital where he later died. Documents he was carrying identified him as Don Julio Lopez Lido, who had only recently arrived in the country.

When the police took a look at the dead man's hotel room, they found material that led them to suspect he had some involvement with espionage. Suspicions were further aroused when they discovered documents revealing his true identity as Ulrich von der Osten, a German army major who was previously unknown to either US or British intelligence. Then the discovery of documents discussing the size, equipment, location and morale of US Army units and details of the routing of convoys between the US and England left no doubt that the man was worthy of further investigation.

The arrangements for the von der Osten's funeral were organised by a US citizen, Kurt Ludwig, been with him at the time he was rundown by a New York taxi. This excited a certain amount of interest within the FBI but it became significantly more important when, a few days later, they were informed about a letter that had been intercepted by British censors in Bermuda referring to the accident. The letter, written with *Geheimtinten* (secret ink), included a reference to someone called 'Joe K' who, apparently, was the man who had been with von der Osten when he was killed.

'Joe K' had, for some time, been someone of interest to both British intelligence (MI6), and the FBI who were now working together on a broad front monitoring the movement of international travellers and mail crossing the Atlantic. Under the command of Military Liaison and Security Officer Montgomery Hyde, the British were routinely scrutinising mail carried on ships that called at Bermuda, Jamaica and Trinidad for refuelling. The British had got this down to a fine art and had become recognised masters in this arcane counterintelligence specialty. Envelopes and packages could be easily opened, quickly examined and then resealed without revealing any evidence of tampering. Under great pressure, up to 1,000 specially trained staff would offload mailbags and make note of addresses and postmarks. Any suspicious packages were opened, and the contents noted before they were re-sealed and all were taken back onto the ship before its scheduled departure.

In early 1941, a number of letters with similarly handwritten addresses in Germany, Spain and Portugal were examined by British agent Nadya Gardiner whose instincts told her that there was something odd about them. She pestered Dr Charles Enrique Dent, head of the Bermuda science and technology department, to test them and eventually they discovered messages written in secret ink concerning more detailed information about cargoes destined for Britain. This ink was made out of a mixture of Pyramidon, a headache medication and water. When dry the writing was invisible but could be revealed if treated with iodine and a little heat. All the letters were signed 'Joe K'. Many letters that carried this signature referred to 'Uncle Dave and Aunt Loni'. When the FBI had searched von der Osten's papers in his hotel room, they had come across a telephone number for Dave and Loni Harris and a reference to someone called Fred Ludwig who was apparently their nephew. From this they were able to identify 'Joe K' as Kurt Frederick Ludwig, who had been born in Freemont, Ohio at the turn of the century but had gone to Germany with his parents when he was only 6 years old. He returned to the US in 1925 but only for a few years before returning once again to Germany in 1933. The date is significant because Ludwig would boast of having been involved in Hitler's abortive Beer Hall Putsch and always claimed to be friendly with a number of leading Nazis who had just taken power in Germany. It was even said, mostly by him, that it had been Reichsführer (SS leader) Heinrich Himmler, personally, who had suggested that he work for the Abwehr. Records show that Ludwig was active in Spain during the Spanish Civil War under the command of von der Osten and it was he to whom Ludwig had been reporting back after he became operational in the US when he arrived there in March 1940. Ludwig quickly organised a, mostly young and inexperienced, group but under his leadership, they became proficient and soon started providing a regular feed of intelligence.

The commander of *Abteilung II,* Colonel Erwin von Lahousen, was concerned that von der Osten's death might be a thread that the FBI could pull to unravel both the Sebold and Ludwig spy rings but Ludwig assured him that the accident had not compromised him. He was wrong. The FBI placed him under immediate and close surveillance. By following him, they discovered the identities of two of his agents, the teenage Hans Pagel and Karl Victor Mueller. Pagel, a German citizen, who had been a member of the German-American Youth Movement and later the Bund, seemed to restrict his espionage conducting surveillance on the New York waterfront and report on shipping.

In April 1941, Ludwig and Mueller set off on a road trip taking in many high-value locations such as the US Naval Academy at Annapolis, Maryland, where they took numerous photographs. On other occasions, Ludwig was accompanied by the 18-year-old Lucy Rita Boehmler, born in Stuttgart, Germany but raised in New York, who was described as his secretary. Later at her trial, she presented herself as a 'Teutonic image of uncommon beauty' and told the jury that she had joined Ludwig's spy ring because 'it sounded like a lot of fun' but it did not prevent her from getting a five-year sentence.[2] The two of them had visited nearly every army camp and airfield on the East Coast and employed a number of subterfuges to gather intelligence. They used various means of engaging soldiers in conversation after perhaps picking them up as they hitch-hiked away from camps on weekend passes. They would act as innocents by feigning ignorance of all things military and asking silly questions that often got revealing answers. One of Boehmler's most important functions was to maintain a card file containing information on US Army camps, the disposition of American military forces, troop movements and arms production.

Other agents Ludwig had recruited were Dr Paul Theodor Borchardt-Battuta, a former German army major who lectured at Seton Hall University, Helen Pauline Mayer, a Long Island housewife, US-born Frederick Edward Schlosser, Rene Charles Froehlich, born in Germany, but granted US citizenship through the naturalisation of his father, and a Miami-boat captain, and Carl Herman Schroetter, former deputy sheriff in Louisiana and Pennsylvania.

Froehlich was a soldier stationed at Governor's Island in New York Harbor and supplied Ludwig with lists of the admissions and discharges from the military hospital there. From this information, Ludwig was able to work out where specific military units were stationed. He had also established a magazine and bookselling business through which he was able to procure technical magazines, as well as army and navy publications concerning aviation and defence production. Mayer had been born in Brooklyn and made herself useful to the group by striking up friendships with people employed in the defence industry and extracting intelligence from them.

Paul Borchardt-Battuta was the exception in the group. Born in 1886, he was much older than the others. He was an archaeologist by profession and had been incarcerated in Dachau concentration camp in 1938, supposedly because of his Jewish ancestry, but was released after two weeks and given a visa to travel to the US. His imprisonment had apparently been a ruse to deflect from the fact that Borchardt-Battuta had been on the Abwehr's books for a number of years and needed a cover to shield him from scrutiny when he arrived in the US. Once there he took up a post lecturing and later quietly established himself as Ludwig's technical adviser.

Ludwig passed on information acquired through his agents by a variety of means. He wrote letters several times a week, ostensibly on the subject of a thriving leather goods business he was running, to Emanuel Alonzo in Madrid, Spain and Isabell Machado Santos in Lisbon, Portugal. He also had access to a long-range transmitter and a much smaller one in his car, which he used to transmit to South America or U-boats lying off the coast. Records of his communications show that he was an 'extraordinarily industrious spy'.[3] It was a time of great productivity for Pheiffer's organisation. Not only had Ludwig built his network in record time but Sebold and Wheeler-Hill were beavering away in New York and Duquesne was still working with Lang and Roeder at Norden. It was not to last, however.

It was a revelation that von der Osten had been active running other agents in the US, some of them freelance without links to the Abwehr, that infuriated Thomsen at the German Embassy in Washington DC and threatened to undermine all German efforts. One of them, calling himself Walter von Hausberger had come to the embassy claiming that the Abwehr had sent him on a sabotage mission and then left him without funds. He wanted Thomsen to give him money. Another, who presented himself to Thomsen as Julius Bergman, turned up at the embassy with a similar claim but bringing with him samples of explosives that he claimed to have been furnished with. This was intolerable for Thomsen. It was at a time when the German diplomatic staff were frantically trying to curb all illegal activity in the US fearing that it was having a serious adverse effect on public opinion and pushing the US to take a more active role in support of Britain Thomsen demanded clarification from Berlin. Von Lahousen disingenuously told him that there were no saboteurs active in the US. Thomsen then ran off a series of names of the men claimed had trained and instructed them ending with that of von der Osten. von Lahousen denied that the men were saboteurs and had been sent merely as observers. The matter ended up on Canaris's desk when Thomsen cabled to say that it was 'imperative and urgent that the Abwehr refrain from any such [sabotage] activities in the United States'.[4]

Von Lahousen, of course, had been conducting sabotage, insurrection, sedition and propaganda operations since early 1939. Major Richard Astor had been assigned to list possible targets while a small group of officers, including von der Osten and Walter Kappe had been given the job of formulating plans and overseeing their implementation. Pieckenbrock had been called upon to draw up maps of all major cities and strategic locations such as reservoirs.

Hausberger had been one of the first agents to be sent. To avoid suspicion, he had taken his wife and child with him. When he got down to business, he procured a quantity of explosives but came up against a blunt refusal to cooperate from people whose names were on a list of potential agents that Kappe had given him. Only Duquesne had shown willing and was actually deemed over-enthusiastic by coming up with an idea to bomb Roosevelt's church in Hyde Park. It was some time before Hausberger had recruited enough suitable agents in locations such as the Harrison Gas Works, the New York Liquidometer Plant, and a number of factories in New York and Detroit.

A second team was set up under Georg Busch, a fanatical Nazi who had worked with von Lahousen over a number of years in Czechoslovakia and Romania. As part of his evolution as an agent, Busch changed his name to Julius Georg Bergman and had arrived in the US in January 1939. Despite his background with the Abwehr, he proved to be spectacularly incompetent. He began by causing an explosion while one of his recruits, a Pole called Mike, was filling home-made bombs blowing off several of the man's fingers. When Bergman sought medical help not from a hospital but from a back-street doctor, Mike saw an opportunity to relieve Bergman of much of his cash in return for not reporting him to the police. It was after Mike continued to demand money that Bergman went to Thomsen. The vehemence of Thomsen's objections forced von Lahousen to recall both Hausberger and Bergman.

As if that was not bad enough, the diplomatic channels between Washington and Berlin froze on 30 June 1941 when news broke in Berlin of the arrest of Duquesne's spy network. Thomsen was barely able to restrain himself from a 'told you so' signal. Abwehr strategy, based on the smug assumption that US counterintelligence was virtually non-existent, was thrown into turmoil. Ludwig was ordered to remain in place but steer clear of Sebold who they believed was still active on their behalf and had not been exposed. Ludwig panicked, however, and made plans to leave the country. He had been unnerved by seeing Paul Scholz arrested by FBI agents just moments after he had held a conversation with him outside a bookstore in New York on 28 June 1941. He knew that the agents must have seen him talking to Scholz and could not understand why he had not been picked up also unless it was because he was already known to them and deliberately allowed to walk away.

He suspected that the FBI on the East Coast might be onto him and know his face so he decided to cross the country and try to get out through San Francisco but first he tried to 'lose' himself in a Bund summer camp in Pennsylvania to throw off any surveillance. It would not be so easy to avoid the FBI however, who had spies in all the Bund camps. They searched Ludwig's room and found incriminating evidence including the secret ink kit. To communicate with its agents, the Abwehr used a number of secret inks of which three – Apis, Pyramidon and Beate – were particularly effective. They were developed by the *Chemisch-Technische Reichsanstalt* (German Bureau of Standards).[5] Their formulations were one of the Abwehr's most closely guarded secrets. Agents were encouraged to use them freely in the belief that messages would be completely secure. Unaware that he was being followed, Ludwig changed his plans and, leaving the camp on 2 August 1941, headed south to Miami, Florida, US where he made contact with a man known to the world as John Charles Post, otherwise known on the Miami waterfront as 'Captain Jack'.[6] This 'fortyish, heavy-set [man] with close-cropped hair and a conspicuous scar on his cheek' had operated a not very successful fishing, sightseeing and charter business with his boat *Echoes of the Past* but was forced to sell up and now worked as a cook at the Greyhound Club, a popular spot for servicemen from the nearby Opa-Locka naval air station. Swiss-born and German-educated Post was none other than Carl Schroetter who Ludwig now called on to find him a boat to get him to Cuba without getting travel papers. There was no way that Schroetter could do that and so Ludwig was forced back onto his original plan and set off across-country. He abandoned his car at Bute, Montana and continued by bus, but Hoover's men were right behind him and when it was clear that Ludwig's only intention was to get to San Francisco and board a ship as soon as possible, they stepped in and arrested him on the dockside. As soon as Ludwig was in custody, the FBI arrested Schroetter at his home address of 220 Northwest 33rd Avenue, Miami.

The trial of Kurt Ludwig and his eight associates began on 3 February 1942 when all nine were indicted on charges of conspiracy to violate the espionage statutes, and all were convicted. Sentenced to ten years in Atlanta Federal Prison for espionage, Schroetter slashed his wrists with the diaphragm of a radio headset and hung himself with a bedsheet attached to a water pipe.

There was heavy media coverage of both the Duquesne and Ludwig trials. Books, magazines and newspapers were full of stories both true and fanciful making it hard for readers to decide whether or not the country was overrun with Nazi spies and saboteurs. People were fascinated by the spies and could not get enough of them. Roosevelt thought it was prudent to dampen the public mood by showing that the FBI was firmly in charge. Local police authorities across the country were instructed to give the FBI all possible assistance. Harper's magazine was quick to reassure the nation that the FBI agents were

> young, intelligent, sure of themselves in a quiet, competent way. All of them seemed to be college graduates, and each man had had special training in the work he was assigned to do. They had the straight, clear eyes, the firm jaws, the steady look of men to whom life is a perilous adventure and who are not afraid of it.[7]

Thomsen was livid. He wrote to the *Auswärtiges Amt* saying,

> Intelligence agencies in Germany indiscriminately trained totally unqualified persons and sent them to the United States. The operations of the German agencies were marked by naivete, carelessness and lack of coordination.

He had his own agents running in the field and he was desperate to shield them from unwanted attention.

A handsome, debonair man with exquisite cosmopolitan manners,[8] the German consul in Washington DC, Herbert Wilhelm Scholz, was enormously popular in diplomatic circles but he had a secondary role as the resident director of Reinhard Heydrich's *Sicherheitsdienst* (SD – intelligence agency of the *Schutzstaffel* (SS) – Nazi paramilitary organisation) and as such was no friend of the Abwehr. He had already proved himself to be a very astute agent who was able to identify suitable recruits from organisations such as Father Charles Coughlin's Christian front and steer then towards a Nazified philosophy.

At one of Washington's many diplomatic cocktail parties, soon after Scholz had been appointed in early 1938, he had been approached by an American actress, Mary Elizabeth 'Madcap Merry' Fahrney, who was also heir to $100 million fortune. She was already almost done with the second of what would be eight husbands and just how much she knew of Scholz's SD affiliation is unclear but over lunch at Pierre's on Connecticut Avenue, Fahrney offered her services as a spy for Germany. Scholz found her extremely anti-Semitic, 'exceptionally intelligent' but someone whose 'ideas were somewhat marred by her erratic way of thinking'.[9] Born to wealth and privilege and by nature indiscrete, Fahrney had never been one to keep her opinions to herself. Her pro-Nazi sentiments were well known and acknowledged by the FBI but generally ignored within her own social circles as an eccentric foible of no importance.

Scholz would later describe her as a source of invaluable intelligence material whose prominent position in American public life gave her invaluable access to people of influence both politically and economically. It was with some regret, therefore, that when he was transferred away from Washington and somewhat removed from the beating heart of American government, he was obliged to offer

Fahrney not to the Abwehr but to Thomsen who found her rather overpowering and someone who brought unwanted attention to the clandestine side of his work.

Throughout his tenure in Washington, Thomsen would repeatedly complain about the lack of proper supervision of Abwehr agents in the US who were liable to draw attention to themselves and bring the German diplomatic mission into disrepute. This was in stark contrast to the way that he ran his own separate intelligence networks. His first had been a coterie of foreign correspondents of countries such as Switzerland, Spain and Portugal who were expected to remain neutral during any future war. Each was given a secret payment of $350 each month.[10] Next he set about creating a network of informants all across America that he hoped would remain active in the event of the US entering a war against Germany.

Overall, however, Thomsen considered his primary responsibility was to follow events in the White House and maintain close surveillance on the public mood regarding interventionism. He worked with those in the US government who opposed Roosevelt and who were anxious to keep the US out of the Second World War. Having succeeded in creating a network of well-placed informants whose inside knowledge far exceeded anything the likes of Fahrney could produce, he had access to cabinet minutes through a source close to Attorney General Homer Cummings but this was not quite the summit of his achievements. He had actually got a source in the notoriously insecure code room of the Department of State through which all diplomatic telegrams were sent. Over a period of some seventeen months, Joseph P. Dugan, the technical operating chief of the code room, passed along to a friend copies of confidential telegrams between Roosevelt and the US ambassador in London, Joseph Kennedy. He thought his friend was no more than just concerned about the war situation but the copies found their way to Thomsen and subsequently to Berlin.

Ulrich von Gienanth was Heydrich's own personal representative in the US and arrived in the US in 1934 as a military attaché to the German Embassy in Washington DC. His first visit had been four years earlier as a student but now he was back on a mission to keep a close eye on the embassy and report back to SS headquarters. He might well have had a number of virtues from a social and diplomatic aspect, given his Nordic good looks, aristocratic background and high-society manners, but he was a poor fit for espionage. In Berlin, his overt Nazism might have been a virtue and a sure guarantee of approval but von Gienanth's failure to temper his views made him acceptable to only the extreme right-wing fringe of Washington's elite, of whom only one had access to useful intelligence.

Laura Houghtaling Ingalls was a renowned aeronaut who had risen to fame for a number of notable feats including being the first American woman to fly solo over the Andes in 1934. After the fall of France in June 1940, she offered her services as a propagandist to von Gienanth who was impressed by her speechmaking prowess. For a monthly allowance of $300, the 'pasty-faced, cherry-lipped'[11] Ingalls was a regular speaker at Charles Lindberg's America First rallies where she frequently used quotes from Hitler's *Mein Kampf.* After she had unwisely boasted to a friend about her well-paid sideline, the friend, Sylvia Comfort, told the FBI who started to keep a close watch on Ingalls and when she was on the point of taking off for a flight to Berlin on 17 December 1941, agents stepped in and arrested her at Los Angeles airport. On 12 February 1942, Ingalls was charged with violation of the 1938 Foreign Agents Registration Act by undertaking the work of the German government and secretly receiving payment for her services, all without filing the necessary paperwork with the US government. A jury found her guilty of spreading Nazi propaganda at the direction of the German government and the judge sentenced her to between eight months and two years in prison.

Chapter 11

OPERATION PASTORIUS

'The biggest blunder that ever occurred in Abwehr II'[1]

By March 1941, the prospect of the US being drawn into the war in Europe was growing almost to the point when it would become inevitable. Abwehr attention was directed across the Atlantic by the highest authority in Berlin to plan offensive sabotage operations. Colonel von Lahousen was assigned to covertly introduce sabotage units to the East Coast of the US to strike a blow against public morale. They came up with Operation Pastorius, named after Franz Daniel Pastorius, the leader of the first community of immigrant Germans in the United States who settled in Germantown in 1683.

As commander of *Abteilung II* since 1 January 1939, the aristocratic Austrian-born von Lahousen had been tasked with conducting sabotage operations to destroy communications lines, basic industries, warships, airports and railways as well as contacting discontented minority groups in foreign countries for intelligence purposes. After more than two years in which to develop its expertise, *Abteilung II* was highly organised and efficient but carrying out espionage on the other side of a 3,000-mile-wide ocean was something that was beyond its experience. After years of being told to tread carefully with the US, pressure had built on *Abteilung II* rapidly during 1941, and intensified after Pearl Harbor, to develop a strategy for dealing with the US as an enemy nation from an intelligence and espionage perspective. This meant that the plans for Operation Pastorius were hatched over a much shorter timescale than would have been optimal. They had no time to liaise effectively with reliable agents already inside the US who might have been able to prepare the ground.

Walter Kappe was the man von Lahousen chose to organise the mission. When he was 17, Kappe had left the University of Göttingen to join the *Deutsche Freikorps* (German Free Corps) and was also for nine months a member of the Black Reichswehr, the illegal German army which existed in defiance of the Versailles Treaty. It was a natural move for him then to join the newly formed Nazi Party. He boasted of having taken part in Hitler's Beer Hall Putsch in 1923 and, in the aftermath of its failure, had emigrated to the US in 1925 where he had become very involved with German-American groups such as the Friends of New Germany. He had been given responsibility for the *Bundnachrichtenstelle* (the group's intelligence section), and it had been through this that he had developed close links to the Abwehr by setting up a network of informants within the German-American community and also in other pro-fascist groups in the US. When he lost the battle for leadership of the German-American Bund to Fritz Kuhn, he had returned to Germany in 1937 and set about establishing an organisation, *Kameradschaft USA* (Companionship), in Stuttgart under the auspices of the *Deutsches Ausland Institut* (DAI – German Foreign Institute).

By 1941, he was running a small, somewhat independent, unit from a third-floor office at Rankestraße 8, Berlin. It was there that he hatched his plans with the objective of establishing a permanent espionage organisation with headquarters in Chicago, a city which had been characterised as having a particularly anti-war culture. Kappe began recruiting people who had, like him, lived in the US and had been active in the various German-American organisations before being repatriated. All would have to be able to avoid detection in American cities by speaking fluent English and by being very familiar with American culture. They would also need to have skills that would allow them to find employment easily in the US and they would all be required to exhibit loyalty to the Nazi Party. Then they would need to be evaluated according to their aptitude for clandestine operations. Some would need to show leadership while others would be required to follow orders with strict military discipline. Kappe travelled extensively across Germany interviewing potential candidates and, as an indication of the importance of the mission, was given authority to negotiate their release from their industrial or military roles for secondment to the Abwehr.

The final selection of twelve saboteurs was made in March 1942 and their targets were meticulously selected. They included bridges, power plants, factories and Jewish-owned businesses. Special attention was given to the light metals industry such as the Aluminium Company of America in Alcoa, Tennessee, US and Massena, New York, critical for contemporary aircraft manufacture, and the Philadelphia Salt

Company's cryolite plant. The hugely ambitious project even marked down vulnerable waterways and railroad hubs. Kappe looked first for men to lead the operation and he came up with George John Dasch and Edward John Kerling.

Kappe had known Dasch for some months before he had started recruiting for Pastorius and was familiar with his sharp mind and ease with American slang. Dasch was born in Speyer am Rhein, Germany on 7 February 1903. At the age of 13, he entered a convent to study for the priesthood but when the First World War came, he managed to enlist in the Germany army at the age of 14 serving in northern France for eleven months. After the First Word War, he looked to escape from the shame and ignominy of the French occupation of his hometown by stowing away on a ship bound for Philadelphia in 1922. After only a few weeks, he was arrested and deported but was more successful in the following year when he was able to enter the country legally. For a year, he served as a private in the US Army then the thin-faced, skinny Dasch lived in the US for the next fifteen years working in a variety of low-level restaurant and hotel jobs until he achieved respectability as a waiter in San Francisco and then night manager of a hotel in Sacramento. It was still way below the level of employment he felt he was entitled to though and complained of feeling a sense of degradation by having to live off tips. By 1939, he was seeking repatriation to Germany where he could find 'the dignity and pride in work which had eluded him in the United States'.[2]

In January 1941, both he and his wife applied for, and were given, German passports but when their documents came through for passage to Germany, his wife was too ill to travel so he returned alone to Berlin, via Yokohama, arriving on 13 May 1941. His wife had tried to follow him but her ship was stopped by the British and she was interned in Bermuda for the duration of the Second World War. Back in Germany, Dasch struggled to find a position that suited him until he was interviewed by Kappe who thought him suitable for employment by the *Sonderdienst Seehaus* (German Monitoring Service), which monitored foreign broadcasts. When Kappe started recruiting for Operation Pastorius in March 1942, he remembered Dasch and had him transferred from *Sonderdienst Seehaus* to *Abwehr II*.

In March 1941 also, Kappe selected Kerling as a potential leader for his 'strength of character [and] intense loyalty to the Nazi cause'.[3] Kerling had been born in Wiesbaden-Biebirich on 12 June 1909. Frustrated by the economic and political struggles of the Weimar Republic, he joined NSDAP in 1928. He went to the US in the same year and found work in Brooklyn in a packaging business. After a couple of years, Kerling took a job as a chauffeur to Henry Dicks who had estates in both New York and Florida, and he was sufficiently settled by 1931, to marry a German immigrant, Marie Sichart. In October 1939, he wanted to return to Germany but there were restrictions on travel so, along with Hermann Neubauer, Joseph Nussbaum, Ernest Nettin and Richard Ernest Heinz, purchased a two-masted yawl the *Lekala*, which they hoped to sail to Germany, but they only got as far as Miami before abandoning the idea. Neubauer would also later be recruited by Kappe for the Pastorius mission. He had stayed in Miami, and Kerling returned to New York but they joined up again in July 1940 when Kerling, Neubauer and Nussbaum departed for Lisbon, Portugal on the SS *Exocorda* of the American Export Lines. From Lisbon they took a flight to Rome, Italy before taking a train to Hamburg, Germany. There, Kerling was taken on by the army as a translator. Moving on to a job in the Ministry of Public Enlightenment and Propaganda, he was approached by Kappe and recruited to Pastorius.

In woods just outside Brandenburg 40 miles west of Berlin was a huge estate, Quenz Farm, that might once have epitomised rural tranquillity, but which had now been taken over by the Abwehr and turned into a military campus and school for sabotage. Here had been constructed bridges of various styles and materials and lengths of railway. A nearby lake was available for training in boat handling and a nearby airport for practicing parachute drops.

The twelve candidates arrived on 7 April 1942, along with two instructors, an assistant from the Abwehr laboratory in Berlin, and four observers. On the first day, they were divided into three four-man teams and established a routine of physical exercise, lectures, demonstrations and discussions centred round recent US magazine content, American slang, recent American laws and news events, and the lyrics of standard American songs. There were field exercises in the correct placement of the explosives in tracks, bridges and towers. They were taught how to mix chemicals to make incendiary bombs using saltpetre, sawdust, aluminium powder and plaster of paris, all of which were easily purchased in the US. They learned how to make crude timing devices by soaking dried peas in water and using their expansion to force a contact with battery leads. Another method was using a small medicine bottle half full of sulphuric acid and stoppered with piece of paper held securely in place by paraffin. When the bottle was turned upside down, the acid burned through the paper and fell onto a mixture of calcium chlorate and powdered sugar mixture, which ignited. Next came the use of explosives to damage power lines, railyards and factories. Two experts, Dr Walter Schulz and Dr Helmuth

König demonstrated one of their own inventions, which was a stable material that looked like bricks of yellow plasticine. It could be dropped, cut, hammered, burned or drilled full of holes and could only be detonated with a special device that required intense heat.

At the end of the first week, two trainees had failed to impress Kappe and they, along with a third who was called away for personal reasons left the programme. Consequently, the men were now split into just two teams, Dasch had Ernest Peter Burger, Heinrich Harm Heinck, Richard Quirin and Joseph Schmidt while Kerling's group included the young Herbert Haupt, his fellow sailor, Hermann Neubauer and Werner Thiel.

Ernest Peter Burger was born on 1 September 1906 in Augsburg, Germany. A man not averse to dealing out physical violence, he had joined the *Freikorps Oberland* (right-wing paramilitary) when he was 15 and claimed to have taken part in the 1923 Beer Hall Putsch. He emigrated to the US in 1927 under a quota immigrant visa and was given US citizenship after which he joined the Michigan National Guard on 17 June 1931. After an honourable discharge, he joined the Wisconsin National Guard on 6 November 1931. In 1933, he returned to Germany and rejoined the Nazi Party to become an aide-de-camp to Ernst Röhm, which was not the best move he could have made since Röhm was murdered along with many of his followers on Hitler's orders in the Night of the Long Knives on 30 June 1934. It was not in his nature to do so, but Burger was forced to keep a low profile to avoid being caught up in the purges following that and he quietly took a minor posting in the political division of the *Reichsleitung* (Reich leadership) attending courses in journalism at the University of Berlin. He was arrested on 4 March 1940 after writing an article critical of Gestapo methods in occupied Poland. As punishment he was drafted into the infantry and posted to work as a prison guard. Perhaps impressed with Burger's obvious physical presence and conscious that his teams would be working on foreign soil in a hostile environment carrying out acts of destruction, Kappe was well aware that there was a high risk of violent confrontation. Burger was a man who could be relied to act in such a situation.

Heinck and Quirin had been working together at the Volkswagen plant in Braunschweig, Germany and were recruited from there. They had known each other in New York when they had both been members of the German-American Bund. Heinck was born in Hamburg on 27 June 1907 and had entered the US illegally in 1927. He had worked his passage on the Hamburg-American Line's SS *Westphalia* as an oiler and machinist's helper and jumped ship in New York. Once there he stuck closely to the German communities of Yorktown in New York to avoid exposure. He had a series of low status jobs; from busboy to handyman to elevator operator and finally learned a trade as a machinist.

Quirin was born in Berlin in 1908 and had been brought up by foster parents. On leaving school he worked at the Schulte Machine Company before being laid off in 1926. He struggled to find work after that and so, with money borrowed from his uncle, emigrated to the US in 1927, the same year that Heinck arrived, but unlike him had done so legally. He had worked as a tinsmith in Schenectady before joining the maintenance department of General Electric. The Great Depression saw him laid off and he found his way to New York where he found work as a house painter. Both men found it hard to settle into American life and discovered solace in the camaraderie of the Bund. Both applied for assisted passage back to Germany in 1939. Kappe had got his leaders and now he was looking for foot soldiers. When he interviewed Berger, Heinck and Quirin Kappe was impressed by their straightforward, uncomplicated approach to life. Their obvious devotion to the Nazi Party was proof that they could be relied upon to follow orders dutifully.

Dasch's fourth man, Joseph Schmidt, was the odd one out. It was soon clear that he had a low opinion of Dasch and was reluctant to obey his orders. He had gone to Canada in the mid-1920s where he lived something of a solitary life farming, fishing and trapping as well as making and selling wood alcohol to local indigenous peoples. Kappe saw that, apart from the fact that he thought he should lead the group instead of Dasch, Schmidt had positive qualities of self-reliance and courage and he decided to keep him on and give him a chance to show his colours.

In Kerling's group was the young, tall, broad-shouldered Herbert Johannes Wilhelm Haupt. He had been born in Szczecin, Poland on 21 December 1919, but had moved to the US with his mother in 1924 and was brought up there. Even in the German communities of Chicago, the young Haupt grew up heavily influenced by American culture which gave him a very different outlook to those in the group who had lived in Germany during the First World War and had experienced the turbulence of at least some of the Weimar years. His habit of wearing jewellery and his brash, confident demeanour grated with them and made him rather unpopular but, as with Schmidt, Kappe saw that this young man's physical stature and his pugnacious character could be assets in a dangerous mission. He was further convinced by Haupt's capabilities when Haupt told him how, as a young man in 1941, he had taken off to Mexico with a friend looking for adventure and from there had gone to Yokohama in Japan hoping to find work. What Kappe may not have known was that Haupt had become involved with a widow Gerda Melind who was using her maiden name of Stuckmann at the time. Both sets of parents had objected to the relationship. When Gerda had become pregnant, she wanted Haupt to marry her, but Haupt had gone to Mexico to avoid having to deal with the situation. He told Gerda he would send for her as soon as he found work but the last she heard from him was a postcard from St Louis three days after he had left saying that he was on his way to California. At his trial he would later accuse Gerda of being a drunk and of 'running around with other men'. From Japan, the two men worked their passage back to Germany on a freighter. When Kappe interviewed Haupt, he got an impression of a physically strong and cunning individual who was obsessed by making money but someone who was not particularly intelligent. He also had the advantage of being a US citizen and one who would be totally comfortable in a US environment.

When Kerling and his crew had abandoned the *Lekala* in Miami, Hermann Otto Neubauer had stayed there and married Alma Wolf, a German-American girl he had known in Chicago. Born in Fuhlsbuttl, Hamburg on 5 February 1910, Neubauer had taken his first job as an apprentice cook on the SS *Hamburg* of the Hamburg-America Line then jumped ship in New York in July 1931. He was able to secure a permanent residency permit under an immigrant quota visa on 23 November 1931 and remained in the US working at his occupation as a cook in various hotels and restaurants and occasionally obtaining employment on an ocean-going vessel. He joined the German-American Bund in Chicago in 1935 and became a member of the NSDAP in Chicago. With a $50 subsidy from the German Consulate in New York, Neubauer left New York on 11 July 1940, and returned to Germany via Lisbon and Rome. He was drafted into the German army and wounded in action in Poland after which he spent six months in hospital. During his time in the US, he had been interviewed by the FBI because of his affiliation with the Bund so he was on their files.

The fourth member of Kerling's group was Werner Edward Thiel, born in Essen on 29 March 1907. He arrived in Detroit from Germany on 26 April 1927, on a German immigrant quota visa. He found work at the Ford plant and then at General Motors before moving to New York spending three years as a porter at the Home for the Aged and Infirm on Central Park West. In 1933, he joined the Friends of New Germany and later the German-American Bund. Having joined the NSDAP, he returned to Germany on 27 March 1941, on a German passport, departing from San Francisco, California, on a Japanese liner proceeding to Germany via Japan, Manchuria and Russia.

It is clear that many of these men had at various times experienced poverty and alienation while living in the US so it was no great feat for Kappe to persuade them to embark on a mission that would allow them some measure of payback for their humiliation. Now that Germany was in the ascendent Kappe was offering them an opportunity to recover their self-esteem and to take pride in striking a blow for the fatherland.

The men were now given more specialised training They toured railyards in Berlin where engineers pointed out vulnerable spots in the engines such as the bearings, oil systems, brakes, engines, signals and switches. Reinhold Barth, Dasch's cousin by marriage, who had worked for nine years on the Long Island Rail Road, explained that sand or some other abrasive material thrown into the bearings or the oil filter would cause significant damage and dynamite disguised as coal and dropped into the tender would sooner or later blow up a valuable engine. Next, they visited aluminium and magnesium plants in Germany to be shown the most vulnerable points to attack. High-tension power lines were the easiest to damage and only an eight-hour power cut to the plants would destroy all the stoves and baths in which the aluminium was manufactured.

Finally the men were issued with false identities. Dasch became George Davis, born in San Francisco and Kerling, became Edward 'Eddie' J. Kelly. Five years were added to his age, so he could also be born in San Francisco before the earthquake. Thiel's resemblance to a Pole got him the role of a Polish immigrant, Billy Thomas, born in the coal-mining area of Pennsylvania, which has a large Polish population. Heinck became Henry Kaynor, with a Polish mother and a German father, from Wilkes-Barre, which he had left at an early age. Quirin was given the name Richard 'Dick' Quintas, born in Lisbon, but emigrating to the United States with his parents at the age of 3. Neubauer became Henry Nicholas, born in Lithuania and brought to Chicago as a small boy. Joseph Schmidt had a Scandinavian appearance and so became Jerry Swenson. Haupt and Burger, as US citizens, retained their own identities which meant that they would have to register for the draft.

The men were issued with German military uniforms which they would wear while executing the landing so that if they were caught setting foot on US soil they would be interned as prisoners of war and not shot as spies. Their equipment was held in eight wooden crates, each with an inner container made of galvanised sheet steel, which was soldered to make it waterproof. Six of the boxes were filled with the dynamite Schulz and König had invented now formed into the shape of bricks, apart from some disguised as pieces of coal, and all wrapped in heavy paper. The other two boxes contained a variety of timing devices, coils of wire, incendiaries and sulphuric acid.

They now signed contracts to authorise payments and a pledge of secrecy. There was some argument over payments since not all were paid the same amount and there was also a little personal friction between some members of the team so Kappe brought forward the departure to divert attention away from that. On Wednesday, 20 May 1942, Kappe gave them forty-eight hours' notice of departure and treated them all to a high-class dinner at Berlin's swanky Tiergarten restaurant as an official farewell. First stop for them was Paris where Kappe Dasch and Kerling, as group leaders were given $50,000 each for general expenses, travel, the establishment of fronts, the purchase of materials and bribes, if needed. In addition to that, each man would get $9,000 of which the group leader would hold $5,000.The remaining $4,000 was in money belts which the men would receive just before leaving on their mission. All the money would be in genuine American banknotes in denominations of no more than $50. Kappe's efforts for verisimilitude, however, were almost undone when Haupt noticed that some of the notes were of a type that had gone out of circulation in 1933 when the US came off the gold standard. Dasch inspected his and found that mixed in with the genuine notes were some with oriental lettering on the back which immediately made them look suspect. All the money was hastily sorted to eliminate the duds which, fortunately amounted to only a small proportion of the whole. Even so, it was also noted that many of the notes had consecutive numbers, which could link the men in any investigation if, indeed, the notes were queried when they tried to spend them.[4] The incident, and the rather offhand way that Kappe had dealt with it was not conducive to raising the morale of the saboteurs who were now getting wound up as the mission approached. From that point, the men questioned whether they would ever be able to use the money safely and if not, how would they survive on US soil.

From Paris, they travelled to Lorient in Brittany, France where they prepared to board U-boats but before they could do that Schmidt started showing symptoms of gonorrhoea and was hospitalised for treatment. He had never been the most popular and his departure was not lamented. Kerling's group were going to the Florida coast as since they had the furthest to travel they boarded first. Their transport across the Atlantic would be the Type VIIC U-boat, *U-584*, skippered by Lieutenant Commander Joachim Deecke. They departed on 26 May 1942, but it was two days before Dasch's team, now reduced to four, was able follow in *U-202* 'Innsbruck' captained by Lieutenant Commander Hans-Heinz Lindner.

U-202 ran on the surface at night and submerged by day. Every day there was a practice alarm when the submarine crash-dived deep into the water as each man raced to his station. During the first week, Dasch and his men suffered from seasickness and were disturbed by the claustrophobic conditions on board. For another two weeks they endured the sort of atmosphere that none of them could have been prepared for. It would have come as relief, therefore, when Lindner told them that they were approaching the Newfoundland Banks, Canada but the thought of what was coming next would soon have had their pulses racing. They became increasingly nervous, endlessly checking their kit and equipment and practicing getting into the rubber dirigible that would take them from ship to shore. Persistent thick fog off Nova Scotia, Canada and the threat of US coastal patrols ratcheted up tension within the rest of the U-boat crew who were now much closer to the US coast than they had ever been before.

Then on the evening of 12 June 1942 the skies cleared and Lindner was able to take bearings which he thought put his ship off Long Island at East Hampton, New York. He was out by 3 miles, actually lying off Amagansett, New York which, under the circumstances, was still a remarkable feat of navigation. Dasch and his men changed into military uniform and checked their gear one last time. The U-boat inched its way towards the shore and surfaced into another fog bank that had descended with the dusk. The dirigible was inflated and tied with a towline that was meant to guide it back to the boat in the fog after landing the saboteurs. Just after midnight, the four men and two crew loaded the boxes and *U-202* quickly disappeared in the fog as they pulled away. It was something of a bare-knuckle ride. The water was choppy and threatened to dump them all into the water as they rode the surf towards then shore. It was a huge relief when they ran aground on the sandy beach and the boxes could be quickly unloaded while the two crewmen emptied the dirigible of water ready for their return to the submarine. Dasch remained with the sailors while the others carried the four boxes up the beach and changed into their civilian clothes.

When Dasch followed them some moments later he was surprised by a man walking along the beach with a flashlight. Dasch quickly approached the man to prevent him observing the sailors in the boat and realised that he was a member of the Coast Guard. The guard, John Cullen, asked Dasch what he was doing on the beach in the fog and Dasch told him that he had just landed a fishing boat and was trying to work out which part of the beach he had arrived at. Cullen suggested that he accompany him to the Coast Guard station, but Dasch was obviously disinclined to do that. In the moment he had to decide whether to follow the instructions Kappe had given him in the event of being discovered, which was to lure the man down to the water's edge where he could be overpowered by the sailors. Dasch could see that the guard was little more than a youth and he baulked at the thought of killing him. He tried instead the option of bribing the man to go away. He was not having much luck with this when Burger appeared out of the fog dragging a duffel bag full of discarded uniforms and speaking to Dasch in German. He saw Cullen and gave him a hard look. Cullen became aware that Dasch was wearing a kind of uniform and when the other man had spoken German it dawned on him that they were probably engaged in some sort of illegal activity. Dasch sensed that Cullen was now quite scared and played on that. The best Cullen could do, he told him, was take some money, go away and pretend he had never seen them. He thrust a handful of notes into Cullen's hand. Cullen took what turned out to be $260, turned and quickly left. The saboteurs now buried the boxes in the sand and Dasch hurriedly changed into his civilian clothes. Dasch would later boast to the FBI that he had 'fooled that little navy boy' but the distant sound of a U-boat engine fading away in the fog brought to all four of them the cold reality that what they were now involved with was no longer a theoretical exercise.

The FBI had been alerted by the Amagansett Coast Guard on the morning of 13 June 1942. Alerted by Cullen they had searched the beach for signs of the mysterious strangers and discovered tracks that led them to the buried boxes. When they described the contents to Hoover at FBI headquarters, he thought it important enough to send Connelly, the man who had broken the Duquesne spy ring. Investigations showed that four strangers had boarded the New York train earlier that morning but there were no clues as to who they were or where they might be by now.

Four days later and 850 miles to the south, Deecke was having better luck with the weather. On a clear night his *U-584* crept towards Ponte Vedra beach at Jacksonville, Florida and surfaced just 50 yards from shore but the crossing had not been without incident. Deecke had taken a long south-west sweep of the Atlantic but had still been spotted by a British aircraft. An emergency dive to avoid eight bombs rocked the U-boat but did no damage except for severely disturbing the morale of Kerling and his men.

The sea was much calmer off the Florida coast and Kerling's group were rowed to shore without mishap. Once on land they took their four boxed high up the beach and buried them in the sand next to a clump of three palm trees so that they would be able to locate the spot again in the future. They changed into their civilian clothes and the next morning joined the highway and took a bus into the town where they split into two pairs. Haupt and Thiel booked into the Hotel Mayflower on West Bay Street while Neubauer and Kerling went to the Hotel Seminole on the corner of Hogan and Forsyth streets registering as Nicholas and Kelly.

After two days, on 19 June 1942, Neubauer and Kerling took a train to Cincinnati, Ohio, US. Neither man was confident that they could carry out their assignment. It was one thing playing at being saboteurs in Germany but quite another faced with the real thing cast adrift in a far-off land with no support agency to fall back on. Once in Cincinnati, they went their separate ways and arranged to meet again on 6 July 1942 in Chicago. Neubauer went on alone to Chicago on 20 June 1942 where he met up with Haupt whose somewhat dull imagination had allowed him to settle quickly. Back on his home turf. Haupt felt more at ease than the others. His US upbringing had ingrained deep within him a high regard for money and a sense of what it did for self-esteem. He celebrated by using some of the $4,000 Kappe had given him to buy a gold watch and some fancy clothes and run around the city in taxis. He even registered for the draft. Seeking to establish some sort of contact with his old life, he had looked up his uncle, Walter Freehling, whose address Kappe had given him and persuaded him to take him in as a lodger with an assurance that his compliance would ease the pressure on a brother who was being held in a German concentration camp. Later at his trial, Haupt would claim that he never had any intention of going through with sabotage operations. While in Germany, he said, he had been hounded by the Gestapo and the police and had decided long before he had left Germany that he would turn himself into the authorities when he got to the US.

Neubauer, on the other hand, was showing distinct signs of nervousness. He had brooded all during his U-boat confinement having argued with his wife just before leaving Germany. He decided to contact her when he landed and arrange for her to get passage to the US through Sweden. He told Haupt that he was sure he was being followed. A day later, his sense of insecurity led Neubauer to the home of a friend Harry Jaques at 211 West North Avenue, Chicago where he gave him the contents of his money belt, about $3,600, which he asked Jaques to keep for him until he called for it.

Meanwhile, Kerling met Thiel and both men went on to New York and booked into the Commodore Hotel. They stayed there for three days until, on the evening of 23 June 1942, Kerling was on his way to meet his wife when he was stopped by FBI agents. Thiel had caught up with an old friend, Anthony Kramer to whom he also gave the contents of his money belt for safekeeping. They spent a couple of days together but when Thiel left Thompson's restaurant on the evening of 23 June 1942, he was also detained by FBI men. What had put the authorities onto them so quickly?

On the Long Island beach, Dasch's encounter with Cullen had shown just how precarious their position was. They got away as quickly as they could and walked inland until they came across a railway line which they followed until they got to Amagansett station. There they waited there on the platform until daybreak. When the train arrived, they bought tickets for Jamaica, Long Island, where they split up. All four booked into hotels using aliases. Dasch and Burger went together to the Governor Clinton Hotel while Henck with Quirin checked into the Hotel Martinique

Henck and Quirin moved out of their hotel after one night's stay, having found it too expensive, and found lodgings at 149 West 76th Street a few blocks away from where Duquesne had lived. All four met together again at Grant's Tomb and discussed what they were supposed to do but they were unable to formulate any plans. They had been told by Kappe to settle in for a few months before beginning their sabotage activities and they were quite content to do that. It seems clear that no one had much idea of how to go about carrying out their instructions and they showed little enthusiasm to get started. They had money to live off in the meantime.

Discipline was eroding by the minute. With money in their pockets and time on their hands, the bars and clubs of New York were too much of a temptation and arguments, mild at first, broke out. Dasch had never been a popular leader from the start and now he seemed to have gone off on his own and was out of touch which concerned Quirin and Heinck. They would have been a lot more bothered if they knew what Dasch was up to, however. There had never been much love lost between Dasch and Burger either although there was a sort of bond between them that overrode their antipathy. Neither was enthusiastic about Nazism. Burger had been imprisoned for his criticism of the regime and Dasch hated what Germany had become when he had returned in 1941. During their training period, both had looked upon the mission as a way of escaping Germany and each had sensed that in the other.

Dasch would later claim that he had never been committed to the mission even before leaving Quenz Farm and the confrontation with

Cullen, who had clearly seen his face, cannot have helped his morale. Whatever the truth of that assertion, Dasch had now decided to give himself up to the US authorities and he risked taking Burger into his confidence. On Sunday, 14 June 1942, Dasch called the FBI from a phone booth and spoke to agent Dean F. McWhorter. The agent was not impressed with Dasch's story of how he had just arrived from Germany and was assigned to carry out a sabotage mission. How would he like to come into the FBI offices and give a bit more detail? Not at all was Dasch's reply, he wanted to speak to Hoover himself, and he hung up. Perhaps relieved that McWhorter had not taken him at his word, Dasch took a pause to think about what he was doing and did not follow up on this call for another four days.

Then he decided to go to Washington DC and make another approach to the FBI. He arrived there in the late afternoon of 18 June 1942. The next day he called the FBI again and this time spoke to agent Duane L. Traynor who, unlike McWhorter, knew about the find of boxes at Amagansett beach. When Dasch told his story about coming to the US on a U-boat to carry out sabotage, it seemed plausible that there was a connection and so he sent a car to bring him in. Dasch then underwent exhaustive questioning before revealing the location of his three group members who were arrested. Soon the other four were located and arrested also.

Hoover called a press conference in the Federal Court House in New York on 27 June 1942 after the last one, Neubauer, was taken into custody. He gave a brief account of the arrests along with cursory details of the saboteurs but little more was heard from him until the trial. Before that, however, the DOJ had to work out what the charges would be and how to frame them so as to justify the harshest possible sentence.

President Roosevelt wanted the saboteurs tried by a military tribunal because a civilian court proceeding might have resulted in acquittal. At the time, it was not a crime to merely buy a gun or plan to use it in a murder, and the saboteurs had done little more. A military tribunal would also offer a crime with which to charge the saboteurs. When enemy combatants are found behind enemy lines in civilian clothing, as they were, it is a serious violation of the laws of war. It also offered the death penalty.[5] Defence counsel pointed out that none of the eight men had, in fact, committed any act of sabotage, and all had confessed their actions and, indeed, had claimed they never intended to carry out such acts. They had only agreed to come to the US to escape from Germany.

The eight men were brought to trial on 8 July 1942 in a makeshift courtroom on the fifth floor of the DOJ despite there being a challenge to the court's authority. Each of the eight defendants was charged with four crimes.

- Charge I accused the Germans of secretly and covertly entering the United States in civilian dress, contrary to the law of war, for the purpose of committing acts of sabotage, espionage, and other hostile acts.
- Charge II accused the defendants of knowingly communicating with and giving intelligence to each other and enemies of the United States.
- Charge III said the men were found lurking or acting as spies in civilian clothes in or about the fortifications, posts, and encampments of armies of the United States and elsewhere.
- Finally, Charge IV accused the defendants of plotting, planning, and conspiring with each other and the German Reich to commit each of the crimes specified in the first three charges.

Twenty days later, all eight were found guilty and sentenced to death. Attorney General Francis Beverley Biddle and J. Edgar Hoover appealed to President Roosevelt to commute the sentences of Dasch and Burger because of their cooperation. Dasch then received a thirty-year sentence, and Burger received a life sentence, both to be served in a federal penitentiary. Within hours, the other six men were executed by electric chair.

Ever since, there had been much debate about the legality of the court and the sentence. The constitutional scholar Edward S. Corwin claims that the court's ruling was 'little more than a ceremonious detour to a predetermined end.' Another, John P. Frank, wrote that the court 'sent the defendants to their deaths some months before Chief Justice [Harlan] Stone was able to get out an opinion telling why.' Frederick Bernays Weiner, an expert on military justice concluded that the court had been 'careless or uninformed [in its] handling of the Articles of War' – a source of law that should have been central to the court's ruling.[6] In 1948, Dasch and Burger had the remainders of their sentences commuted, and were sent back to Germany.

Chapter 12

WILHELM ALBRECHT VON PRESSENTIN GENANNT VON RAUTTER

'I cannot tell from the record how many of our boys went to their deaths on your information.'

Brooklyn Federal Court Judge Grover M. Moskowitz, at the trial of Wilhelm Albrecht von Pressentin genannt von Rautter, 10 October 1944

Shortly before the entry of the US into the Second World War, as part of their routine examinations of mail, British chemists at the luxurious Princess Hotel, the headquarters of the Bermuda censorship station, became interested in a letter sent from Havana, Cuba to a firm in Lisbon, Portugal. The contents seemed innocent enough but there was something that prompted them to make a copy before sending it on its way and then a few days later the sorters picked out another letter going to a Lisbon firm and written in a similar handwriting. Another was spotted weeks later in the same handwriting, this time going to an address in Bilbao, Spain. The contents of the letters were requests for a commercial agent of a Havana firm to acquire representation in Europe. Investigations revealed that one of the addresses the letters were going to was owned by a known German Abwehr agent but there was no trace of either of the others in any business directory.

Working with the Cuban police, the FBI identified the sender as Heinz August Luning, a German-Italian who arrived in Havana just weeks before his first letter was intercepted. He was arrested and tried before a Cuban military court on charges of espionage and, on 10 November 1942, 'dropped before a firing squad of the Cuban army'.[1]

The names of all intermediaries and addresses linked to the Luning letters were monitored for future contacts and, in early February 1942, a letter to one of the addresses in Bilbao had a signature 'Fred Lewis' and was postmarked New York. Another with the same handwriting was intercepted on 6 April 1942 going to Walter Hirzel, a lawyer living in Winterthur, a small village in north-east Switzerland near the German border but this one was signed 'Gerson'. Close analysis of the letter uncovered a secret writing message containing cryptic details about technical matters that could prove useful to German military planners. Based on analysis of the Lewis letter, handwriting experts concluded that the letters were written by two different people suggesting that there might be two separate spy rings reporting to the same handler in Switzerland. The FBI sent an urgent signal to Hyde in Bermuda asking him to look out for any more messages sent by 'Gerson'. Over the course of the following year, British censors found twelve more letters with the same handwriting going to various known mail drops in in Switzerland and other neutral European countries, but return addresses remained fictitious or were not included on the envelope at all. The letters sometimes signed 'Rogers' or 'Count from New York', contained information about a range of topics such as the rate of manufacture of military aircraft, the number of navy shipyards, details of the 'Allison 2400 H.P. motor', data about a Ford Motor Company plant that was building the B-24E bomber and a Bell Aircraft Company aircraft with detachable fuel tanks. There were even details about Allied operations planned in North Africa and the Balkans but the FBI was still no closer to identifying 'Gerson'.[2]

All the FBI and British investigators could determine from the letters was that Lewis had probably received espionage training in Germany and had recently been in Lisbon so must have arrived in the US within the past few months. Having no alternative, FBI personnel started the laborious process of comparing Lewis's handwriting with thousands of baggage declarations of travellers arriving from Europe within that time.

Eventually, a match was found. The mysterious 'Lewis' was tentatively identified as Ernest Frederick Lehmitz of Tompkinsville, New York who had passed through Bermuda in March 1941 when he had described himself as a rubber salesman returning to the US where he had been naturalised in 1924.

He would be arrested on 27 June 1943 on a charge of violating the Wartime Espionage Act. Since his arrival he had lived in Staten Island, New York where he ran a boarding house for sailors as well as working as a waiter at a restaurant frequented by naval personnel. Lehmitz's arrest would lead the FBI to Erwin Harry de Spretter, a mechanical engineer and former lieutenant in the German army. Both men would plead guilty and, on 28 September 1943, were handed down thirty-year prison sentences, the maximum allowed under the law.

Also in April 1942, the censors had spotted another letter going to the Winterthur address but the handwriting indicated an entirely new correspondent. This time the letter was signed 'R.O. Gerson'. Then another letter with the same handwriting as the 'Gerson' letter was intercepted a few weeks later. This time the sender was given as 'R.L. Erskine' and signed 'Roger'. He was eventually identified as Wilhelm Albrecht von Pressentin genannt von Rautter. He was arrested at his Portland Avenue apartment on 11 January 1944 and quickly made a full confession to the FBI. This was not surprising since some of his letters had contained indications that he had been having grave misgivings about his espionage role and was constantly in fear of exposure and prosecution. When he appeared the next day before US Commissioner Jacob A. Visel, charged with espionage, he broke down and claimed that he had been 'forced into [spying] almost at pistol point.' Visel ordered him to be imprisoned in lieu of $25,000 bail.[3]

Under questioning, von Rautter gave a full account of his life and recruitment by the Abwehr. He had been born the son of Count Earl von Rautter and his English-born wife, Countess Bertha von Rautter, previously known as Bertha Brayley-Fisher, on a vast estate in the Prussian village of Wilkamm. When his parents separated during the First World War, he found himself in England but as soon as he was able, he set out to travel the world. He arrived in New Orleans, Louisiana, US from Valparaiso on the tramp steamer *Lake Pithica* and from there travelled north to Sharon, Pennsylvania where he found work at the Standard Tank Car Company. Having entered the country illegally he was denied citizenship and returned first to England and then to Germany.

From Germany he returned as a legal alien to New York, where he took up employment on Wall Street in the foreign loan department of the investment banking firm Dillon Reade & Company, analysing European and South American loans. He had later joined National City Bank of New York and then the First Boston Corporation, which sent him to Colombia. After spending a year in Germany, he returned to the US in 1933 and lived in Washington DC, working for the Resettlement Administration. His fluency in German, Spanish, Russian, French and Portuguese proved to be a valuable asset and he made regular trips to Mexico. When this assignment came to an end he went once again to Germany to oversee the administration of the family estate then back to the US where he was granted citizenship in 1938.

It was around the same time that Sebold was just starting to find his way into the Duquesne spy ring that von Rautter went once more to Germany. This time, he was approached by Hans Blum, an Abwehr major and owner of Remy and Company, inviting him to meet for a discussion about business opportunities in the US. Blum described his company's chemical export and import business and explained that he wished to appoint von Rautter as his company representative in the US. Agreeing to think about it, von Rautter was approached again by Blum who abruptly informed him that he had been selected as an agent for German military intelligence. It would not involve anything dangerous, he was told, it was simply a matter of gathering helpful 'information' about industrial production in the US. When von Rautter protested he was told that it was his duty as a Prussian aristocrat to serve his country and he was given none too subtle indications that his family estate might be subject to takeover by the state.

Von Rautter was instructed in the basics of espionage including the use of secret solutions such as buttermilk, urine and pyramidon, a common headache remedy effective for secret writing when combined with pure alcohol. He received instruction on radio construction, along with transmitting, receiving, coding and decoding using a standard work of fiction. Next, he studied the creation of microdots hidden on common everyday letters sent from Europe and then how to read them using a local store-bought microscope.

When he received letters from Germany containing microdot instructions and information, he was told that he must take careful note to see if the dateline included the word 'of' and if it did, he was to carefully examine all the letters 'O' appearing in the sixteenth line of the text for a microdot that could be read through a 110- or 125-power microscope. His codename on his secret writing messages to Europe would be 'Rogers', and was to send his letters to three mail drops: Mr A John in Lisbon, Portugal, Mr Walter Hirzel in Winterthur, Switzerland and Apartado 1006, Mexico, D.F. Mexico. For his cover he received a thirty-two-page list of chemical companies engaged in business with Remy and Company that he was to contact to establish his credentials.

His responsibilities would include making regular crossing of the Hudson River on the Brooklyn-Staten Island Ferry, taking note of ships of all kinds in New York Harbor, taking note of their names, and making mental notes of markings on crates bound for Europe while casually strolling along docks and wharves. Other included observing factory facilities of United States Steel, Remington Arms Corporations, and the twelve leading aircraft companies such as the Douglas and

Boeing companies. For his services, Blum gave him $1,200 in cash before departing and arranged to pay him $300 a month through a Mexican bank.

When he returned to the US, von Rautter rented an apartment in Brooklyn at 18 South Portland Avenue near De Kalb Avenue and Fort Greene Park right next to the Brooklyn Navy Yard. As instructed by Blum, he set up a mail drop through an old friend Mrs Clara von Der Goltz who lived across the East River at 465 West Avenue on Manhattan's Upper West Side near Riverside Drive. One of the first contacts he made was with Heinrich Ludwig Suhl, a New York businessman with offices in the Singer Building, a Lower Manhattan office complex located at 149 Broadway in Manhattan's Financial District.

Suhl was a 55-year-old German-born US citizen who had built up a lucrative business as an importer of cork. He would later claim that he had been forced to cooperate with the Abwehr when Blum had propositioned him in Lisbon and threatened that harm might come to his young son still living in Germany if he did not. Suhl's assignment would be to act as a paymaster for German agents in the event of war disrupting the international movement of funds. This Suhl-von Rautter operation had first started to fall apart when the Abwehr had asked Sebold to act as a relay between Germany and another espionage cell, which turned out to a major one operating in Mexico. One message Sebold was asked to pass on to the Mexican ring was an order to improve the quality of reports coming from the 'Count from New York' and another 'Rogers'. Alarms went off at FBI headquarters and another link was established when a cheque for $50,000 that Blum sent to Suhl, drawn on the Lisbon account of a German agent named Herman Zum Hingate, was questioned by American banks and referred to them. Suhl was arrested and Rautter's detention soon followed. Von Rautter was brought to trial on 10 October 1944 when the Brooklyn Federal Court Judge Grover M. Moskowitz said

> I cannot tell from the record how many of our boys went to their deaths on your information. I could impose the death sentence, but that might mean that revenge would be meted out to American citizens in Germany. That's the only reason why I hesitate to impose the death penalty and sentenced him to twenty-nine years [*sic*] imprisonment.[4]

Chapter 13

GIMPEL AND COLEPAUGH

'The only way that the agencies charged with the internal security of this country can cope with the problem is to ask for the cooperation of every loyal American in reporting any suspicious characters to the FBI.'

J. Edgar Hoover,
after the trial of Gimpel and Colepaugh[1]

On 24 September 1944, one of the newer, larger and long-range standard class of Atlantic submarine, the 252-foot IXC/40-class U-boat *U-1230* slipped out of Kiel Harbour and proceeded by slow stages and several delays along the coast of Norway, putting in at Horton and Kristianson. Then on 6 October 1944 it set off on its long slow cruise across the Atlantic towards Frenchman's Bay on the Grand Banks, off the coast of Maine, US. On the night of 21 November 1941, Kapitänleutnant Hans Hilbig took radio bearings on Atlantic coast stations and fixed his position as being off Mount Desert Rock. Coast Guard activity constrained the U-boat to remain there, sitting on the seafloor which gave it time to repair its damaged sonic depth-finding instruments. After a week of maintaining silence and enduring the bitter cold, with all heating shut down to save fuel, on 28 November 1941, the U-boat screws came to life and the vessel slowly rose from the seabed and steered north towards the US naval patrol base at Bar Harbor.

Hilbig had received an urgent message from Berlin advising him to abandon the Frenchman's Bay approach because of enhanced US patrols in the area but he stuck to his original orders and took a bearing on lights at Great Duck and Baker Island. He proceeded to enter the deep inlet of Crabtree Creek advancing at little more than 2 knots by slow manoeuvres between Ironbound Island, Jordan Island and Long Porcupine Island towards Hancock Point, a remote region with minimal local population and little urban development. The U-boat ran in until approximately 11.00 pm, when it was only 300 yards from shore. Hilbig surfaced and put an inflatable rubber boat into the water. Two of the regular forty-eight-man crew had been left behind in Kiel and their place taken by two others, whom the rest of the crew were led to believe were an engineer and a war correspondent. These were the men who, wearing light topcoats and suits, now stepped into the dinghy to be rowed ashore by two sailors.

As they made their way up the beach, on a cold, stormy night with snow swirling around, the US-born William Curtis Colepaugh, also known as William Caldwell or William Koller, and the Belgian Erich Gimpel, alias Edward George Green, had concealed about them $60,000 in small bills and packages of ninety-nine small diamonds for commercial distribution as a contingency measure. The men were quite unsuitably dressed for the bitterly cold weather and so did not escape notice, especially in a region where strangers were rare. The 17-year-old Harvard Hodgkins spotted them as he was making his way home from a school dance in the storm and told his father, a deputy sheriff, who called the FBI. Mary Forni also took note of them as she was driving home from a card game. She almost offered them a lift but decided against it. The men managed to hail a taxi in the village and made it to Bangor where they caught a train to Boston. By 1 December 1941, they were in Grand Central Station, New York.

Colepaugh and Gimpel had been paired together at the special espionage training school of A-Schule West in the Netherlands run by Hitler's 'favourite commando', Otto Skorzeny, where German intelligence prepared field operatives destined for the North American theatre. Since Colepaugh had very little German, he had been paired with Gimpel, a German radio technician who also spoke English.

Colepaugh was a US citizen but, since childhood, had been made conspicuous by his pro-German sympathies possibly derived from his German grandparents and a mother who raised him single-handed after his father died when he was 8 years old. After attending military prep school in New Jersey and failing to gain admittance to the naval academy in Annapolis, Maryland, US he enrolled in the Massachusetts Institute of Technology to study marine engineering, but he never finished his degree. He became obsessed with Nazism after reading about it and listening to media broadcasts about the Third Reich, and the Blitzkrieg attacks launched by the Wehrmacht in the beginning months of the Second World War. Encouraged to do so by the consul general in Boston, Dr Herbert Scholz, with whom he had become friendly, he agreed to join a British vessel as a crew member and report back on British convoys. Going to Halifax, Nova

Scotia, he signed up with the *Reynolds* and sailed for Scotland. When he got back, the German Consulate had closed and he was drafted into the US Navy but, after only a year was honourably discharge for his pro-Nazi views. In 1944, he went to sea again, this time as a mess boy aboard the Swedish relief vessel *Gripsholm*. In port in Portugal, he jumped ship and contacted the German Consulate telling him of his wish to be conscripted into the German army. The Lisbon Consulate officials suspected that they might be looking at an American double agent and got him off their hands as quickly as possible by sending him to Berlin. There he was subjected to questioning and surveillance for three months before he was judged suitable for training for espionage. It was not what he wanted. His ambition had been to join the German army but the Abwehr decided that he would be of much more use to them as a spy. After all, he could pass himself off in the US with no trouble at all.

Gimpel was a different case altogether. Born in Merseberg, Germany in 1910, he had gone to Peru in 1934 working as an electrical engineer for Telefunken and had been recruited there by the Abwehr as a radio operator communicating with U-boats offshore at Lima. When Peru severed diplomatic relations with Germany in 1942, along with many other German nationals, Gimpel was first interned and then deported to Camp Kennedy in Texas leaving his wife and two children behind in Peru. From there he got passage on the Swedish ship *Drottningholm* and returned to Germany on 1 August 1942. The following year, he was seconded to *Amt IV* where he was initially employed as a courier between Berlin and Madrid and then as an engineer producing radio and electrical equipment for various government agencies. He was deployed to Operation Pelikan, a plan to cripple the Panama Canal and so limit the US naval capabilities but when Pelikan was abandoned, he was transferred to Operation Elster (Magpie) a mission to gather information about the US Manhattan Project to develop an atomic bomb and was then that he met up with Colepaugh.

Once in New York, the two men rented an apartment at 33 Kenmore Hall Hotel in Manhattan as they settled in to get acclimatised to the environment. They soon moved to other accommodation at 39 Beekman Place that did not have steel construction, which made radio transmission easier but discord seeped into their relationship. Gimpel was the professional and applied himself to sourcing material for the radio but he was essentially an alien who was extremely uncomfortable in a country that was now so anti-German and where his German-accented speech singled him out for attention. Colepaugh, however, was back home and seduced by the ebullient and carefree New York lifestyle after the austerity of Germany. He was displaying alarmingly little interest in performing his espionage duties. Gimpel was furious when Colepaugh started spending lavishly on entertainment in local bars which made him very popular with the ladies. Meanwhile the FBI had gone to Crabtree Creek to follow up on the report about strangers filed by Hodgkins especially since there had also been reports of U-boat activity in the area. They interviewed Hodgkins and Forni but could get no further with the investigation. It did, however, heighten their awareness of possibly having two aliens on the loose.

Gimpel had the radio transmitter up and running by 21 December 1942. He now set about contacting agents in the city according to instructions he had been given. Colepaugh, however, was beginning to think that the spy game was not for him. Already wavering and considering how to extricate himself from what might well be a suicidal mission, he was further disturbed by the news from Europe that the German army had suffered a major defeat at the Battle of the Bulge and the Allies were advancing towards the Rhine. He was very much on the wrong side of history now. While Gimpel was out, he made his decision. He fled the apartment taking all the cash and diamonds with him. He kept a prearranged rendezvous with a woman he had befriended, and together they moved into a midtown hotel. By Boxing Day 1942, Colepaugh had convinced himself that he was now in a very precarious position. He saw no future for himself working for an organisation that might cease to exist within a few months but, having no doubt that the Abwehr still had many agents in the city, he worried that it would not be long before they tracked him down. The result, if that happened, was barely worth thinking about. He chose to hand himself in to the FBI who initiated an immediate and widespread search for Gimpel. As soon he realised that Colepaugh had gone, Gimpel had feared the worst and fled the Beekman Place apartment checking into the Pennsylvania Hotel as George Collins.

Special agents of the New York Field Division contacted all the known operating hotels in the counties of Manhattan, Queens, Bronx, Brooklyn and Richmond comprising metropolitan New York in an attempt to locate Gimpel through comparison of known samples of his handwriting with all registrations in such hotels made between 21 December 1942 and the date of investigation. In large hotels where such comparison with all registrations was not feasible, the comparison was made with all registrations in the name of Green and Caldwell. When nothing was turned up, agents canvassed all furnished rooming houses in Manhattan County and especially the area bounded on the north by 59th Street, on the south by 13th Street, on the west by the North River, and on the east by the East River. On 30 December 1942, they began another canvass of hotels in metropolitan New York. Baggage rooms in all railway stations, bus stations and airline terminals were examined in an effort to locate the bags that Gimpel was thought to have with him. Colepaugh had told them of Gimpel's compulsive habit of buying daily newspapers which led to his arrest by FBI agents on 30 December 1942 at the Times Square newsstand.

Both men were tried by a military court on Governor's Island in February 1945 accused of offences under the 82nd Article of War. If his plan was to win leniency by turning himself in, Colepaugh failed. Both men were convicted and subsequently sentenced to death with no appeal. The executions were scheduled for 15 April 1945 but when Roosevelt suddenly died, they were postponed and when Germany surrendered in June 1945 the sentences were commuted to life terms in prison. Colepaugh was paroled in May 1960 and Gimpel was repatriated to West Germany and released in 1955. Up until his release in 1960, Colepaugh served his time in Leavenworth Prison, where he was a model prisoner and learned the trade of metalworking. After being granted parole, he opened a business in King of Prussia, a a suburb of Philadelphia, before marrying, acquiring a passion for fishing, and volunteering with local Boy Scouts. He became highly regarded in his community, known mainly for his volunteer work as a Rotarian.

Chapter 14

DOUBLE AGENTS

'The subject is not amenable to direction or control and is utterly devoid of any patriotic motives.'

Letter to J. Edgar Hoover from Arthur N. Thurston,
23 October 1943

Jorge Mosquera, a short, stocky Latino man with black hair, greying at the temples, walked into the American Embassy in Montevideo, Uruguay in July 1941 and told the first secretary there, Selden Chapin, that he had been sent to South America to set up a radio station and spy for the Abwehr. As evidence, he produced a number of microphotographed instructions and letters of introduction from the Abwehr to three Americans. Mosquera seemed eager to places himself entirely at the disposal of the FBI. His information was certainly in line with known German intelligence procedures and secret writing chemicals he produced matched those used in other cases. On 18 November 1941, Mosquera slipped into New York off the SS *Argentina* and went straight to FBI headquarters at Foley Square. He was questioned over a number of days by William G. Friedman, a fluent German speaker who had played a central role in the Duquesne case.

Mosquera told him that he had been born to Spanish immigrants in Rosario, Santa Fe, Argentina in 1895 and when he grew up, he had begun a sales career buying and selling agricultural products in Buenos Aires, Argentina before starting his own business importing German products. In 1927, he had moved to Hamburg, where he opened an import-export business between Germany and Latin America. When he sold his business in 1936, he was ready to return to Argentina but the stringent financial regulations now in place in Germany meant that he was unable to arrange for the transfer of his capital out of the country. Finding ways round that restriction now became his overriding priority. When a friend in the chemical export business, Herbert Krug, introduced him to a Hamburg Nazi Party official named Julius Steinert, Mosquera saw an opportunity to ingratiate himself with the authorities who might be able to assist him with moving his money. So when Steinert suggested that, as a good friend of Germany, Mosquera could be relied upon to contribute to the party in its time of need, he readily agreed.

Mosquera was given a few tasks to test his suitability and commitment to the cause. In September 1939, he was sent to deliver two letters to someone in Amsterdam and when he had done this efficiently, he was instructed to go to Berlin and meet a man called Herr (Mr) Boewig, who sent him on an assignment to the Canary Islands to report on a British submarine base in the region. A year later Boewig sent him on a posting to Czechoslovakia where he was instructed in the use of explosives at the Bruenner and Skoda munitions works. Mosquera had no stomach for such things and flew back to Berlin saying that while he was still willing to play his part, he was sure he was not cut out for the destructive side of espionage work.

After a few months of idleness, he was approached in March 1941 by Abwehr major, Hans Blum, whom he knew from earlier business dealings. Blum suggested that Mosquera might like to return to South America and do some work for the Abwehr there. The prospect appealed greatly to Mosquera who was anxious now to get out of Europe with or without his money. He readily agreed to attend an espionage school in Hamburg to study secret inks, codes, radio construction and telegraphy. Six weeks later he received microdots containing Abwehr instructions and requirements that were stitched into the lining of his tie. Blum warned him that he was being sent on a long-term mission that required patience and extreme caution. Money for his living expenses would be sent through the US with his personal savings and a substantial reward awaiting him in Germany at the end of the Second World War.

What he would be required to do was enter the US and search out any information concerning 'experiments performed in the United States relative to shattering of atoms.'[1] Having no idea what that meant, he left Hamburg by train on 15 June 1941 and arrived in Bilbao where he booked into the Hotel Excelsior. The next day he was approached by an Abwehr agent, Jose Boogen, who would be his cutout for cables and secret writing messages to be forwarded to Blum. Days later he was on the SS *Cabo de Esperanza* bound for Uruguay.

When the FBI examined Mosquera's microphotographs in New York they found a huge amount of information. These tiny items were known as *Mipu* or *Mikropunkt* (microdots). They had been invented by Professor Emanuel Goldberg of Internationale Camera Actiengesellschaft in Dresden as early as 1925. Using this method, a whole page of print could be reduced to about 1 millimetre across. On Mosquera's microdots were details of how to construct a short-wave radio along with details of frequencies, call letters, emergency keys and codes to use. There were also, in breach of all basic espionage protocols, the names of sixteen espionage agents or potential agents located in Spain, Portugal, Switzerland, Sweden, Germany, Argentina and, most importantly, New York City. Given the amount of credible evidence Mosquera put before them, there was every reason for the FBI to believe his story and they began running him as a double agent with the codename 'ND98'.

Three of the agents exposed by Mosquera were of special interest, and Mosquera was directed by his FBI handlers to sound them out. Alexander Semmler had been born in Dortmund, Germany on 12 November 1900. A musical prodigy, he had begun performing as a concert pianist when only 15 years old. He had emigrated to the US on 23 October 1923, aboard the SS *Muenchen*. After joining the Columbia Broadcasting System's symphony orchestra as a pianist, he later worked for RKP-Pathe Film Company becoming a US citizen on 17 July 1930. Mosquera contacted Semmler at his New York studio, 51 West 53rd Street, where he formed the opinion that Semmler was still very pro-German but the musician claimed that he far too busy to have much time to devote to the old country.

Mosquera next contacted Elmer H. Carlton, owner of Remle-Carlton Company, a manufacturer's representative and chemical import/export company in midtown Manhattan. Carlton was US-born but had lived in Berlin for twenty years. He was known to have open Nazi sympathies and was a regular guest at the German Embassy in Washington DC. Remle-Carlton imported Bund uniforms from Germany for his friend, Fritz Kuhn. Carlton also had financial interests in Germany through his close friendship with Hjalmar Schacht, Hitler's Minister of Economics.

Mosquera went to see Carlton at his New York City office on 18 December 1941 but was given a polite rebuff when he suggested that Carlton might assist him in his espionage work. He wanted to know nothing about Mosquera's mission. 'The situation here has been radically changed', he warned. He trusted no one and advised Mosquera to be very cautious. Mosquera was not having much luck recruiting agents and he was further disappointed by Max Fritz Ernst Rudloff when he too refused to cooperate. It was natural that, given all the publicity over spy trials in the US, that all three men were acutely aware that they might be being duped by US intelligence.

FBI agent, Richard Millen, had worked on the building and operating of Sebold's Centerport radio station and, together with Sam Foxworth, was now running a similar but larger one at Wading River also on Long Island. It was through here that agent ND98 made his first transmission to Hamburg on 28 January 1942.

'On Carlton, Semmler and Rudloff I cannot rely. First one refused entirely. The others too. But they appear to me to be unsuitable', he informed Blum. The rapid increase in security measures with mass internment of Germans, Italians and Japanese was a major problem now and although the men were sympathetic to the cause Axis sympathisers were 'very apprehensive'. 'I need the assistance of two or at least one important good [reliable] worker', he pleaded 'Do everything you can to execute my wishes. It is necessary. Many thanks.'[2]

Hamburg replied by reminding Mosquera of the importance of collecting atomic research information about 'Uranium 235'. Nobody knew what they were talking about so FBI agents in New York began scouring public journals and newspapers for any scraps of information about the subject. Despite nuclear research being conducted under the utmost secrecy in the US, they found several articles in the public domain that were cleared for transmission to the Germans. There was one lengthy *Fortune* magazine article on atomic fission and a *Washington Evening Standard* article covering a speech given by the Nobel Prize-winning physicist Ernest O. Lawrence on cyclotron particle accelerators. Other useful information came from a November 1941 edition of *Review of Scientific Instruments*, which contained the 'complete plans of an electrostatic generator for nuclear research at the Massachusetts Institute of Technology.'[3]

Meanwhile Mosquera was getting ample funds through his friend Ricardo Gioscia in Montevideo, Uruguay who was acting as the conduit for finance from Germany, which Mosquera channelled into an FBI bank account in New York. Money was either wired from Europe to Gioscia or delivered to Mosquera by German consular officials. The large sums of money sent by the Germans were clear reflections of Mosquera's importance to them as a source. From May 1942 to March 1944, he was paid a total of $46,875.90.[4]

He was, however, proving to be a headache for his FBI controllers. He had settled into a New York lifestyle as the owner of a front called La Plata Commercial Company and he had started a relationship a somewhat talentless vocalist with dreams of becoming an opera diva. Mosquera began pestering Friedman for money to pay for his girlfriend's singing lessons, publicity photographs and a manager. When Friedman refused, Mosquera threatened to tell Gioscia in Montevideo to stop sending the money to the FBI's bank account without first getting his permission.

This put Friedman in an unenviable position. The Joint Security Control of the Military Intelligence Division had just created a central deception staff whose mission was to carry out planned measures for disguising or concealing an operation directed against an enemy. In other words, use all means to provide the enemy with false information while persuading them that it was genuine. Mosquera was, by this time, a vital cog in that machine and, in order to retain his services, Friedman was forced to grant him a salary of $500 a month.

To get maximum benefit from the investment, beginning in April 1942, Friedman called for the expansion of material sent by Mosquera, but he was mindful of the need not to raise German suspicions about how one man could acquire such a volume of intelligence. Four new fictional sources were created. One was a Department of War employee in Washington DC code-named 'Wasch', another was 'Nevi', a New Yorker working at the Brooklyn Navy Yard, a friend of 'Nevi' codenamed 'Osten', and a fourth 'Rep' who was working in a critical department at the Republic Aviation Company on Long Island.[5]

The expanded volume of intelligence Mosquera was now sending was divided into two categories. 'A' messages were both true and false reports created by JSC as part of a larger integrated deception campaign jointly coordinated and approved by London and Washington and 'B' messages concerned mundane information most of which could be found in public sources but which might be altered in certain details. When Hamburg complained of slow delivery, Mosquera blamed the heightened security that was causing even the most loquacious dock workers to 'button their lips' knowing that FBI agents were active amongst them now listening for loose talk.

In July 1943, Mosquera was incorporated into the Allied 'Cockade' deception plans. This operation was designed to reduce German operations in Sicily by persuading them that an attack in Western Europe was imminent. 'Wasch' in Washington, he told Hamburg had heard rumours that a large part of the 101st Airborne Division had been sent to England together with the First Army headquarters 'under great secrecy.' A month later 'Wasch' reported on increased activity along the East Coast involving training and troop preparations where drivers of all types of vehicles were being trained for left-hand driving. Other messages were designed to mislead and misdirect the enemy such as ones that greatly exaggerated American airpower. They told of 'remarkable new engines' on the B-29 Superfortress bomber enabling it to carry greater bomb loads, heavier armour and more fuel. Right up until the end of the Second World War, the Germans had no idea that Mosquera had been turned.

Hellmuth Siegfried Goldschmidt was Jewish, born in 1895, in Groningen, the Netherlands. When his parents divorced, his mother remarried Gustaf Blum, and they settled in Munich. At that time Goldschmidt renounced his Jewish faith and was disinherited by his family. He spent eight months studying at the University of Oxford before returning to the Netherlands, where he became a first-year infantry cadet at the Royal Military Academy in Breda. After a short time, Goldschmidt left and was transferred from infantry to cavalry and joined the 3rd Hussars regiment in February 1915 as an apprentice cornet. He was made up to reserve second lieutenant in 1916.

In 1922, he passed his master's degree in law at the University of Leiden. As a qualified lawyer, he left for the Dutch East Indies to join the Tax Service of the Colonial Government where he was assigned to the Royal Netherlands East Indies Army as a reserve officer. Three years later he travelled to the US, joining Shell Oil Company in Tulsa, Oklahoma and later Dallas, Texas. He returned, penniless to the Netherlands in 1929. He rejoined the Hussars practicing map reading, aerial photography and communications before being assigned to the army air force.

Goldschmidt tried and failed to carve out a career in law before borrowing money from a fellow reserve officer of the cavalry and setting off on his travels again ending up in the Dutch East Indies again. A year later, he returned to Amsterdam and joined the Fokker aircraft company but was fired after only six months. In autumn 1936, he co-founded the *Nederlandsche Automobiel Fabrieken N.V.* (Netherlands Car Factory) hoping to emulate the success of the German Volkswagen company but again the venture came to a disastrous end.

With war fever mounting in 1939, Goldschmidt was called up to the 1st Aviation Regiment, then in May 1939, he returned to the cavalry as commander of the Staff-squadron of the recently reorganised 4th Hussar Regiment in Ede. When the Germans attacked, he was accused of desertion by his 'deliberate unauthorised absence in time of war, committed in Utrecht from 14–19 May 1940'. Dismissed from the service, out of work, awaiting court martial and desperately in need of money, he was also, as a Jew facing persecution under the Nazi occupation. By late summer 1941, with his court martial still pending, he was desperately trying to leave the country and get to England but met up with an old German acquaintance, Mathias Janssen, who told him that he was employed in economic espionage. Janssen was also a recruiter for the Abwehr and had been tasked with building an espionage network. He was able to delay the court martial proceedings further and suggested to Goldschmidt that he could make it go away altogether if he agreed to work for him. Goldschmidt was not enthusiastic about that prospect and tried again, unsuccessfully, to arrange for an escape to England through contact with Dutch resistance workers.

It had now become compulsory for Jews to wear the yellow Star of David but Goldschmidt had not registered as a Jew and now faced deportation to the east if he was found out. Then, in May 1942, the attorney general decided not to refer Goldschmidt's case to the Court of Justice of the Peace, but to the Military Chamber of the District Court in The Hague who sentenced him to three months' imprisonment. The next day, Janssen came to Goldschmidt telling him that arrangements had been made for him to go immediately to Nijmegen and then on to South America where he would be employed in economic espionage with a salary of 50 guilders a month. His destination would be Barranquilla, Colombia to which he would go via Portugal, then clipper (seaplane) to the US. Once in place, his remuneration would be $150 a month with an initial cash payment of $5,000 to be used to establish a spy ring. Goldschmid's position was further crystallised by the beginning of the deportation of Jews from the Netherlands to Auschwitz.

Before he could go on his mission, however, Goldschmidt was to receive training in Branch I M (Marine) in Hamburg where he was given new identity papers in the name of Hans Muth, a German lawyer. He remained there for six months learning about secret inks, Morse Code, radio transmitting, receiving, encoding, searching and setting frequencies and lastly but most importantly, he learned how to build a shortwave radio. At the end of the training, the assignment to Colombia was cancelled and the destination changed to the US. The Abwehr now presented him with an extensive list of the sort of intelligence he would be expected to provide. This somewhat ambitiously included coastal defence and guns, use of aircraft carriers for coastal defence, ports and everything that happens there, loading and unloading of armaments and aircraft, the number and types of warships in harbour and the mood among sailors and crew members.

His orders were to take it easy for the first few months after arriving in the US, find a nondescript detached house with trees next to it for cover. He must then buy radio parts from another district so as not to arouse suspicion and use them to build a transceiver installation. At first, he would only receive and was not expected to transmit.

Photomicrographs with instructions for building a transceiver and codes were sewn into the collar of his coat and the title of the codebook *Lecturao Españolas* agreed upon. Soluble secret ink, known as 'Philip' was sewn into his best suit in small batches. He was shown a map showing the places where everything was hidden: in the collar, in the crotch of his trousers, between two buttons of the back pocket and in the lining of his inner pocket. His espionage trainer, Dr Friedrich Karl now gave him his cover story which he was to repeat many times so that he would get it clear in his mind. He would be a Jewish refugee on his way to England. From November 1942 to May 1943 he had been in hiding with photographer called van Eijsden on the Weteringschans in Amsterdam.

On 5 May 1943, Goldschmidt set off by train to Berlin with an Abwehr minder, called Greiner. His German companion facilitated the crossing of occupied France to arrive at Hendaye on the French-Spanish border. There they were met by a car from the German Consulate in San Sebastian, Spain. Goldschmidt was hidden in the boot of the car as it crossed the border. At the Terminus Hotel in San Sebastian, he was met by two other Germans who recognised him by the tie he had been instructed to wear. They drove him to Salamanca on the Portuguese border but were forced to return to Madrid when their guide failed to show up. Goldschmidt remained there for two weeks awaiting further instructions.

He eventually crossed into Portugal on 27 May 1943 with a letter of introduction to the Dutch consul general in Lisbon, Jonkheer van der Maesen de Sombreff, but instead of posing as a refugee, as ordered, he told the whole story of how he had been trained by the Abwehr and smuggled to Lisbon via Spain with the intention of traveling to North or South America as a German spy. He handed over all the materials he had been given, invisible ink, money and microphotographs. A Dutch security official, Neils Gestramus, now took change of him and allowed him to stay in the Dutch refugee home in Praia das Macas at his own expense. Gestramus passed him over to MI6 agent in Lisbon, Charles de Salis. Neither man knew quite what to do with Goldschmidt but at the same time did not want to leave him in limbo in case his German handlers tried to contact him. The co-director of MI6 operations in Portugal, Kim Philby, suggested that he might find employment for him under cover of a posting as a Dutch consular official in Argentina where he could be run by the FBI. With this in mind, Arthur Thurston was brought into the conversation. He was an FBI agent at the American Embassy in London, and Hoover's representative with the British security and intelligence services. Thurston, in turn, contacted

Washington. He cabled Hoover saying that he thought Goldschmidt had been 'loosely handled by the German authorities and therefore his productivity as a double cross agent would appear to be questionable'. De Salis told him that MI6 had similar doubts given the amount of time he had spent in Lisbon before giving himself up to the Dutch legation. Notwithstanding Thurston's reservations, the FBI cabled back on 8 August 1943 saying, 'Bureau acceptable to utilising subject as double agent in Latin America preferably in Argentina.'[6]

The Department of State was anxious to maintain a good relationship with British intelligence and saw benefits in accepting their offer to use Goldschmidt. There were also a number of significant benefits that might flow from a successful utilisation of him as a double agent. Thurston understood from de Salis that arrangements had been made for funds to be transferred from Germany to Goldschmidt through a New York bank once he was in Argentina. If nothing else, running Goldschmidt as a double at least gave the FBI the opportunity to find out more about how German money was getting into the US to fund other espionage operations. Leaving Golschmidt in play and under FBI control would give unique opportunities to study Abwehr methods of agent handling and present opportunities for giving them bogus intelligence. One of the instructions Goldschmidt had been given was to scout potential sites for landing agents by U-boat, which allowed him quite a large degree of discretion about what sort of activities he could involve himself with.

He also came up with three addresses through which he had been authorised to communicate, which allowed Allied intelligence agencies to put them on a special watch list searching for links to other unknown agents. These were Antonio Concalves Navega, Rua S. Rocque de Lameira 1061, Porto, Sta, Felisa Jimene y Doctor, Castelo 8-3, Madrid and Augusto Strecht, Rua Ribero, Boavista 285, Porto.

With a 'nothing ventured, nothing gained' approach, on 8 September 1943, the US Department of State authorised Thurston to arrange for Goldschmidt's transfer to London for further questioning. In the meantime, Goldschmidt was to tell Hamburg that he had been unable to find passage to Argentina from Portugal and would have to find an alternative route. He was going to London, he said, posing as a Dutch government employee. Goldschmidt flew to London from Lisbon on 16 September 1943 on DC-3 G-AGBD of the BOAC/KLM with Dutch crew and upon arrival was taken to the Royal Victoria Patriotic School for questioning and given £10 per week plus an expense allowance.

The more Thurston saw of Goldschmidt, the more he was uneasy about taking him on. After several weeks of intense scrutiny it was concluded that his story was credible but that he was unreliable and would most likely, if picked up by his German handlers, he would 'play open cards with them'. Likewise if he taken on and run as a double agent there was no way that he could be controlled sufficiently to prevent him from indiscretions that would quickly expose him. He recommended that he be sent to the US on a fast ship as soon as possible and accompanied at all times by tight security. Despite the 8 August 1943 telegram, Washington did not reply immediately to Thurston. He was forced to ask several times for guidance on what to do. In an urgent and 'double-coded' telegram to Thurston dated 18 October 1943, Hoover personally authorised the running of Goldschmidt as a double agent but wanted the British to arrange for a suitable cover story for his travel to the US rather than Argentina and one that Goldschmidt was to explain to Hamburg. Also, the British would have to cover all expenses.

Meanwhile Goldschmidt had messaged the Strecht address in Porto on 16 October 1943 saying that he was still in Portugal but that he had obtained a position with the Dutch government arranged through the Dutch (government in exile) Foreign Minister Eelco van Kleffens. This would require him to go to Britain to get the appropriate travel visa.

Thurston was now having serious doubts about the prospect of letting Goldschmidt loose in New York. He reported that, in his opinion, Goldschmidt was acting purely out of selfish motives believing that the FBI would reward him handsomely alongside any money he received from the Abwehr. He had also started giving his MI5 handlers some serious headaches. As well as unreasonable demands for money, he was exhibiting a penchant for romance. He had started a relationship with a woman working for the US Army Paymaster at the American Embassy, but this was alongside a situation where he had been forcibly removed from an MI5 safe house after propositioning a chambermaid, and even had been arrested by local police for engaging in sex with a woman in a public park.

Thurston was now of the opinion that moving such a 'completely worthless and irresponsible individual whose mentality is certainly well below average' to the US would give the FBI unacceptable problems. Thurston's assessment of Goldschmidt is somewhat subjective and may have shielded other prejudices given that the man was a law graduate of the University of Leiden, which could hardly be reconciled with someone of low intelligence. He recommended that, because of Goldschmidt's 'appetite for women which made him a continual administrative problem', it should be left to the British to keep him under control, but they must not, under any circumstances, try to make use of him themselves if the FBI put him into play. On 24 October 1943, they advised that 'Goldschmidt remain in England and that the Bureau continue this operation in the United States by simulating his secret ink letters and faking radio transmissions'.[7] To forestall any problem should the Germans attempt to make personal contact with Goldschmidt in New York, it was decided to find an FBI agent with the necessary language qualifications who, after through briefing, could impersonate him if need be.

Goldschmidt was held in isolation in London while FBI radio specialists scanned the airwaves for transmissions on 14,179 kilocycles on 10 November 1943 at 3.30 and 4.00 pm with the call sign DFO, which is how Hamburg had arranged to make contact. In London, MI6 created fake messages using the secret ink materials that Goldschmidt had been trained to use. This involved using a material, ammonium vanadate, that he had been provided with which he referred to as 'Philip'. This had been sown into the lapels, seams and collar of his best suit before leaving Germany. Using a matchstick as a pen and 'Philip' as ink a message was written on ordinary business newspaper, or even newspaper cuttings, laid out on a sheet of glass. When receiving secret messages, the procedure was to heat the paper with a hot iron, not so hot that it scorched the paper, when the writing would appear in brown.

All the indications were that Hamburg had complete faith in Goldschmidt and that his cover was still intact so Thurston thought it was worth the risk of putting him into play but told MI5 that the FBI did not accept that his double-agent work would guarantee Goldschmidt US citizenship at the completion of his service.

FBI agent Mark Felt thought that Goldschmidt could still be useful and together with Thurston worked out a plan to exploit him without risk. It was entirely possible to send shortwave radio messages from the US using Goldschmidt's frequency and codes without the Dutchman ever leaving British soil. All he would have to do is describe the sort of intelligence he had been called upon to provide and the FBI could concoct seemingly authentic replies without compromising US security. A Post Office Box (number 720) was rented in New York City for secret ink correspondence, while an FBI radio operator began practicing Goldschmidt's 'fisting' his distinctive transmitting style using recordings supplied by MI5. The fictional agent in the US, who was in fact an amalgam of several people, was given the codename 'Peasant'.[8]

On 20 January 1944, the FBI simulated a letter in secret ink that was sent to a maildrop in Portugal according to instructions that Hamburg had given Goldschmidt. It read,

> Upon arrival found that position which Van Kleffens promised was no longer here. Have no job and no money. Can your New York man still contact me? Password same. Have found equipment for my transmitter is available in New York. Am looking for suitable bungalow but can't do much without funds. Please hurry. My mailing address is John Gold, PO Box 720 New York City.[9]

Posing as Goldschmidt, Ralph A. Sanders contacted Hamburg informing them that he had made it to North America and had taken employment with the Shell Oil Company office in Washington DC. Goldschmidt was now assigned to agent Felt, a young headquarters supervisor, who decades later would be exposed as 'Deep Throat' in the Watergate investigation.

Hamburg was informed that Goldschmidt had moved to Washington DC and found work at the Shell Oil Company, for whom he had worked previously in Oklahoma. All Shell Oil Company employees had, in fact, been seconded to one of two government agencies. Goldschmid's fictional position in the company would seem to offer him access to valuable information, rumours and gossip about 'restricted and confidential information concerning almost every phase of the uses and needs of petroleum by the Army and Navy.'[10] 'Peasant' radioed Hamburg within days with fabricated 'intelligence' saying that he had heard from a friend in the patent office that the Boeing Company in Seattle was producing a four-engine double-deck cargo plane similar to the B-29 with a larger fuselage. Ensuring that morale in Hamburg would not recover, a few days later 'Peasant' went on to say that the oil industry was producing 'over 700,000 barrels of 100 octane aviation gasoline daily' with a large part 'in excess of 100 octane for use in B-29 and B-32'.[11] The FBI now proposed that 'Peasant' supply details of East Coast defences and the use of aircraft carriers and aerial coastal patrols in anticipation of the arrival of more U-boat saboteurs.

In October 1944, they also authorised 'Peasant' to tell Hamburg that,

- An aircraft fighter plane manufactured by Bell was entirely jet-propelled.
- The latest aircraft carriers were fitted out with automatic guns to replace the 50 calibre type.
- Curtiss were producing 18-foot, 4-blade hollow steel propellors with automatic synchronisation and reverse thrust.

- The US Air Force was experimenting with rockets to assist aircraft launch in tight spaces.
- North American Mustang aircraft now powered by 1500hp supercharged engine had a top speed of 425mph and a range of 2,000 miles.

'Peasant' continued to remain in contact with Hamburg until 2 May 1943 when British forces took the city. All this time Goldschmidt had been in London in the care of MI5 who, by now, were pleased to be rid of him but before sending him on his way telling him that he was now on his own, he was warned that for his own safety he should remain forever silent about the entire affair. Felt sent a message to MI5 a few months later to say that 'the Peasant affair' was closed and they should dispose of 'Peasant' 'as they see fit.'[12]

All this time, Goldschmidt was kept in the dark about the 'Peasant' operation. As far as he knew, he had been ignored and left out in the cold. Then on 3 November 1943, he was picked up from the MI5 safe house at Rugby Mansions in Hammersmith by a British major called Cussen who told him that it had been officially decided that he was no longer required. The British were grateful for the formation he had provided but he would now be handed over to the Dutch authorities at 82 Eaton Square. Arriving there he was taken in by Baron Steengracht von Moyland and Lieutenant Colonel Oreste Pinto who agreed that Goldschmidt should be sent to court martial and to prison but, in reality, wanted nothing to do with him and suggested that the British intern him for the duration.

Goldschmidt now began to make a total nuisance of himself complaining endlessly to the Dutch that he had been badly treated and had been left to find a job and fend for himself. He ended up writing to both Dutch Queen Wilhelmina, British Prime Minister Winston Churchill and even Hoover but all to no avail. Interrogated after the Second World War, Herbert Christian Wichmann, head of *Abwehrstelle Hamburg*, said that results of Goldschmidt's spying were considered to be 'poor' and that there was often 'trouble with the W/T (radio) traffic'.[13]

On 12 November 1940, a report arrived in Bremen from the US and checked in the log as number 6079/40/Ig – Agent R.2232.[14] This had been sent by a long-time Abwehr agent and resident of the US, the German-born chemist Alfred Hohlhaus. His job took him all across the US and it was in Amarillo, Texas, that he had filed this report which concerned the production of helium gas. This had been produced in small quantities by the US Navy for a number of uses including the inflation of dirigibles but, for some reason, Hohlhaus noticed that it was suddenly being produced in significantly higher quantities and knew enough about nuclear physics to postulate that it might have something to do with experiments that were currently being carried out in US universities to harness atomic energy. Bremen thought this piece of information of vital importance but when the report was passed on to the German military they brushed it off as containing 'nothing new'.

Recalled to Bremen a year later, Hohlhaus wrote a paper entitled 'Production of heavy uranium from helium, probably for the US Air Force'. Again, the military dismissed this as fantasy and told Bremen not to bother them with the subject any more. Luftwaffe intelligence chief, Joseh Schmid, a man not usually associated with insight or good judgement, did take note, however, and passed the paper to Colonel von Roeder, the Wehrmacht Ordnance chief of research. As a result, Bremen was asked to follow up on Hohlhaus's paper and try to find more about US nuclear research. If possible, an agent with specialised scientific knowledge should be assigned but the best Bremen could offer was the 'balding, myopic and pudgy' Dutchman Alfred Meiler. This shy, unremarkable man at least had all the physical attributes of a spy in that he passed pretty much unnoticed wherever he went.

Meiler was Jewish and from the small town of Nijmagen, the Netherlands. During the First World War, he had been a member of the Dutch police but also operated as a double agent working for the Germans who were using neutral the Netherlands as a centre of espionage. During the 1920s, he became active in right-wing politics and, despite his Jewish background, joined the Dutch Nazi Party in 1932 but he also had a criminal record. A six-month sentence for theft had left his fingerprints on file at Interpol, which were likely to have been shared with the US. Despite moving away from extreme politics, he became friends with Udo von Bonin who worked in German naval intelligence, and it was this relationship that saved him when the Nazis were registering Dutch Jews after they occupied the country in May 1940, but it came with strings attached. Many of Meiler's family were living under the threat of persecution but von Bonin assured Meiler that he could protect them by agreeing to undertake an espionage mission for him. Meiler had little choice but to agree. It would be no straightforward mission, however. The Abwehr had special plans for him that would place him in a unique position within their spy operations.

A jeweller by trade, his scientific knowledge was limited but the Abwehr thought they could bring him up to speed sufficiently for him to serve their needs. He was given a new name, Alfred Koehler, a crash course in the rudiments of nuclear physic and a routine of basic agent training in The Hague and later in Paris where he spent six months undertaking advanced espionage courses at Abwehr headquarters in the Hotel Lutetia concentrating on shortwave radio construction, communication and secret writing.

The plan was for Meiler and his wife, Elizabeth, to enter the US via Spain and Argentina but when they arrived in Madrid, Meiler went straight to the American Consulate and told them straight out that he had been recruited as a spy by the Germans. To convince them he put on display all the spy paraphernalia he had been given including radio parts and described in detail the system of codes he was supposed to use. He also showed them the $38,000 in cash he was carrying.[15] The consulate contacted Washington and got authorisation from the FBI to send him along but first they told him to contact von Bonin to tell him that he had not been able to get a visa for Argentina so he was going directly to the US via Lisbon. A wry smile may well have played across von Bonin's lips when he got that signal.

Arrangements were made for Meiler to go to Lisbon and take a Portuguese ship *Guine* which put to sea on 5 May 1942. The couple did so but when FBI agents met the ship in New York, Meiler was not on board. He had been taken off by Florida Coast Guard who had responded to an emergency call. Meiler was in the Sunny South Hospital and Sanatorium where he was being treated for pneumonia and typhoid. A month later the couple were escorted to New York by FBI agents and set up in a suite at the Hotel Mayflower while he continued to recuperate. Meiler sent a letter to a maildrop in at the Hotel Continental in San Sebastian to inform von Bonin of the safe arrival of him and his wife.

Within weeks a radio facility was set up at Benson House in Wading River, New York, from where the Mosquera operation had also been run. The Abwehr had issued Meiler with a copy of a Dutch bible and the Dutch national anthem, 'Wilhelmus', for use in encoding and decoding his messages.[16] Hamburg urged Meiler to secure employment that would offer him 'as much freedom as possible' to pursue anything that could glean insights into American war plans. They told him to get information from public sources such as journals and magazines such as *Aeronautics, Electrical Engineering, Flying and Aero Progress*, and newspapers. 'We are interested in all details about new equipment and methods for directional finding of ships, U-Boats and airplanes.' They seemed pleased with what he sent. 'Uncle is highly pleased. He declares his approbations and well wishes', they told him.[17]

Once established as a reliable source, Meiler became an important part of Allied deception. There were many different ways of misleading Hamburg with false information that appeared to be genuine. One of the easiest was for Meiler to report on conversations he claimed to have overheard in dockland bars. For instance, he might say he had heard dock workers grumbling about extra security permits on particular wharves and then he would say which ships were moving in and out there. All of it false. He might also report on military convoys moving into the docks, giving registration numbers and unit insignia. These would be fictitious and correspond to other deceptions designed to mislead the Germans into believing that there was a fourth US Army with its headquarters in Edinburgh, Scotland. This all went to support untruths disseminated by two British double agents 'Cobweb' and 'Beetle', who had been warning the Germans about preparations that were underway for the imminent departure of American troops to Scotland. Officers with 'five sided blue and gold' shoulder patches, he observed, were part of the US 55th Division, a phantom army division that would become part of the equally non-existent British Fourth Army order of battle.

While the FBI might have thought they had been smart, von Bonin had actually been smarter this time. Bremen took little notice of the signals coming from Meiler using the Dutch prayer book he had been issued with for coding. They knew that they had been doctored because it had been their plan, right from the start, for Meiler to give himself up and offer his services as a double agent. What he was, in fact, was a triple agent still working for the Abwehr and he had set up his own radio unknown to the FBI who, apart from bugging his hotel room, had left him pretty much to his own devices having taken over all his communications with Bremen. At least they had taken over all the ones they knew about.

After the Second World War, the writer Ladislav Farago examined Abwehr files held in the National Archives and Records Centre in Washington DC and discovered that as well as the reports von Bonin had received from Meiler a similar number had gone to a handler called Wagg in Paris using a different code. These had been sent from a radio station in Rochester financed by Meiler. When Paris fell to the Allies in 1944, Meiler continued to send messages to a new case officer, Rauh, in Wiesbaden. While Meiler was extremely productive as a spy, he was able to inform Bremen very little about atomic research because of the security blanket that fell over it. His work as a triple agent was never uncovered by the FBI.[18] In April 1945, just days before the final surrender, the Germans told him,

> Because of present situation we must consider the temporary disruption of our connection. Uncle will protect your interests in the future as before and will care for you. He thanks you many times for that which you have done up to present time.[19]

Another double agent about whom little has been written was Walter Nipken who had been approached by Carl Reuper in late 1940. With arrogance typical of many German agents whose contempt for US counterintelligence agencies was profound, Reuper boasted to Nipken, an engineer at Air Associates in Bendix, New York, about his espionage activity and encouraged him to join his spy network. Reuper had targeted Nipken believing that, having been born in *Mülheim*, he retained an enduring loyalty to his native land but Nipken had taken US citizenship in 1936 and, by this time, was much more American than German. He went straight to the FBI who told him to play along with Reuper. They provided Nipken with bogus drawings and blueprints, which Reuper duly passed along to his couriers for Hamburg. From that day, Reuper was blown and his connection with the Jahnke and Wheeler-Hill radio station exposed. The FBI would now have access to most of the clandestine radio traffic between the New York and Hamburg. Thanks to Nipken, Reuper was swept up along with the rest of the Duquesne network at the end of 1941.

POSTSCRIPT

German diplomats in the United States had consistently appealed to Berlin that the US political administration was fundamentally hostile to Nazism, that the country as a whole was essentially sympathetic towards the British and that US industry and was capable of massive restructuring to create a formidable armaments industry. Right at the top of the Nazi regime, however, Hitler despised military intelligence that was always telling him things he didn't want to hear. He also had a low opinion of the US calling it a 'feeble country with a loud mouth' weakened by 'racial decay'; this conveniently allowed him to virtually ignore it while he concentrated on making plans to conquer Eastern Europe. All of this meant that Abwehr was left very much to its own devices as to how to conduct its operations in the US but that inevitably left it with fragile morale and a dearth of first-class leadership.

Against this was a sense that espionage in the US, especially given the country's liberal environment and lack of counterintelligence organisation, presented few difficulties. It was, perhaps, this assessment of the US as a 'soft touch' when it came to espionage that allowed the Abwehr to adopt a less-than-rigorous approach when recruiting agents and to harbour unrealistic expectations of what could be achieved. They did enjoy some success in its early years in the US, but by and large it was forced to deal not only hostility from the US diplomatic mission but with the embarrassment of failure and an eventual realisation that nothing emanating from its US activities ever had very much influence on the outcome of the Second World War.

In terms of recruits, those selected were often, but not always, supremely unqualified for the work. One needs only to think of the Operation Pastorius bunch upon whom so much time and money was lavished but who lacked both motivation and competence anywhere near the levels required of to carry out the tasks allocated to them. Guenther Rumrich was caught because of a schoolboy error and thereafter promptly gave up everyone he knew. William Colepaugh had become a spy because it thought it might be fun and certainly enjoyed himself but hardly in the way the Abwehr intended. He managed to burn through a large part of the money he had been given in the bars and nightclubs of New York before turning himself and his partner into the FBI. The amount of faith invested in Sebold was rewarded by the largest number of mass arrests of alien spies in American history.

Appendix 1

THE GERMAN INTELLIGENCE SERVICES

The German Armed Forces High Command (OKW) drew their intelligence from the *Amt Auslands und Abwehr*, usually abbreviated to Abwehr. This had been created in a second manifestation in March 1921 independent of the three service commands, army, navy and air force. Each of these had their own intelligence staff but restricted them to evaluation and dissemination of information rather conducting their own secret intelligence activities themselves. The original Abwehr had been disbanded under the terms of the Treaty of Versailles but was allowed to re-form as part of the Reichswehr. It was organised into three sections: reconnaissance, cipher and radio monitoring, and counterespionage but was a tiny department having only three officers and seven former officers plus clerical staff. Before the Nazis took power in 1933, the Abwehr commanders were Colonel Friedrich Gempp (1921–1927), Major Günther Schwantes (1927–1929) and Lieutenant Colonel Ferdinand von Bredow (1929–1932). Under Gempp, the Abwehr was mostly occupied monitoring the activities of trade unionists and communists as well as embryonic nationalist organisations such as the NSDAP.

On 7 June 1932, it was reorganised under a naval officer, Captain Konrad Patzig, but remained a backwater and not a place where one might come across ambitious and capable officers. Under Patzig, the Abwehr established lines of communication with all three services: navy, army and air force. He proceeded to divide the service into three basic groups (*Abteilung*): *Abt I*, which was charged with offensive intelligence, including espionage, *Abt II*, which was given sabotage and subversion and *Abt III*, which dealt with counterintelligence and security.

Abt I was broken down into sections for army, naval, air and economic intelligence, plus certain technical sections. These sections were further broken down into geographical subsections, dealing with particular countries or areas. The Abwehr maintained field offices in Germany and abroad, staffed by their own officers. In neutral countries, the Abwehr frequently disguised its organisation by attaching its personnel to the German Embassy or to trade missions. Such postings were referred to as *Kriegsorganisationen* (KOs – War Organisations) and usually acted under cover of the diplomatic mission. In Germany and occupied countries, these field offices were called *Abwehrstellen* (Asts) and their branches called *Nebenstellen* (Nests). Personnel included officers from all three services plus civilians recruited and commissioned directly. The departments responsible for espionage against the US were *Abwehrstelle Hamburg* and is sub-office *Nebenstelle Bremen*. Unfortunately, a lack of communication and mismanagement of Abwehr operations often resulted in the overlapping of targets and sometimes contradictory intelligence. The *Auswärtiges Amt* often had good reason to complain about the large number of Abwehr personnel with diplomatic cover working out of consulates and embassies causing embarrassment for genuine diplomats. The Abwehr drew its agents from a wide variety of sources. From a purely intelligence viewpoint, the most important were military and naval attachés, trade delegations and scientific institutes, which shared industry secrets across borders. Next was the *Deutsches Ausland Institut* (DAI – German Foreign Institute), which kept in touch with German emigrants and those of German heritage and the Nazi Party's *Auslandsorganisation* (foreign organisation) for party members living abroad. In addition to that were freelance agents and those who were coerced by various legal or oppressive means into working for the Abwehr.

On 1 January 1935, it was another navy man, Wilhelm Canaris, who took over from Patzig. The writer Ladislav Farago who met Canaris at the time described him as a 'rumpled, tongue-tied, absent-minded little man', but under his leadership the Abwehr burst into life.[1] Patzig had been worn down by the constant plotting of Heinrich Himmler and Reinhard Heydrich to have the Abwehr taken under the wing of the *Sicherheitsdienst* (SD – intelligence agency of the *Schutzstaffel* (SS) – Nazi paramilitary organisation), the Nazi Party security and intelligence service, but Canaris was determined to get along with these two men and preserve the independence of his service. The SD existed independently of the German military. It was the security organ of the NSDAP, a subsidiary division of Himmler's powerful *Reichssicherheitshauptamt* (RSHA – Reich Security Main Office). While the Abwehr was limited to military intelligence, the SD was free to focus on political and ideological functions both inside and outside Germany.

Canaris was a controversial choice. He was not even a Nazi Party member and was actually nearing retirement age when he, somewhat reluctantly, took on the job. He would never be reconciled to Nazism and recruited many of his staff from outside the NSDAP or at least from those whom he saw as being, like himself, not drawn to fascism, but, like almost all German military leaders, he believed resolutely in the right of Germany to reassert itself as a leading world power and that meant creating a powerful military machine. He was seen by rivals as something of a soft target and had to move quickly to establish himself before Himmler and Heydrich could strike. Emissaries were sent out to establish bases of operations across all areas of interest including the US. For this region Canaris chose the 'round-faced, balding'[2] Kapitänleutnant Hermann Menzel, the Abwehr's director of *Marine Nachrichten Stelle* (German naval intelligence).

Canaris was granted an audience with Hitler to discuss Abwehr operations, an honour never bestowed upon Patzig. When Canaris mentioned the US, Hitler was not interested. He knew very little about the country and showed little enthusiasm to learn. It came as something of a surprise to Canaris, therefore, to discover that there were already a dozen agents active there.

Canaris believed that the industrial power and strategic political importance of the US would make it a decisive factor in any European war and would almost guarantee victory for whichever side it chose to support. When Canaris recruited Erich Pheiffer to head up Abwehr espionage against the US he had to contend with the fact that Heydrich was running agents in the US from Hamburg and resolutely denying the Abwehr any knowledge of their locations or objectives.[3]

Canaris reorganised the agency in 1938, subdividing the Abwehr into three main sections:

Abteilung Z

The *Abteilung* Z or *Zentralabteilung* (Central Division, Department Z), under Generalmajor (General Major) Hans Oster, coordinated the other two sections and handling personnel and financial matters, including the payment of agents.

Amtsgruppe Ausland

The *Amtsgruppe Ausland* (Foreign Branch and later known as Foreign Intelligence Group), which had several functions. They liaised with the OKW and the general staffs of the services, coordination with the German Foreign Office on military matters, including evaluation of captured documents and evaluation of foreign press and radio broadcasts. This liaison with the OKW meant that the Foreign Branch was the appropriate channel to request Abwehr support for a particular mission.

Abts I, II and III

A combination of *Abts I, II and III* the roles of which are described here in more detail:

Abt I

Abt I was commanded by Colonel Hans Piekenbrock and was responsible for foreign intelligence collection with subsections designated by letter:

G: False documents, photographs, inks, passports and chemicals.
H: West – army west (Anglo-American army intelligence).
H: Ost – army east (Soviet army intelligence).
Ht: Technical army intelligence.
I: Communications – design of wireless sets and wireless operators.
K: Cryptanalysis.
L: Air intelligence.
M: Naval intelligence.
T/lw: Technical air intelligence.
Wi: Economic intelligence.

Attached to Abwehr I was *Gruppe I-T* for technical intelligence.

Abt II

Abt II was commanded by Colonel Erwin von Lahousen and tasked with sabotage and contacting discontented minority groups in foreign countries for intelligence purposes.

Attached to *Abt II* was the Brandenburg Regiment, an offshoot of *Gruppe II-T* (Technical Intelligence), and unconnected to any other branch outside of Abwehr II.

Abt III

Abt III was commanded by Colonel Egbert Bentivegni and was the counterintelligence division responsible for operations in German industry, planting false information, penetration of foreign intelligence services and investigating acts of sabotage on German soil. Subsections here were:

IIIC: Civilian Authority Bureau.
IIIC-2: Espionage Cases Bureau.
IIID: Disinformation Bureau.
IIIF: Counter Espionage Agents' Bureau.
IIIN: Postal Bureau.

Appendix 2

MEMBERS OF THE DUQUESNE SPY RING

Paul Bante
A former member of the German-American Bund, Bante served in the German army during the First World War. He arrived in US in 1930 and became a naturalised US citizen in 1938. With Paul Fehse, he passed on information about ships bound for Britain with war materials and supplies. He admitted supplying dynamite and detonation caps to Sebold. Entering a guilty plea to violation of the Registration Act, Bante was sentenced to eighteen months' imprisonment and was fined $1,000.

Max Blank
Blank arrived in the US in 1928 but never applied for US citizenship. He claimed to have access to details about rubberised self-sealing aeroplane gasoline tanks, as well as a new braking device for aircraft, from a friend who worked in a shipyard. He had boasted to Sebold that he had been involved in espionage since 1936 but had lost interest when payments from Germany stopped. Entering a guilty plea to violation of the Registration Act, Blank was sentenced to eighteen months' imprisonment and was fined $1,000.

Alfred E. Brokhoff
Brokhoff had come to the US in 1923 and became a naturalised citizen in 1929. He worked as a mechanic for the United States Lines in New York City for seventeen years gaining information about the sailing dates and cargoes of vessels destined for Britain. Upon conviction,

Brokhoff was sentenced to a five-year prison term for violation of the espionage statutes and to serve a two-year concurrent sentence for violation of the Registration Act.

Heinrich Clausing

German-born Clausing arrived in the US in September 1934 and became a naturalised citizen in 1938. He served as a cook on various ships sailing from New York Harbor acting as one of the principal couriers for this spy ring, transporting microphotographs and other material to South American ports, from where the information was sent to Germany via Italian airlines. Clausing was convicted and was sentenced to eight years for violation of espionage statutes. He also received a two-year concurrent sentence for violation of the Registration Act.

Conradin Otto Dold

Dold came to the US from Germany in 1926 and received his US citizenship papers in 1934. He was chief steward aboard the SS *Siboney* of the American Export Lines and acted as a courier between the US and neutral ports. He was sentenced to ten years in prison on espionage charges and received a two-year concurrent sentence, and a fine of $1,000 for violation of the Registration Act.

Rudolf Ebeling

When he arrived in the US in 1925, Ebeling was employed as a foreman in the shipping department of Harper and Brothers in New York City where obtained information regarding ship sailings and cargoes. He was sentenced to five years in prison on espionage charges. He also received a two-year concurrent sentence and a $1,000 fine for violating the Registration Act.

Richard Eichenlaub

Eichenlaub came to the US in 1930 and became a citizen in 1936, after which he ran the Little Casino restaurant in the Yorkville section of New York City. This became a rendezvous for many members of the spy ring but he also obtained information from his customers who were engaged in national defence industries in the city. He entered a plea of guilty to violation of the Registration Act, and was sentenced to eighteen months' imprisonment and was fined $1,000.

Heinrich Carl Eilers

Eilers arrived in the US in 1923 and became a citizen in 1932. He worked as a steward on ships sailing from New York City. At the time of his arrest by Customs authorities in June 1940, he had in his possession twenty letters addressed to people throughout Europe and books about to magnesium and aluminium alloys. Upon conviction, Eilers received a five-year prison sentence on espionage charges, and a concurrent sentence of two years' imprisonment and a $1,000 fine under the Registration Act.

Paul Fehse

Fehse arrived in the US in 1934 and was naturalised in 1938. He was employed as a cook on ships sailing from New York Harbor but claimed to be head of the marine division of the German espionage system in the US. Having been trained for espionage work in Hamburg, he was one of the leading members of the spy ring arranging meetings, directing members' activities and correlated information before sending it to Germany. He was arrested while trying to leave the country on the SS *Siboney* on 29 March 1941. Pleading guilty he was sentenced to one year and one day in prison for violation of the Registration Act but was later found guilty of espionage and received a prison sentence of fifteen years.

Edmund Carl Heine

Heine had lived in the US since 1914 and had been a naturalised citizen since 1920. He had held various positions in the foreign sales and service department of Ford Motor Company and Chrysler Motor Corporation travelling throughout Central and South America, Spain and Berlin. He was convicted of sending letters to Stein containing technical data regarding military aircraft construction. Upon conviction of violating the Registration Act, Heine received a $5,000 fine and a two-year prison sentence.

Felix Jahnke

Jahnke had served in the German army as a radio operator during the First World War. He arrived in the US in 1924 and became a naturalised citizen in 1930. He transmitted messages about shipping in New York Harbor to Germany using a radio installed in his apartment. After pleading guilty to violation of the Registration Act, Jahnke was sentenced to twenty months in prison and ordered to pay a $1,000 fine.

Gustav Wilhelm Kaercher

Kaercher came to the US in 1923 and becoming a US citizen in 1931. He had served in the German army during the First World War and was a former leader of the German Bund in New York. At the time of his arrest, he was engaged in designing power plants for the American Gas and Electric Company in New York City. He pleaded guilty to violating the Registration Act, received a $2,000 fine and a prison sentence of twenty-two months.

Josef Klein

Klein had come to the US in 1925 but never applied for citizenship. He was a photographer and lithographer, with a keen interest in the building and operation of shortwave radio transmitters. Upon conviction, Klein received a sentence of five years' imprisonment on espionage charges and a concurrent sentence of two years' imprisonment under the Registration Act.

Hartwig Richard Kleiss

Kleiss came to the US in 1925 and became a naturalised citizen in 1931. He was employed as a cook on various ships. He obtained information including blueprints of the SS *America* which showed the locations of newly installed gun emplacements and details of their firing mechanisms. He also obtained details on the construction and performance of new speedboats being developed by the US Navy. He pleaded guilty on charge of espionage and received an eight-year prison sentence.

Herman W. Lang

Lang came to the US 1927 and became a citizen in 1939. He was trained as a machinist and draftsman and was employed as an assembly inspector at the Carl L. Norden Company where the top secret Norden bomb was manufactured. He claimed to have taken part in the 1923 Beer Hall Putsch. The Nazis had offered to transport him safely to Germany, but Lang refused to leave his home in Ridgewood, Queens. Upon conviction, Lang received a sentence of eighteen years in prison on espionage charges and a two-year concurrent sentence under the Registration Act.

Evelyn Clayton Lewis

A native of Arkansas, Lewis had been living with Duquesne in New York City. She was aware of and condoned his espionage activities.

While she was not active in acquiring information, she helped Duquesne prepare material for transmittal abroad. Pleading guilty, she was sentenced to serve one year and one day in prison for violation of the Registration Act.

René-Emmanuel Mezenen

Mezenen was French and had claimed US citizenship through the naturalisation of his father. He was employed as a steward in the transatlantic clipper service and acted a courier, transmitting information between the US and Portugal. He also became involved in the smuggling of platinum. Following a plea of guilty, Mezenen received an eight year prison term for espionage and two concurrent years for registration violations.

Carl Reuper

Reuper arrived in the US in 1929 and became a citizen in 1936. He worked as an inspector for the Westinghouse Electric Company in Newark, New Jersey. He obtained confidential photographs relating to national defence. Upon conviction, Reuper was sentenced to sixteen years' imprisonment on espionage charges and two years' concurrent sentence under the Registration Act.

Everett Minster Roeder

Born in the Bronx, New York, Roeder had been a child prodigy and had he entered Cornell University's engineering school at the age of 15. He had been one of the first employees of the Sperry Gyroscope Company, where he worked as an engineer and designer of classified materials for the US Army and US Navy. He had visited Germany in 1936 when he was recruited for espionage work. In his work he developed long-range artillery trackers that can hit moving targets up to 10 miles away, aircraft autopilot and blind flight systems. He provided Germany with Lockheed Hudson bomber wiring diagram, and Hudson gun mounting diagram. From him, the Abwehr also obtained blueprints for advanced autopilot systems that would later be used in Luftwaffe fighters and bombers. He pleaded guilty to the charge of espionage and was sentenced to sixteen years in prison.

Paul Alfred W. Scholz

Scholz came to the US in 1926 but never gained citizenship. He was employed in German bookshops in New York City, where he disseminated Nazi propaganda. Upon conviction, Scholz was sentenced to sixteen years' imprisonment for espionage with two years concurrent sentence under the Registration Act.

George Gottlob Schuh

Schuh came to the US in 1923 and became a citizen in 1939. Having pleaded guilty to violation of the Registration Act, Schuh received a sentence of eighteen months in prison and a $1,000 fine.

Erwin Wilhelm Siegler

Siegler came to the US in 1929 and obtained citizenship in 1936. He had served as chief butcher and acted as a courier on the SS *America*. He also served as an organiser and obtained information about the movement of ships and military defence preparations at the Panama Canal. He was sentenced to ten years' imprisonment on espionage charges and a concurrent two-year term for violation of the Registration Act.

Oscar Richard Stabler

Stabler came to the US in 1923 and obtained citizenship in 1933. He was employed primarily as a barber aboard transoceanic ships and acted as a courier. He was convicted and sentenced to serve five years in prison for espionage and a two-year concurrent term under the Registration Act.

Heinrich Stade

Stade came to the US in 1922 and became a citizen in 1929. Following a guilty plea to violation of the Registration Act, Stade was fined $1,000 and received a fifteen month prison sentence.

Lilly Barbara Carola Stein

Vienna-born Stein had arrived in the US in 1939 and acted as a go-between for agents and couriers. In New York she worked as an artist's model and she is said to have been active in New York society. Her mission as a German agent was to find targets in New York nightclubs, sleep with them, and blackmail or otherwise lure them into divulging valuable secrets. One FBI agent described her as a 'good-looking nymphomaniac'. She pleaded guilty and received sentences of ten years' and two concurrent years' imprisonment for violations of espionage and registration statutes, respectively.

Franz Joseph Stigler

Stigler arrived in the US in 1931 and became a citizen in 1939. He was employed as a crew member aboard the SS *America* acting as a courier. He also recruited amateur radio operators in the US to send messages to Germany. Upon conviction, Stigler was sentenced to sixteen years in prison on espionage charges with two concurrent years for registration violations.

Erich Strunck

Strunck came to the US in 1927 and obtained citizenship in 1935. He worked as a seaman aboard the ships of the United States Lines acting as a courier. He was convicted and sentenced to ten years in prison on espionage charges. He also was sentenced to serve a two-year concurrent term under the Registration Act.

Leo Waalen

Born in Danzig, Waalen entered the US illegally in 1935 and worked as a painter for a small boat company that was constructing small craft for the US Navy. He gathered information about ships sailing for England and acquired information about government contracts listing specifications for materials and equipment, as well as detailed sea charts of the US Atlantic coastline. He was sentenced to twelve years in prison for espionage and a concurrent two-year term for violation of the Registration Act.

Adolf Henry August Walischewski

Walischewski had become a naturalised US citizen in 1935 and acted as a courier. He received a five-year prison sentence on espionage charges, as well as a two-year concurrent sentence under the Registration Act.

Else Weustenfeld

Weustenfeld arrived in the US in 1927 and became a citizen ten years later. She worked as a secretary for a law firm representing the German Consulate in New York City. She delivered funds to Duquesne that she had received from Germany. She lived in New York City with Hans, the brother of the German spy Nickolaus Ritter. After pleading guilty, Weustenfeld was sentenced to five years' imprisonment on charge of espionage and two concurrent years on charge of registration violations.

Axel Wheeler-Hill

Axel Wheeler-Hill was born in Russia and had come to the US in 1923. He gained US citizenship in 1929 and was employed as a truck driver. Following conviction, Wheeler-Hill was sentenced to fifteen years in prison for espionage and two concurrent years under the Registration Act.

Bertram Wolfgang Zenzinger

Zenzinger came to the US in 1940 as a naturalised citizen of the Union of South Africa. He pleaded guilty and received eighteen months in prison for violation of the Registration Act and eight years' imprisonment for espionage.

Appendix 3

MEMBERS OF THE LUDWIG SPY RING

Kurt Frederick Ludwig
Ludwig was born in 1903 in Fremont, Ohio, but was a resident of Germany most of his life. He was sentenced to twenty years in prison.

Rene Charles Froehlich
Froehlich was a former army private who sold Ludwig defence magazines and gathered ship information. He was sentenced to twenty years in prison.

Dr Paul T. Borchardt-Battuta
Borchardt was a former German army major, who analysed the data collected. He was sentenced to twenty years' imprisonment.

Helen Pauline Mayer
Mayer was a Long Island housewife who was sentenced to fifteen years in prison.

Karl Victor Mueller
Mueller was a machinist who helped collect production figures. He was sentenced to fifteen years' imprisonment.

Hans Helmut Pagel
Pagel was sentenced to fifteen years in prison.

Frederick Edward Schlosser
Schlosser who found out when ships would sail received a twelve year prison sentence.

Carl Herman Schroetter
Schroetter was a Miami-boat captain. He was sentenced to ten years' imprisonment.

Lucy Rita Boehmler
Boehmler was Ludwig's secretary and was sentenced to five years in prison.

Appendix 4

CODING RADIO MESSAGES

A description of the coding method used by Colepaugh (as described by him to the FBI).

1. An easily remembered phrase was chosen. It was the advertising slogan of Lucky Strike cigarettes:

LUCKY STRIKE CIGARETTES ITS TOASTED[.]

2. Using graph paper with at least thirty-one spaces start with the first letter and enter them on the paper leaving one space between every two letters until sixteen letter have been written down.

L		U		C		K		Y		S		T		R		I		K		E		C		I		G		A		R

3. Start counting at the first empty space on the left and count empty spaces up to a number equal to the month of the year the message is being sent. Place the remaining fifteen letters of the phrase in order starting with the empty spaces indicated in the previous sentence. (April=4).

L	T	U	E	C	D	K	E	Y	T	S	T	T	E	R	S	I	I	K	T	E	S	C	T	I	O	G	A	A	S	R

4. Number each letter starting from the left alphabetically i.e. the first A is 1, the second A is 2. There are no Bs so the first C is 3 and the second C is 4, D is 5, and the first E is 6 etc.

L	T	U	E	C	D	K	E	Y	T	S	T	T	E	R	S	I	I	K	T	E	S	C	T	I	O	G	A	A	S	R
16	24	30	6	3	5	14	7	31	25	20	26	27	8	18	21	11	12	15	28	9	22	4	29	13	17	10	1	2	23	19

5. Black out the space before the number of the day of the month on which the message is sent (9th).

L	T	U	E	C	D	K	E	Y	T	S	T	T	E	R	S	I	I	K	T	E	S	C	T	I	O	G	A	A	S	R
16	24	30	6	3	5	14	7	31	25	20	26	27	8	18	21	11	12	15		9	22	4	29	13	17	10	1	2	23	19

6. Print the message to be sent starting to the right of the blacked out square. The blacked-out space is skipped each time. Each sentence must have a number of letters divisible by five so Xs are added to make up the number. The total number of letters in the whole message will then be divisible by five.

   Example of message sent by Goldschmidt on 20 January 1944 using only the first two sentences:

   'Upon arrival found that position which Van Kleffens promised was no longer here. Have no job and no money. Can your New York man still contact me.'

L	T	U	E	C	D	K	E	Y	T	S	T	T	E	R	S	I	I	K	T	E	S	C	T	I	O	G	A	A	S	R
16	24	30	6	3	5	14	7	31	25	20	26	27	8	18	21	11	12	15		9	22	4	29	13	17	10	1	2	23	19
																				U	P	O	N	A	R	R	I	V	A	L
F	O	U	N	D	T	H	A	T	P	O	S	I	T	I	O	N	W	H		I	C	H	V	A	N	K	L	E	F	F
E	N	S	P	R	O	M	I	S	E	D	W	A	S	N	O	L	O	N		G	E	R	H	E	R	E	X	X	X	H
A	V	E	N	O	J	O	B	A	N	D	N	O	M	O	N	E	Y	X		C	A	N	Y	O	U	R	N	E	W	Y
O	R	K	M	A	N	S	T	I	L	L	C	O	N	T	A	C	T	M		E	X	X	X	X						

7. Now start at 1 and read down listing the letters horizontally, then 2 etc.

   ILXNVEXEDROAOHRNXTOJNNPNMAIBTTSMNUIGCE
   RKERNLECWOYTAAEOXHMOSHNXMFEAORNR
   UINOTLFHYODDLOONAPCEAXAFXWONVRPENLS
   WNCIAOONVHYXUSEKTSAI

8. Now list the letters in groups of five.

   ILXNV EXEDR OAOHR NXTOJ NNPNM AIBTT SMNUI GCERK
   ERNLE CWOYT AAEOX HMOSH NXMFE AORNR UINOT LFHYO
   DDLOO NAPCE AXAFX WONVR PENLS WNCIA OONVH YXUSE
   KTSAI

9. Leave blank spaces for the third and fourth groups from the end of the message.

ILXNV EXEDR OAOHR NXTOJ NNPNM AIBTT SMNUI GCERK ERNLE CWOYT AAEOX HMOSH NXMFE AORNR UINOT LFHYO DDLOO NAPCE AXAFX WONVR PENLS WNCIA OONVH *****
***** YXUSE KTSAI

These are left for the key to show the date the message was sent (required for decoding). These groups are filled in as follows:

The letters of the month are listed APRILAPRIL and given numerical values in the same way as in step 4

A	P	R	I	L	A	P	R	I	L
1	7	9	3	5	2	8	10	4	6

For December it would have been:

D	E	C	E	M	B	E	R	D	E
3	5	2	6	9	1	7	10	4	8

10. The word DEUTSCHLAND is now placed in a third row.

A	P	R	I	L	A	P	R	I	L
1	7	9	3	5	2	8	10	4	6
D	E	U	T	S	C	H	L	A	N

The remaining letters of the alphabet after DEUTSCHLAND are removed and are now listed in alphabetical order starting from the left (note only the final digit of 10 is used).

A	P	R	I	L	A	P	R	I	L
1	7	9	3	5	2	8	0	4	6
D	E	U	T	S	C	H	L	A	N
B	F	G	I	J	K	M	O	P	Q
R	V	W	X	Y	Z				

Using the seventh and eighth groups of five, substitute the numbers in the above key which appear above the column listing the letter in question.

S	M	N	U	I		G	C	E	R	K
5	8	6	9	3		9	2	7	1	2

To the above numbers in group seven add a series of numbers representing the day on which the message is sent (26 April) 26026 (day, zero, day; if it had been 9 April then 90909).

S	M	N	U	I
5	8	6	9	3
2	6	0	2	6
7	4	6	1	9

To the numbers under group eight add a group of numbers representing the month in which the message is sent followed by a zero then the number of groups in the message.

G	C	E	R	K
9	2	7	1	2
0	4	0	2	5
9	6	7	3	7

The numerals are then transposed back to the letters in group seven.

S	M	N	U	I
5	8	6	9	3
2	6	0	2	6
7	4	6	1	9
F	P	N	D	W

The numerals are then transposed back to the letters in group eight.

G	C	E	R	K
9	2	7	1	2
0	4	0	2	5
9	6	7	3	7
G	Q	F	T	F

Now add these two groups as the third and fourth from the end. The complete message is now:

ILXNV EXEDR OAOHR NXTOJ NNPNM AIBTT SMNUI GCERK
ERNLE CWOYT AAEOX HMOSH NXMFE AORNR UINOT LFHYO
DDLOO NAPCE AXAFX WONVR PENLS WNCIA OONVH FPNDW
GQFTF YXUSE KTSAI

NOTES

Chapter 1: The First Word War

1 Blum, Howard, *Dark Invasion*, (Scribe Publications, 2014), p.348
2 Feilitzsch, Herbert von, *The Secret War Council: The German Fight against the Entente in America in 1914*, (Henselstone Verlag LLC, Kindle edition), p.15
3 ibid, p.69
4 ibid
5 Price Jones, John, *The German Secret Service in America 1914–1918*, (Gutenberg e-book, 2019)
6 Records of the National Archives and Records Administration NA RG 65 FBI Case Files, Roll 877, File 8000-925, Memo to A. Bruce Bielaski, March 28, 1918
7 Lambert, Nicholas A., *Planning Armageddon: British Economic Warfare and the First World War*, (Cambridge, MA, 2012), p.212
8 Feilitzsch, Herbert von, *The Secret War Council: The German Fight against the Entente in America in 1914*
9 Goltz, Horst von der, *My Adventures as a German Secret Agent*, (R.M. McBride & Co., New York, 1917), p.115
10 ibid, p.168
11 Price Jones, p.72
12 Sperry, Earl Evelyn, *German Plots and Intrigues in the United States During the Period of Our Neutrality*, (The Committee on Public Information, Washington DC, 1918), p.27
13 Feilitzsch, Herbert von, *The Secret War Council: The German Fight against the Entente in America in 1914*
14 Reinhard, R., *Prelude to the Easter Rising: Sir Roger Casement in Imperial Germany*, (Frank Cass Publishers, 2000), p.81
15 NA RG 65 Albert Papers, Box 19, 'Military War Supplies', 11 February 1915
16 Sperry, p.30
17 Price Jones, p.120

18 Feilitzsch, Herbert von, *The Secret War on the United States in 1915: A Tale of Sabotage, Labor Unrest and Border Troubles*, (Henselstone Verlag LLC, Kindle edition), p.77
19 NA RG 65 FBI Case Files, M1085, File 8000-925.
20 Feilitzsch, Herbert von, *The Secret War on the United States in 1915: A Tale of Sabotage, Labor Unrest and Border Troubles*, p.89
21 The Philadelphia Evening Ledger, 21 July 1915, 'Nine Compartments Damaged By Flames on Great Warship'
22 Feilitzsch, Herbert von, *Felix A. Sommerfeld and the Mexican Front in the Great War*, (Henselstone Verlag LLC, Kindle edition), p.6
23 Investigation of Mexican Affairs, Report and Hearing before a Subcommittee Foreign Relations, 66th Congress, 2nd Session (Washington DC: Government Printing Office, 1919–1920), I, 1205
24 Feilitzsch, Herbert von, *Felix A. Sommerfeld and the Mexican Front in the Great War*, p.66
25 NA RG 65 FBI Case Files, M1085, File 8000-174, William Offley to Chief Bielaski, 29 September 1915
26 Feilitzsch, Herbert von, *Felix A. Sommerfeld and the Mexican Front in the Great War*, p.84
27 ibid, p.87
28 Goltz, p.236
29 Feilitzsch, Herbert von, *Felix A. Sommerfeld and the Mexican Front in the Great War*, p.89
30 NA RG 65 FBI Case Files, M1085, File 8000-3089, Captured document from Frederico Stallforth's office, report entry for 13 August 1915
31 *The New York Times*, 'Submarine Sinks British Steamer Without Notice', 21 February 1915,
32 *The New York Times*, 'German Embassy Issues Warning', 1 May 1915
33 Blum, p.339
34 Keller, Phyllis, *George Sylvester Viereck: The Psychology of a German-American Militant*, (The Journal of Interdisciplinary History, Vol. 2, No. 1, 1971), p.59
35 Reiss, Tom, *The Orientalist. Solving the Mystery of a Strange and Dangerous Life*, (Random House, 2005), p.285
36 Feilitzsch, Herbert von, *The Secret War Council: The German Fight against the Entente in America in 1914*
37 Price Jones, p.221
38 Blum, p.391
39 Sperry, p.29
40 Feilitzsch, Herbert von, *The Secret War on the United States in 1915: A Tale of Sabotage, Labor Unrest and Border Troubles*, p.231
41 NA RG 76 Mixed Claims Commission, Box 8, Testimony of Edward Felton, 11 April 1930

42 Feilitzsch, Herbert von, *The Secret War on the United States in 1915: A Tale of Sabotage, Labor Unrest and Border Troubles*, p.242
43 Siegel, Robert and Silverman, Art, *During World War I, US Government Propaganda Erased German Culture*, https://npr.org, 2017

Chapter 2: German Propaganda

1 'Exchange Student Speaks of Nazi Colonial Demands.', Stanford Daily, 26 October 1938
2 Rubenstein, Jared, *Nazi Propaganda in American Universities from 1933 to 1938*, https://mospace.umsystem.edu
3 Spivak, John L., *Secret Armies: The New Technique of Nazi Warfare*, (Gutenberg Press, 1939), p.74
4 Ridley, Norman, *Hitler's Allies*, (Pen & Sword, 2024), p.31
5 Spivak, p.84
6 Frye, Alton, *Nazi Germany and the American Hemisphere, 1933-1941*, (Yale University Press, 1967), p.50
7 Vasey, p.24
8 'German Rules for Newsreels' Variety, 6 November 1934, p.13
9 Spivak, p.119
10 Rubenstein
11 ibid
12 Spivak, p.104
13 Ridley, p.143
14 ibid
15 Rosenzweig, Laura, *Hollywood's Spies: Jewish Infiltration of Nazi and Pro-Nazi Groups in Los Angeles, 1933–1941*, (University of California, 2013), p.31
16 Woods, Gerald, *The Police in Los Angeles* (Reform and Professionalization, Garland, 1993), p.60
17 ibid, p.141
18 Rosenzweig, p.83
19 Ross, Steven J., *Hitler in Los Angeles*, (Bloomsbury Publishing, 2017), p.16
20 Rosenzweig, p.91
21 ibid, p.94
22 ibid, p.251
23 ibid, p.200
24 Farago, Ladislas, *The Game of the Foxes*, (David McKay Company Inc, 1971), p.377
25 Gunther, John, *Inside USA*, (Harper and Brothers, 1947), p.175
26 Farago, p.387
27 ibid, p.388
28 Vasey, p.27

Chapter 3: FBI Background

1 Batvinis, Raymon J., *The Origins of FBI Counterintelligence,* (University Press of Kansas, 2007), p.31
2 Fox, John F. Jr, *The Birth of the Federal Bureau of Investigation,* (FBI Historian, 2003)
3 Elton Morrison, The Letters of Theodore Roosevelt, Vol. 5, Letter 4705 [Theodore Roosevelt] to Joseph Gurney Cannon, 4/29/1908
4 Batvinis, Raymon J., *The Origins of FBI Counterintelligence,* p.38
5 ibid, p.42

Chapter 4: The Griebl-Lonkowski Spy Ring

1 Batvinis, Raymon J., *Hoover's Secret War against Axis Spies: FBI Counterespionage during World War II,* (University Press of Kansas, Kindle edition)
2 Farago, p.18
3 Kahn, David, *Hitler's Spies,* (Macmillan, 1978), p.76
4 Jeffreys-Jones, Rhodri, *Ring of Spies: How MI5 and the FBI Brought Down the Nazis in America,* (The History Press, Kindle edition), p.13
5 ibid, p.141
6 ibid, p.34
7 Batvinis, Raymon J., *The Origins of FBI Counterintelligence,* p.8
8 Kerbaj, Richard, *The Secret History of the Five Eyes: The Untold Story of the Shadowy International Spy Network, Through its Targets, Traitors and Spies,* (Blink Publishing, Kindle edition), p.18
9 Jeffreys-Jones, p.31
10 ibid, p.49
11 Turrou, Leon, *The Nazi Spy Conspiracy in America,* (Westphalia Press, Kindle edition), p.42
12 ibid, p.63
13 ibid, p.101
14 ibid, p.79
15 Jeffreys-Jones, p.80
16 Indictment against Jessie Jordan, 1, JC26/1938/46, SSC
17 Turrou, p.115
18 ibid, p.120
19 ibid, p.138
20 Farago, p.23
21 Turrou, p.153
22 Farago, p.24
23 Vasey, p.28
24 Batvinis, Raymon J., *The Origins of FBI Counterintelligence,* p.14
25 Turrou, p.165

26 ibid, p.176
27 Breuer, William, *Hitler's Undercover War – The Nazi Espionage Invasion of The USA*, (St Martin's Press, 1989), p.29
28 Turrou, p.21
29 Jeffreys-Jones, p.122
30 Breuer, William, *Hitler's Undercover War – The Nazi Espionage Invasion of The USA*, p.44
31 Strassman, W. Paul, *Science, Politics and Migration in Turbulent Times (1793–1993)*, (Berghahn Books, 2008), p.138
32 Breuer, William, *Hitler's Undercover War – The Nazi Espionage Invasion of The USA*, p.88
33 Vasey, p.33
34 Turrou, p.188
35 ibid, p.221
36 ibid, p.226
37 https://antipolygraph.org/articles/article-027.shtml, downloaded 4 November 2023
38 E.A. Tamm, Memorandum for the (FBI) Director, 11 May 1938
39 Jeffreys-Jones, p.149
40 ibid, p.161
41 ibid, p.164
42 ibid, p.196
43 Hoover, Memorandum for Mr Tamm, 26 October 1938, FBIT 1/3/1
44 *The New York Times*, 16 November 1938, p.1
45 Batvinis, Raymon J., *The origins of FBI Counterintelligence*, p.29
46 Kahn, p.100
47 Farago, p.477
48 Beck, Alfred M., *Hitler's Ambivalent Attaché: Lt. Gen. Friedrich von Boetticher in America, 1933–1941*, (Potomac Books, 2005), p.70
49 Kahn, p.81

Chapter 5: Nazis of the West Coast

1 Rosenzweig, p.251
2 Ross, p.158
3 Spivak, p.46
4 ibid, p.134
5 ibid, p.135
6 Rosenzweig, p.302
7 ibid, p.303
8 ibid, p.230
9 ibid, p.296
10 ibid, p.242

Chapter 6: Financial Espionage

1 Batvinis, Raymon J., *The Origins of FBI Counterintelligence*, p.98

Chapter 7: Torkild Rieber

1 Capshaw, Ron, *Doing Big Business with Fascists*, https://www.tabletmag.com, 2018
2 Farago, p.401
3 ibid, p.408

Chapter 8: Ritter, Duquesne and Sebold

1 Documents on German Foreign Policy 1918–1945: Series C (1933–1936), Series D (1937–1941), Washington DC: United States Department of State, 1949–1983, D:IX:636
2 Ritter, Nickolaus, *Cover Name: Dr Rantzau*, (University Press of Kentucky, 2019), p.14
3 ibid, p.27
4 Vasey, p.35
5 Farago, p.479
6 Ritter, p.52
7 Batvinis, Raymon J., *The Origins of FBI Counterintelligence*, p.161
8 ibid, p.162
9 https://www.fbi.gov/history.famous-cases/duquesne/
10 Ritter, p.55
11 Miller, Joan Irene, *Spies in America: German Espionage in the United States, 1935–1945*, (Portland State University, 1984), p.44
12 Vasey, p.105
13 'Espionage Report on William Sebold', FBI Files, RG65 Serial 332, Vol. 1, 3713, NARA, 236
14 Ritter, p.106
15 Batvinis, Raymon J., *The Origins of FBI Counterintelligence*, p.228
16 Vasey, p.93
17 Farago, p.321
18 Ritter, p.109
19 Batvinis, Raymon J., *The Origins of FBI Counterintelligence*, p.234
20 ibid, p.241
21 Hynd, Alan, *Passport to Treason*, (Robert M. McBride and Co., 1943), p.48
22 Vasey, p.107
23 Miller, p.48
24 Farago, p.312
25 Batvinis, Raymon J., *The Origins of FBI Counterintelligence*, p.24
26 Vasey, p.110

Chapter 9: Sleepers

1 Farago, p.499
2 ibid, p.498
3 ibid, p.497
4 ibid, p.496
5 Switsky, Robert, *Wealth of an Empire: The Treasure Shipments that Saved Britain and the World*, (Potomac Books, 2013), p.108
6 Breuer, William B., *The Air-Raid Warden Was a Spy And Other Tales from Home-Front America in World War II*, (John Wiley & Sons, Inc, 2002), p.164
7 Farago, p.500

Chapter 10: The Ludwig Spy Ring

1 Trefousse, Hans L., *Failure of German Intelligence in the United States, 1935–1945*, (The Mississippi Valley Historical Review, Vol. 42, No. 1, 1955)
2 Burnett, Gene M., *Florida's Past: People and Events That Shaped the State*, (Pineapple Press Inc, 1997), p.78
3 Farago, p.429
4 ibid, p.432
5 Macrakis, Christie, *Prisoners, Lovers, and Spies: The Story of Invisible Ink from Herodotus to al-Qaeda*, (Yale University Press, 2014)
6 Burnett, p.77
7 Aswell, Edward C., *The Case of the Ten Nazi Spies*, (Harper's Magazine, CLXXXV.1105, 1942), p.14
8 Farago, p.467
9 ibid, p.468
10 ibid, p.469
11 ibid, p.475

Chapter 11: Operation Pastorius

1 Farago, p.433
2 Rachlis, Eugene, *They Came To Kill The Story of Eight Nazi Saboteurs in America*, (Eumenes Publishing, Kindle edition), p.33
3 ibid, p.40
4 ibid, p.82
5 ibid, p.192
6 Dean, John W., A Timely Account of the Key Supreme Court Military Tribunals Precedent: https://www.findlaw.com, 2003

Chapter 12: Wilhelm Albrecht von Pressentin genannt von Rautter

1 A Report on the Office of Censorship, United States Government Printing Office, Washington DC, 1945 p.46
2 Batvinis, Raymon J., *Hoover's Secret War against Axis Spies*
3 ibid
4 ibid

Chapter 13: Gimpel and Colepaugh

1 *The New York Times*, 2 January 1945

Chapter 14: Double Agents

1 Batvinis, Raymon J., *Hoover's Secret War against Axis Spies*
2 NYO Report of SA J.C. Fellner, 11 April 1942, FBI Mosquera File
3 Batvinis, Raymon J., *Hoover's Secret War against Axis Spies*
4 ibid
5 ibid
6 Thurston cable to Hoover, 3 August 1943 (1180): Hoover letter to Thurston, 8 August 1943, FBI Goldschmidt File
7 Thurston cable to Hoover, 24 October 1943; Thurston letter to Hoover, 23 October 1943, FBI Goldschmidt File
8 Batvinis, Raymon J., *Hoover's Secret War against Axis Spies*
9 Memorandum from R.G. Fletcher for Mr D.M. Ladd, 5 January 1944, FBI Goldschmidt File
10 I.W. Conrad memorandum to Coffey, 22 July 1944, FBI Goldschmidt File
11 Miller, Keith, *How Important Was Oil in World War II*, (George Mason University, History News Network, 2000)
12 Batvinis, Raymon J., *Hoover's Secret War against Axis Spies*
13 US Government memorandum from R.G. Fletcher to D.M. Ladd, 30 October 1945, FBI Goldschmidt File
14 Farago, p.646
15 ON22/ND7, AS-5: EF3O signal from District Intelligence Officer, SEVENTH Naval District to The Chief of Naval Operations, 27 June 1942
16 Batvinis, Raymon J., *Hoover's Secret War against Axis Spies*
17 ibid
18 Farago, p.645
19 Batvinis, Raymon J., *Hoover's Secret War against Axis Spies*

Postscript

1 Farago, p.9
2 Jeffreys-Jones, p.116
3 Breuer, William B., *The Spy Who Spent the War in Bed: And Other Bizarre Tales from World War II*, (John Wiley & Sons, Inc, 2003), p.5

SOURCES

Aswell, Edward C., *The Case of the Ten Nazi Spies,* Harper's Magazine, CLXXXV.1105, 1942

Batvinis, Raymon J., *Hoover's Secret War against Axis Spies: FBI Counterespionage during World War II,* University Press of Kansas, Kindle edition, 2014

Batvinis, Raymon J., *The Origins of FBI Counterintelligence,* University Press of Kansas, 2007

Beck, Alfred M., *Hitler's Ambivalent Attaché: Lt. Gen. Friedrich von Boetticher in America, 1933–1941,* Potomac Books, 2005

Blum, Howard, *Dark Invasion,* Scribe Publications, 2014

Breuer, William, *Hitler's Undercover War – The Nazi Espionage Invasion of The USA,* St Martin's Press, 1989

Breuer, William B., *The Air-Raid Warden Was a Spy And Other Tales from Home-Front America in World War II,* John Wiley & Sons, Inc, 2002

Breuer, William B., *The Spy Who Spent the War in Bed: And Other Bizarre Tales from World War II,* John Wiley & Sons, Inc, 2003

Burnett, Gene M., *Florida's Past: People and Events That Shaped the State,* Pineapple Press Inc, 1997

Capshaw, Ron, *Doing Big Business with Fascists,* https://www.tabletmag.com, 2018

Cushman, Robert E., *The Case of the Nazi Saboteurs,* The American Political Science Review Vol. 36, No. 6, 1942

Dean, John W., A *Timely Account of the Key Supreme Court Military Tribunals Precedent,* https://www.findlaw.com, 2003

Farago, Ladislas, *The Game of the Foxes,* David McKay Company Inc, 1971

Feilitzsch, Herbert von, *Felix A. Sommerfeld and the Mexican Front in the Great War,* Henselstone Verlag LLC, Kindle edition, 2015

Feilitzsch, Herbert von, *The Secret War Council: The German Fight against the Entente in America in 1914,* Henselstone Verlag LLC, Kindle edition, 2016

Feilitzsch, Herbert von, *The Secret War on the United States in 1915: A Tale of Sabotage, Labor Unrest and Border Troubles,* Henselstone Verlag LLC, Kindle edition, 2015

Fox, John F. Jr, *The Birth of the Federal Bureau of Investigation*, FBI Historian, 2003

Frye, Alton, *Nazi Germany and the American Hemisphere, 1933–1941*, Yale University Press, 1967

Goltz, Horst von der, *My Adventures as a German Secret Agent*, R.M. McBride & Co., New York, 1917

Gunther, John, *Inside USA*, Harper and Brothers, 1947

Hasian, Marouf A., *Franklin D. Roosevelt, Wartime Anxieties, and the Saboteurs' Case*, Rhetoric and Public Affairs, Vol. 6, No. 2, 2003

Hynd, Alan, *Passport to Treason*, Robert M. McBride and Co, 1943

Jeffreys-Jones, Rhodri, *Ring of Spies: How MI5 and the FBI Brought Down the Nazis in America*, The History Press, Kindle edition, 2020

Kahn, David, *Hitler's Spies*, Macmillan, 1978

Kahn David, *The Code-Breakers*, Scribner, 1967

Keller, Phyllis, *George Sylvester Viereck: The Psychology of a German-American Militant*, The Journal of Interdisciplinary History, Vol. 2, No. 1, 1971

Kerbaj, Richard, *The Secret History of the Five Eyes: The Untold Story of the Shadowy International Spy Network, Through its Targets, Traitors and Spies*, Blink Publishing, Kindle edition

Lambert, Nicholas A., *Planning Armageddon: British Economic Warfare and the First World War*, Cambridge, MA, 2012

Linder, Douglas O., *The Nazi Saboteurs Trial*, https://famous-trials.com, 2019

Macrakis, Christie, *Prisoners, Lovers, and Spies: The Story of Invisible Ink from Herodotus to al-Qaeda*, Yale University Press, 2014

Meyer, Michael C., *The Mexican-German Conspiracy of 1915*, The Americas, Vol. 23, No. 1, 1966

Miller, Keith, *How Important Was Oil in World War II*, George Mason University, History News Network, 2000

Miller, Joan Irene, *Spies in America: German Espionage in the United States, 1935–1945*, Portland State University, 1984

Paehler, Katrin, *The Third Reich's Intelligence Services*, Cambridge University Press, 2017

Price Jones, John, *The German Secret Service in America 1914–1918*, Gutenberg, e-book, 2019

Prior, Leon O., *German Espionage in Florida during World War II*, The Florida Historical Quarterly, Vol. 39, No. 4, 1961

Rachlis, Eugene, *They Came To Kill The Story of Eight Nazi Saboteurs in America*, Eumenes Publishing, Kindle edition, 2019

Reinhard, R., *Prelude to the Easter Rising: Sir Roger Casement in Imperial Germany*, Frank Cass Publishers, 2000

Reiss, Tom, *The Orientalist: Solving the Mystery of a Strange and Dangerous Life*, Random House, 2005

Ridley, Norman, *Hitler's Allies*, Pen & Sword, 2024

Rintelen, Franz von, *The Dark Invader: Wartime Reminiscences of a German Naval Intelligence Officer*, Lovat, Dickson, 1933

Ritter, Nickolaus, *Cover Name: Dr Rantzau*, University Press of Kentucky, 2019

Rosenzweig, Laura, *Hollywood's Spies: Jewish Infiltration of Nazi and Pro-Nazi Groups in Los Angeles, 1933–1941*, University of California, 2013

Ross, Steven J., *Hitler in Los Angeles*, Bloomsbury Publishing, 2017

Rubenstein, Jared, *Nazi Propaganda in American Universities from 1933 to 1938*, https://mospace.umsystem.edu

Siegel, Robert and Silverman, Art, *During World War I, US Government Propaganda Erased German Culture*, https://www.npr.org, 2017

Sperry, Earl Evelyn, *German Plots and Intrigues in the United States During the Period of Our Neutrality*, The Committee on Public Information, Washington DC, 1918

Spivak, John L., *Secret Armies: The New Technique of Nazi Warfare*, Gutenberg Press, 1939

Strassman, W. Paul, *Science, Politics and Migration in Turbulent Times (1793–1993)*, Berghahn Books, 2008

Switsky, Robert, *Wealth of an Empire: The Treasure Shipments that Saved Britain and the World*, Potomac Books, 2013

Trefousse, Hans L., *Failure of German Intelligence in the United States, 1935–1945*, The Mississippi Valley Historical Review, Vol. 42, No. 1, 1955

Turrou, Leon, *The Nazi Spy Conspiracy in America*, Westphalia Press, Kindle edition, 2013

Vasey, Christopher, *Nazi Intelligence Operations in Non-Occupied Territories: Espionage Efforts in the United States, Britain, South America and Southern Africa*, McFarland & Company, Inc., Publishers, Kindle edition, 2016

Woods, Gerald, *The Police in Los Angeles*: Reform and Professionalization, Garland, 1993

INDEX

Afanassieff, Peter (aka Prince Peter Kushubue, Peter V. Armstrong), 41, 42, 52
Albert, Heinrich Friedrich, 2–8, 13, 15–18, 29–32, 34
Alberts, Hans, 130
Alexander, Kenneth, 52
Alexander, Thomas, 44
Allen, Bert, 49, 52
Allen, Henry Douglas (aka H.O. Moffet, Howard Leighton Allen), 52, 95–101
Allendorf, Nella Florence, 14
Armstrong, Peter V., 41, 42, 52
Aubert, Marc, 81

Backhaus, Irwin, 78
Bante, Paul, 123, 124, 190
Barth, Reinhold, 148
Bauer, W.P., 52
Baumgarten, Baur, 66
Becker, Ernst, 19, 34
Behn, Sosthenes, 106
Bensmann, Carl Hermann Nicholas 'Niko', 106, 107, 130
Benton, William S., 22
Berliner, Heln, 81
Berliner, Isadore, 81
Bernstorff, Count Johann Heinrich Andreas Hermann Albrecht von, 2, 4, 6, 16, 17, 27, 30
Biddle, Francis Beverley, 155
Bischoff, Johannes, 127–130
Blank, Max, 190
Blanquet, Aureliano, 23
Blomquist, Guiri, 69
Blum, Hans, 159–160, 167, 169
Bode, Enno, 19, 34
Boehmler, Lucy Rita, 133, 199
Boetticher, Friedrich von, 62, 93, 106, 110
Bohle, Ernst Wilhelm, 93
Böhme, Eleanor, 74
Bonaparte, Charles, 56–57
Bonin, Udo Wilhelm Bogislav von, 69, 77, 81, 82, 86, 87, 88, 179–181
Bopp, Franz, 16
Borchardt-Battuta, Paul Theodor, 134, 198
Boy-Ed, Karl, 3–6, 8, 16, 17, 22, 23, 26, 32, 36
Brincken, Wilhelm von, 16
Brokhoff, Alfred E., 190
Bryan, William Jennings, 22
Buchanan, Frank, 25
Buenz, Karl, 8
Bülow, Bernhard Ernst von, 52
Burger, Ernest Peter, 145, 148, 151, 153, 154, 155
Burghardt, Joachim, 109
Burke, Frank, 29–30
Burke, John W., 90
Busbee, C.M., 67
Busch, Georg (aka Julius Georg Bergman), 135, 136
Busch, Katherine 'Kate' Moog, 72–74, 81–82, 86–87, 136
Bush, Guy, 50
Buss, Gregor, 42
Busse, Frederick A., 12
Butler, Nicholas Murray, 44

Cárdenas, Lázaro, 95, 97
Carlton, Elmer H., 168, 169
Carranza, Venustiano, 21–24
Chandor, Louise A. (aka Leslie Fry), 99, 100, 101

Chapin, Selden, 166
Churchill, Winston, 178
Clausen, Heinrich, 124
Clausing, Hienrich, 191
Colepaugh, William Curtis (aka William Caldwell, William Koller), 162–165, 183
Collins, Seward, 90
Comfort, Sylvia, 140
Connelly, Earl, 118, 119, 124, 126, 151
Coolidge, Calvin, 59
Cornell, Margaret W., 16
Coughlin, Charles, 45, 104, 138
Covani, Constante, 12, 13
Craig, Mailn, 94
Crowley, Charles C., 16
Cullen, John, 150–151, 153, 154
Cummings, Homer, 139
Curran, Mary, 65, 73
Czolgosz, Leon, 56

Daeche, Paul, 32
Dalton, Joseph N., 67, 68, 70, 80
Danielsen, Christian F., 75
Dasch, George John (aka George Davis), 143, 145–146, 149–151, 153–155
Davis, James, 47, 48
Davis, Pablo, 35
de Salis, Charles, 173, 174
de Sombreff, Jonkheer van der Maesen, 173
de Wanger, Senta (aka Senta Dirlewanger), 78, 79
Deatherage, Georgs, 97, 98, 100
Debrowski, Wilhelm Georg, 114
Deecke, Joachim, 149, 151
Dent, Charles Enrique, 132
Dernburg, Bernhard, 2, 3, 16
Devoy, John, 12
Díaz, Felix, 23
Dicks, Henry, 144
Diebel, Hans, 52
Dieckhoff, Hans, 53, 90
Dilger, Anton, 33–34
Dilger, Carl, 33
Dix, George C., 90, 92
Dold, Conradin Otto, 191
Dreschel, William, 70, 86, 87
Dugan, Joseph P., 139
Dunigan, Lester C., 90
Duquesne, Frédéric 'Fritz' Joubert (aka Frederick Fredericks, George Fordam, Piet Nicaud, Frank de Trafford Craven), 110–126, 130, 135–137, 151, 153, 159, 166, 182

Ebeling, Rudolf, 191
Eckardt, Heinrich von, 36
Ecker, Otto, 3, 6
Eglin, Henry W.T., 66–68, 71, 91
Eicehlaub, Richard, 191
Eilers, Heinrich Carl, 192
Eitel, Karl, 63, 76, 77, 81, 82, 84, 88
Ellsworth, James C., 118, 119
Emerson, Edwin, 39–41, 45, 90
Evans, Hiram, 100

Fahrney, Mary Elizabeth 'Madcap Merry', 138, 139
Fay, Robert, 32
Fehse, Paul, 123, 125, 126
Fellner, John G., 124
Felt, Mark, 176–178
Fetzer, Friedrich, 105
Finch, Stanley W., 57
Fish, Hamilton, 53
Flynn, William, 30, 58
Ford, Edsel, 106
Ford, Henry, 99
Fowler, H. Robert, 25
Freehling, Walter, 152
Friedmann, William G., 124, 166
Friske, Franz, 88
Fritzen, Alfred E., 12
Froehlich, Rene Charles, 134, 198
Fuehr, Karl Alexander, 3
Fürholzer, Edmund, 40

Gardiner, Nadya, 132
Garrison, Lindley Miller, 22
Gauseback, August T., 104
Gempp, Fritz, 61, 62, 76,185
Gestramus, Neils, 173
Gienanth, Ulrich von, 139, 140
Gilbert, Dan, 44, 45
Gimpel, Erich (aka Edward George Green), 162–164
Gioscia, Ricardo, 169, 170
Gissibl, Fritz, 42, 75
Glaser, Erich, 71–72, 88, 90, 91, 93

Goebbels, Joseph, 39, 40, 45, 46, 48, 74, 75
Goldschmidt, Hellmuth Siegfried, 171–178
Goltz, Clara von Der, 160
Göring, Hermann, 106
Griebl, Ignatz T., 71–78, 80–88, 90, 92–93, 117
Grimm, Hans, 130
Grogan, Stanley, 79
Gudenberg, Werner Georg, 63, 79, 85, 88
Guellich, Gustav, 82, 83
Gyssling, Georg, 46, 50–52

Haddow, William, 64–65
Hardy, Lamar, 88
Harris, Dave, 133
Harris, Loni, 133
Haupt, Herbert Johannes Wilhelm, 145–149, 152
Hausberger, Walter von, 131, 135
Hausmann, Ulrich, 80
Heinck, Heinrich Harm (aka Henry Kaynor), 145–146, 148, 153
Heine, Edmund Carl, 121, 192
Heins, Otto, 10
Heinz, Richard Ernest, 144
Helbing, Hans, 96
Herman, Richard, 16
Herrmann, Karl Friedrich Wilhelm 'Willi', 84, 86, 87
Heydrich, Reinhard, 138, 186, 187
Hilken, Paul, 34
Himmler, Heinrich, 133, 186, 187
Hinchley Cooke, William Edward, 65, 72, 73
Hindenburg, Paul von, 40
Hingate, Herman Zum, 160
Hinsch, Frederick, 33
Hintze, Paul von, 21
Hirzel, Walter, 157, 159
Hodgkins, Harvard, 162, 164
Hofmann, Jeni (aka Ruth Hofmann, Johanna Hofmann), 71–73, 88, 91, 92, 93
Hohlhaus, Alfred, 178, 179
Holleuffer, Hans Heinrich von, 96
Hollzer, Harry, 98, 100
Homburg, R.A., 130
Hoover, Herbert, 40
Hoover, J. Edgar, 58–60, 67, 72, 78, 86, 87, 88, 89, 90, 92, 93, 102, 103, 117–119, 124, 125, 137, 154,155, 161, 166, 174, 175, 178
Horn, Werner, 15
Houghton, W.H., 29
Huerta, Victoriano, 21–25
Hulbert, Murray, 89
Hull, Cordell, 99
Hunter, Edward H., 41
Hyde, Charles, 44
Hyde, Montgomery, 132, 157
Hynes, William 'Red', 47, 48

Igel, Wolf Walter Franz von, 3, 4, 15
Ingalls, C.F., 97
Ingalls, Laura Haughtaling, 139, 140

Jagow, Gottlieb von, 2
Jahnke, Felix, 116, 123, 182, 192
Jahnke, Kurt, 35–36
Jänichen, Karl Herbert, 88
Janssen, Matthias, 172
Jarosch, William, 16
Jewett, W.K., 100
Jimene y Doctor, Felisa, 174
Jordan, Jessie, 64–67, 71–73, 81, 88
Jordan, Karl Friedrich 'Fritz', 65
Jordan, Marga Wilhelmina, 65
Josephs, Morris, 79
Jung, Harry A., 41, 42, 45
Justice, Edmund, 12, 31

Kaercher, Gustav Wilhelm, 193
Kaltschmidt, Albert Carl, 15, 16
Kappe, Walter, 135, 141–149, 151–153
Karl, Friedrich, 173
Kaufmann, Emilie 'Milly' von, 17
Kayville, Victor de, 41, 42
Keating, John P., 14
Keeler, Leonard, 86
Keitel, Karl, 113
Kell, Vernon, 64, 72
Kennedy, Joseph, 139
Kerling, Edward John (aka Edward J. Kelly), 143–144, 147, 149, 151–153
Kerrigan, F.J., 41
Killinger, Manfred von, 52
Kleffens, Eelco van, 175, 177
Klein, Joseph, 123, 193

Kleiss, Hartwig Richard, 193
Knox, John Clark, 90, 92
Koechel, Johann, 63
Koedel, Simon Emil, 127–130
Koeler, Marie Hedwig, 128
Koenig, Paul W., 9–13, 15, 27, 29, 31, 34
König, Helmuth, 145, 148
Kositsin, Vladimir, 100
Kramer, Anthony, 153
Kraus, Paul, 75, 114, 115
Kristoff, Michael, 35
Krug, Herbert, 167
Kueck, Otto, 12
Kuhlenkampff, Gustav B., 5, 8
Kuhn, Fritz, 93, 97, 98, 100, 142, 168

LaGuardia, Fiorello, 73
Lahousen, Erwin von, 133, 135–136, 141
Lamar, David, 25, 26
Lang, Hermann, 111, 112, 117, 118, 119, 135
Lansing, Robert, 32
Lee, Raymond E., 64, 67
Lefler, William, 16
Lehmitz, Ernest Frederick, 157
Leibl, J.K., 42
Lewis, Evelyn Clayton, 113, 126
Lewis, John L., 54
Lewis, Leon, 47–51, 100
Leyendecker, Richard Emil, 31
Lindner, Hans-Heinz, 150
Lonkowski, Auguste 'Gunny', 62
Lonkowski, William 'Willi' (aka William Schneider, Willie Meller, William Sex, William Sexton and William Lonkis), 61–94
Lorentz, Heinrich, 70, 88
Louden, Max Lynar (aka Max Scheimangk), 13, 14
Ludwig, Kurt Frederick 'Fred' (aka Joe K.), 131–137, 198
Luederitz, Karl A., 12
Lundeen, Ernest, 53
Luning, Heinz August, 156, 157
Luther, Hans, 42, 44

MacArthur, Douglas, 94
MacGarrity, Joseph, 14
Madero, Francisco, 11, 21
Mahler, Dale, 115
Marshall, George C., 94
Martini, José, 42
Matthews, Benjamin, 91
Maurer, Otto, 71
Mayer, Helen Pauline, 134, 198
Mayer, Robert C., 104
McAdoo, William Gibbs, 30
McLoughlin, John T., 90
McWhorter, Dean F., 154
Meiler, Alfred, 179–181
Meiler, Elizabeth, 180
Melind, Gerda, 146
Meloy, Andrew, 23–26
Menzel, Hermann, 69, 81–82, 86, 88
Merck, Ernest von, 96, 97
Metcalfe, John C., 43
Metzler, Frederick, 12, 31
Mezenen, René-Emmanuel, 125, 194
Millen, Richard, 169
Mondragón, Manuel, 23, 24, 25
Mooney, James D., 106
Morgenthau, Henry, 73, 102, 103
Moseley, Gesorge van Horn, 100
Moskowitz, Grover M., 156, 160
Mosquera, Jorge, 166–170, 180
Mueller, Karl Victor, 133, 198
Mueller, Nick, 42
Mueller, Tony, 42
Mundt, Karl E., 53
Murray, John S., 68

Nadolny, Rudolf, 14
Navega, Antonio Concalves, 174
Ness, Neil, 52
Nettin, Ernest, 144
Neubauer, Hermann Otto (aka Henry Nicholas), 144–145, 147–148, 152, 154
Nicolai, Walter, 11, 69
Norden, Carl Lucas, 111–112
Northe, Heinrich, 96
Nussbaum, Joseph, 144

O'Brien, Charles, 41
O'Brien, Rose, 14
O'Leary, Jeremia [sic], 14
Orgell, Guenther, 41
Orozco, Pascual, 24, 25
Osten, Ulrich von der (aka Don Julio Lopez Lido), 131–133, 135
Ostjes, Hans, 66
Othmer, Maximilian Gerhard Waldemar, 129, 130
Otto, Theodor, 10

Pagel, Hans, 133, 198
Palmer, A. Mitchell, 58, 59
Pape, Robert, 46–50
Papen, Franz Joseph Hermann Michael Maria von, 2, 3, 4, 9, 10–15, 17, 18, 26, 30–32, 35, 36
Pelley, William Dudley, 40, 41, 52
Pfaus, Oscar, 42
Pheiffer, Erich, 68–70, 76–78, 80–84, 88
Philby, Kim, 173
Phillipbar, Charles W., 90
Piekenbrock, Hans, 77, 109, 115, 126, 188
Plochmann, George, 31
Polis, Albert, 3, 6
Potocki, Jerzy, 54
Prager, Robert, 36
Price, Morris H., 119

Quirin, Richard (aka Richard 'Dick' Quintas), 145–146, 148, 153

Rautter, Bertha von (aka Bertha Brayley-Fisher), 158
Rautter, Wilhelm Albrecht von Pressentin genannt von (aka R.L. Erskine, Roger), 158–160
Reiswitz, Count Kurt von, 16
Respa, Charles Francis, 16
Reuper, Carl Alfred, 123, 182, 194
Reynolds, Robert Rice, 128
Ribbentrop, Joachim von, 54
Rieber, Torkild, 105–107
Rifkind, Simon, 89
Rintelen, Franz Dagobert Johannes von (aka Emil Victor Gasché), 5, 6, 17, 18, 19, 24–26, 31, 32
Ritter, Hans, 113
Ritter, Katharina Francis, 108
Ritter, Klaus Haveland, 108
Ritter, Mary Aurora (Evans), 108
Ritter, Nickolaus (aka Hans Rankin, Alfred Landing), 108
Robbins, Patrick, 65
Rodriguez, Nicholás, 95, 96
Roeder, Everett Minster, 116, 118, 119, 122, 135, 194
Röhm, Ernst, 145
Rossberg, Ewald Fritz, 84, 85
Rudloff, Max Fritz Ernst, 168, 169
Rumrich, Günther Gustav Maria, 68–73, 80, 84, 85, 86, 88, 91, 93
Sanders, Ralph A., 177
Schacht, Hjalmar, 168
Schack, Baron Eckhart H. von, 16
Schade, Martin, 71
Schaeffer, Franz, 42
Scheele, Walter, 18–20
Schimmel, Karl Max, 19
Schleindl, Frederick, 10, 31
Schlosser, Frederick Edward, 134, 199
Schlütter, Karl, 63, 69, 70, 71, 72, 73, 74, 76, 79, 81, 86, 88, 93
Schmidt, Emma, 42
Schmidt, Hugo, 6
Schmidt, John, 48–49
Schmidt, Joseph (aka Jerry Swenson), 145, 146, 148
Scholz, Herbert Wilhelm, 138, 162, 194
Scholz, Walter, 32, 136
Schroetter, Carl Herman (aka John Charles Post, Captain Jack), 134, 137, 199
Schuh, George Gottlieb, 195
Schulz, Walter, 144, 148
Schütz, Theodor, 85, 88
Schwieger, Walter, 28
Schwinn, Hermann, 45, 46, 49, 50, 52, 95–98, 100–101
Scott-Ford, Duncan Alexander Croall, 129
Sebold, William Gotlieb (aka Harry Sawyer), 114–126, 133, 135, 136, 159, 160, 184
Seeckt, Hans von, 61
Semmler, Alexander, 168, 169
Shishmarev, Feodor Ivanovich, 99
Sichart, Mary, 144
Siegler, Erwin, 119, 125, 195
Silberberg, Mendel, 50
Silk, Arthur J., 68
Skorzeny, Otto, 162
Slocombe, Charles, 52, 98, 101
Socha, Max, 49
Sommerfeld, Felix A., 10, 11, 12, 21–24
Spalthoff, Herman Heinrich Rullhausen, 130
Spanknöbel, Hans, 46, 49, 60, 75
Spretter, Erwin Harry de, 158
Stabler, Oscar Richard, 195
Stade, Heinrich, 195
Stallforth, Frederico, 5, 22, 23, 26, 32, 34
Starziczny, Josef Jacob Johannes, 116
Stein, Lilly Barbara Carola, 121

Steinberg, Gustav, 18
Steinert, Julius, 167
Steuer, Johannes Karl, 63
Stigler, Franz, 125, 196
Stone, Harlan Fiske, 59
Strassburger, Ralph Beaver, 106
Strecht, Augusto, 174, 175
Streicher, Julius, 44, 45
Strunck, Erich, 196
Suhl, Heinrich Ludwig, 160
Sunderland, Carl, 49–50

Tamm, E.A., 87, 89
Tauscher, Hans, 3, 12, 22
Taylor, Bridgeman H., 12, 13
Textor, Fred, 130
Themlitz, Paul, 46, 49
Thiel, Werner Edward (aka Billy Thomas), 145, 147, 152, 153
Thomsen, Hans, 53–54, 108, 131, 135–136, 138–139
Thurston, Arthur, 173–176
Tietgens, Paul, 6, 7
Traynor, Duane L., 154
True, James, 45, 52, 98
Tuchendler, Charles (aka Charles J. Tucker), 12
Tuite, Thomas P., 12
Turner, Bill, 28
Turrou, Leon (aka Leon Turovsky, Leon Petrov), 67–68, 70–74, 76, 78–80, 83, 84, 86, 87–90, 92

Ubico, Jorge, 97

Vetterli, Reed, 86–90, 92
Viereck, George Sylvester, 28, 29, 53–55
Villa, Pancho, 21–23
Visel, Jacob A., 158
Voss, Otto Hermann, 63

Waalen, Leo, 196
Wachendorf, Franz R., 11–13
Walischewski, Adolf Henry August, 196
Weidemann, Frederich 'Fritz', 52, 100
Weigand, Karl, 85
Welles, Sumner, 90, 126
Wendt, Amelia, 14
Werner, Robert, 90
Weston, Edward, 68
Westrick, Gerhard Alois, 106, 107
Weustenfeld, Else, 121, 196
Wheeler, Burton Kendall, 54
Wheeler-Hill, Alex, 116, 123, 135, 182
Wichmann, Herbert Christian, 178
Wickersham, George, 57
Wilson, Woodrow, 1, 6, 7,23, 27, 28, 30, 32, 36, 58
Winrod, Gerald Burton, 44, 45, 52
Winterhalder, Hans, 46, 47, 49
Witzke, Lothar (aka Harry Waberski, Hugo Olsen, Pablo Davis), 35
Wolf, Alma, 147
Wolpert, Otto, 19, 34
Woodring, Harry Hines, 94

Yocupicio, Ramón, 95

Zakrewski, Teresa, 67
Zenzinger, Bertram Wolfgang, 197
Zimmermann, Arthur, 14, 36